The World of Children's Sleep

Parents' Guide
to Understanding Children and their Sleep Problems

Alexander Z. Golbin, M.D., Ph.D.

© 1995, 1994 by Michaelis Medical Publishing Corp.

Michaelis Medical Publishing Corp.
2274 South 1300 East, #G8-288
Salt Lake City, UT 84106
Salt Lake   Chicago   Athens

Cover illustrated by: Etola Zinni

Inside illustrations by: Eric Melander
                               Nikos Linardakis
                               Nancy Lu Rosenheim
Cover Designed by: Nikos Linardakis

Library of Congress Catalog Card Number: 94-75432

ISBN 1-884084-09-5

This book is dedicated to my beautiful daughters
and my best friends
Yana, Dina, and Ilana
and devoted to all children on the earth.

ACKNOWLEDGMENTS

In my work at Cook County Hospital and at the Sleep and Behavioral Medicine Institute, I have always been impressed with how knowledgeable, experienced, and creative my colleagues were in taking good care of our little patients. Drs. Gabrielle Woloshin, Jaime Trujillo, Elina Manghi, and other physicians and psychologists are my strong critics and my friends. Their wisdom and invaluable advice seeped into these pages.

My special thanks to Anne Seiden, M.D., whose continued support of my work and willingness to share her experiences as an author of a book for parents made this book possible.

My deep gratitude to Stephen Sheldon, M.D., pediatrician and author of *Pediatric Sleep Medicine*, to Chicago pediatrician Veronica Kroin, and professor of public health, Bernard Baum, Ph.D.

Dr. Rosalind Cartwright, Head of the Sleep and Research Center at Rush-Presbyterian St. Luke's Hospital, is one of the pioneers in sleep medicine. She has been a great support and has shaped me as a scientist.

Much of this book is owed to my friends: Silvia and Floyd Gerber, Irina and Arthur Raff, Larisa and Boris Vayner, Irena and Zin Fooks, Mary Kay Jenkner, Dr. and Mrs. Arthur Block, and many others, who enthusiastically supported me for many years and encouraged me in times of despair. Our efforts finally culminated in the organization of the *Foundation for Children's Sleep Disorders*. They impressed upon me the obligation to parents to spell out clearly what medicine knows about sleep in children, to describe its nature, possible deviations and give guidance to prevent disorder.

Prof. Louis Keith of Northwestern University, President of the Center for Multiple Births, has provided continuous support throughout this endeavor.

My gratitude to another friend of mine: Larry Weintraub, journalist and philosopher. He helped me to verbalize briefly and clearly my vague concepts, define arguments and put things into perspective.

I would also like to express my heartfelt gratitude to Irena Nemchonok and Victor Peppard who provided me with their wonderful stories and fairy tales for children.

My very deep appreciation to Nikos Linardakis, doctor and businessman, a writer and indiscouragable negotiator—in short, the kind of editor and publisher any writer would pray for. He performed a miracle by overcoming all of the barriers in publishing this book.

This book would have lost much of its impact without the audiovisual materials provided by Anthony Cargile, Al Cato, George Sanetra, Elena Levine, Sameer Shamsi and the artwork done by Nancy Lu Rosenheim and Eric Melander.

I would like to emphasize the immense help of our support staff. The word "secretary" originated from the word "secret". Terry D'Souza, Beverly Burbridge, Cathy Lipsey-Hill, Mary Bosworth, Irene Godin and Anna Roytman know all my secrets and do their best to organize me, make my writing readable, and keep my work on schedule. Also, a big thank you to Ms. Wilson of M&M Secretary Services. And, last but not least, my deep gratitude for Nina, Ilya and Elisabeth Genn, and Alla Crowder, who helped me sort out my material and edit the book.

Very special thanks to my family, especially my children Yana, Dina, and Ilana, who are my constant source of inspiration. Their sleep and alertness, their dreams and fantasies, worries and joys give me enormous material to think about. Their help in preparation of this book makes me a very proud father.

Finally, and most importantly, my deep appreciation to the patients whose heartbreaking stories keep me going in search for cures. The details of these patients' lives are, of course, scrambled for the purposes of confidentiality, but the essence of their stories is, to my knowledge, presented accurately.

Alexander Z. Golbin, M.D.
Chicago, Illinois

FOREWORD

You are about to read a book like no other. It introduces the reader, whether parent or physician, to the world of sleep so important to the health and well-being of the developing child. Dr. Golbin has given us a wealth of material from his own twenty years of work with children suffering from a great variety of sleep disorders and covers the international literature as well. Some of this has never before been brought together to inform the reader on the state of knowledge about the what, the why, and how to cope with problems of the night.

The problems of sleep are especially vexing. They happen when the pediatrician is not there to observe and the parents are on their own to cope. They can disrupt a household, yet vanish with the morning light and leave no trace.

Dr. Golbin's *Guide for Parents* is a source book that can help the parent feel less alone. Like Dr. Spock's famous book, it can reassure the reader that the problems they face have occurred to others and there is knowledge available. Often there is not enough, but that is so in much of medicine.

What this book does is bring together the folk tales, the research, the case studies and bring the attention of the reader to an area often ignored, but crucial to our physical growth and psychological functioning, and give it its due.

This book covers a wide range of problems, from the normal effects of pregnancy on sleep of the mother-to-be, the problems of organizing the sleep-wake rhythm in the newborn with and without colic, SIDS, and the debate over co-sleeping (sharing the bed with the baby), when enuresis becomes a problem, night terrors and sleepwalking, narcolepsy and other kinds of daytime sleepiness and what is known about them.

Perhaps most important is the range of ways to treat these disorders discussed here What the parent can do without drugs to help the child sleep well and to increase their own understanding of the disorder and acceptance of the sleep disturbed child. Better basic understanding of sleep troubles helps the parent observe the problem and be able to inform the pediatrician, who in turn can turn to the research literature for a more focused approach. This is an area where parents, physicians and researchers need to keep up good communication for progress toward more peaceful nights and active days for the child.

This book points the way.

Rosalind Cartwright, Ph.D.,
Diplomate, American Board of Sleep Medicine
Chairperson of Department of Psychology and Social Sciences
Director of Sleep Disorder Service and Research Center,
    Rush-Presbyterian-St. Luke's Medical Center, Chicago, Illinois

TABLE OF CONTENTS

PROLOGUE

Sleep, particularly sleep in children, is a world by itself. Like many doctors and parents, I didn't notice this world until it painfully hit me professionally and personally.

That day, incidentally, the fourth of July, started gloriously. As the new chief of the pediatric unit, I began my first evening rounds. A large group of medical personnel: nurses, residents, and students followed me. The sense of omnipotence, (the feeling of knowing everything) was overwhelming. I was the happiest person on the earth. Among other children, I saw a three month old baby who was peacefully sleeping in a crib in a funny position. He was a handsome boy, admitted with a slight fever and questionable breathing and irregular pulse. Nothing major was found during a thorough evaluation. The child seemed to be perfectly healthy. I ordered this child to be discharged the next morning and went to see other children. A few minutes later, the frightened nurse reported that this child was found dead in his crib.

Imagine how I felt and what I went through emotionally, professionally, and legally! Now, incompetence was my overwhelming feeling. I was the most miserable person on the earth. This was my first encounter with Sudden Infant Death Syndrome. Since that time, more than twenty years ago, I have been wildly awakened to the sleeping world. Like many other sleep watchers, I didn't sleep for many nights, trying to find out what was going on in the child's life under the cover of night.

My eyes opened to the strange positions, funny movements, and the many inexplicable things that happened to children in their sleep. My ears opened to parents' frustrations and questions, which I considered trivial and unimportant before. I was professionally intrigued, emotionally scared, and intellectually fascinated. To put it simply, I was hooked to sleep phenomena and felt the rush of the geographer discovering an unknown world.

Modern medical science has made the amazing discovery that sleep is not a passive state, but a very active process. We are born in sleep, we keep growing in sleep, and we are dying in sleep. The world of children's sleep hides the secrets of how our brain works, how we move from yesterday to tomorrow, from restful sleep to active wakefulness, from disordered sleep to disordered wakefulness. The secrets of our daytime behavior, our personality, our physical health or sickness are all rooted in sleep. Maybe knowing the secrets of childhood sleep will lead us to the secrets of adults' daytime success and problems, secrets of our biological destiny!

When parents asked me, "Doctor, just tell me clearly why my child wets the bed, or bangs his head, pulls his hair, chokes, screams, and has hundreds of sleep problems that destroy our family's sleep, relationship, and finances. What is the nature of that and how do we treat it?" I was embarrassed. I just didn't know the answers.

Searching for answers, I read hundreds of professional books and analyzed my colleagues' heartbreaking stories of sudden death, a wide variety of behaviors and symptoms in sleep I also observed the sleep of normal children and the results of sleep deprivation of parents of sleepless children. I compared different theories to come up with my own.

Practical results are the final truth of any theory. We respect what really works and helps, even if it is against a fashionable theory. We learn from our patients. It does not matter how young they are. Patients are the doctors' best teachers, and parents know their children better than any doctor. We learn from parents' tragedies, from their "tricks" to help their child make it through the night.

One day I received a letter from the parents of a child who died in his sleep from severe headbanging. Enclosed was a check for twenty dollars with a short handwritten note: "Dear Doctor, Our child died while he was banging his head in his sleep. His heart stopped. So has ours. We are sending you a check for your research on why children die like our son did. We need a book to prevent other children from dying this way." The twenty dollars and the small note did what a million dollar grant couldn't—it touched my heart, showed me my mission, which is to communicate to parents what we know and what we don't know at the present time about children's sleep and its disorders. This letter cured me of my fear of book writing.

One famous writer, I believe it was Alexander Dumas, once remarked that a writer writes only one book, the Book of His Life. He can produce hundreds of volumes, but all of them are just a search for THAT BOOK, the book of his life. Similar to the myth about Stradivarius, who had to produce 900 violins in the sleepless search for the secret of THAT violin, the Violin of His Life.

Sufferers cannot wait for the final truth when we know everything. Yet we don't. But we do know some helpful strategies. This book is the first step in a search for the Book of My Life. It's a book for parents. By sharing with them some of the history of sleep research, the basic strategies and techniques used to identify the nature of so-called normal sleep and sleep disorders, we tried to help parents better orient themselves in the complex world of sleep. We hope that learning more about present-day research into sleep will assist them in dealing with their children's sleep problems. It will also help them choose, with their doctor's guidance, the best possible course of treatment.

The intention of this book is to guide the parents toward a certain logic of thinking and, inasmuch as possible, to provide them with helpful, direct recommendations.

This book is not a monologue of a "know it all" doctor to a "know nothing" naive mom or dad. It is a dialogue. It is an honest sharing of what we know, or believe to know. It is an attempt to answer parents' questions, based on treatment of actual cases of children with sleep disorders, and an honest admission of not knowing all the answers. This book has many success stories and just as many unsuccessful ones.

The book is devoted to everyone—to patients with the message that they are not alone and their experience is shared by others, to doctors, students, researchers—everyone who is open-minded, eager to learn, and looking for answers. We offer many prescriptions, but it is not a menu book. This book is an invitation to open communication between health professionals and parents, to create a team between formal knowledge and emotional experience, for the benefit of our children's health.

"Those who claim to sleep like a baby, do not have one."
–A parent

PART
1

SLEEP PROBLEMS THROUGH THE EYES OF THE FAMILY

What the Family is Going Through

Siblings

Sleeping Twins

Sleeping With Pets

Harm My Child? Oh, No!

WHAT THE FAMILY IS GOING THROUGH

The world of children's sleep is not independent from our lives as adults. In fact, it is very close, and oftentimes occupies all our wakefulness. It is like air that we do not see, but that permeates everything. If this air is healthy, the family breathes easily, and their sleep is peaceful and undisturbed. But if the air is unhealthy, the family feels suffocated, and nighttime becomes a nightmare, both literally and metaphorically. Childhood sleep disorders usually mean disorders for the whole family.

Dear Reader, if you are a parent of children who sleep well, consider yourself blessed. Perhaps knowing what other families go through will give you a feeling that your life is actually not so bad. If you are a parent who really knows how miserable the night can be, this chapter is for you, to tell you that you are not alone.

At one time or another, most of us, parents, got into real fights with our children in an attempt to put them to bed. Being awakened several times during the night and getting up exhausted in the morning is something many of us remember as an unavoidable part of child-rearing. And, as if that were not enough, the night war is prolonged in the morning, when we have to wake up our child so that he or she is not late for school. The natural result of this is a growing sense of anger and frustration, a typical example of which is expressed in the following letter:

Dear Doctor:

I am writing before our next visit to your office just to let you know what we have been going through lately with Jane. She is a big girl already. She will be ten in October. It might be hard for you to imagine what she is like at home . When she is around people, during the day, they see a sweet, adorable child. During the night, she transforms into a little monster and the continuous stress is almost impossible to live with.

We have ongoing problems with her sleep. For hours, she can't fall asleep alone, and bangs on our door to come in or asks me or my husband to stay with her while she holds our hands tightly. When she finally falls asleep, and we attempt to leave the room, she immediately wakes up and starts to scream, awakening the whole house.

If she does fall asleep, she wakes up every hour, upset and scared. She says she hears noises outside and inside the house, and she is so afraid that she can't stay in her bed. Talking to her is no help. I just want someone to tell me why she can't sleep through the night. Any advice will be highly appreciated.

Needless to say, this torture has affected ours lives tremendously. I just don't know what to do anymore. There doesn't seem to be any end to the problem. It destroys our night sleep and we do not know how much longer we can take it. We have almost resigned ourselves to letting this child run our lives.

I have never heard of anything like this before. Please help.

Sincerely,

Bob and Susan Thomas

Many known sleep disorders are associated with difficult morning arousal, excessive day dreaming, daytime fatigue, decrease in attention, or hyperactivity. All of the above interfere with academic performance and cause absences from school. They also create mistaken assumptions of laziness or stupidity, which, in turn, have a detrimental effect on children's self-esteem. After proper treatment, children can move from behavior disorder and learning disability into regular classes, sometimes even advanced programs.

Chronic bedwetting, headbanging, severe sleepwalking problems, night terrors and nightmares prevent the child from normal relationships with peers, staying overnight at other people's houses or going to camp. As a result, the child feels isolated and inadequate, develops socially unacceptable patterns of behavior, and in extreme cases, has suicidal tendencies. This puts enormous stress on families.

Sleepless nights put tremendous strain on a marriage and challenge the sense of closeness. Unable to solve the problem, a couple may resort to fault-finding. What can be easier than putting the blame on one's spouse for spoiling the child, giving bad genes, or putting his or her job above the child's needs, etc. Such pressure, combined with lack of sleep and frustration, can lead to divorce.

Sleep disorders do not come cheaply.   Many insurance companies refuse to cover sleep disorders and consider them psychological concerns.   Bedwetting, headbanging, nighttime terrors, and sleepwalking could be extremely dangerous.   However, they are not accepted by insurance companies as medical problems.   Looking for the right doctor, taking time off from work, changing job shifts to accommodate such situations, purchasing multiple medical devices from alarms to custom made beds—all of these become quite costly.   We have a case where one very successful owner of a restaurant lost his business due to his child being hospitalized a number of times with severe headbanging problems, which were misdiagnosed as convulsions.   The insurance company did not cover the child's illness.   After his son was successfully treated, this person decided to change his career and become a sleep technician.

Divorce, in itself, before, during and after, is the most stressful event in a child's life.   Sometimes paradoxically, after the divorce, children accommodate quickly and feel better since there is no constant fighting between the parents.   For children who have sleep disorders, there are a million logistic questions.   If the child is a bedwetter or has nocturnal asthma, then sleeping in different homes, on different beds, or with an altered schedule, might be a problem.

SIBLINGS

Now that we have briefly analyzed the different types of socio-economic problems caused by children's sleep disorders, we would like to focus on some specific concerns voiced by parents of siblings. It is important to note here that problems with siblings are both qualitatively multiplied and quantitatively different.

Recently our office received a letter from the mother of two patients of ours:

Dear Doctor:

You asked me to describe a parent's perspective on living with not just one, but two children, who rock and bang their heads when falling asleep. I would like to start by saying that I live with a man who also rocked to fall asleep when he was a child. My biggest concern is that my children may grow up with the same lifelong problems as my husband. When our daughter started to bang her head at the age of six months, my husband and I never thought of it as a sleep disorder. We knew that my husband did it when he was little, so we just let our little girl do it. As the years progressed, we consulted a few pediatricians, who told us it would pass, she would outgrow it. When she grew older, she started to share her bedroom with her sister. Because of the size of the room, they had bunk beds. My older daughter heard her little sister bouncing her head every night and shaking the bed to fall asleep. It usually ended up in a fight. It tears my heart apart, because she does not know why she bangs her head. She tells me, "it's the only way I can sleep". Now she is eight years old, and I worry about her academic abilities at school. She does not want to spend the night over at friends' houses. And if she does , she forces herself not to bang her head.

When our daughter was six, I had another baby, a boy, who at the age of approximately six months also started to bang his head. At the age of two, he does not cry when he wakes up, but rocks his crib. When he was one, his room had hard wood floors. I would go into his room at night or in the morning, and his crib would be in the middle of the room. We have since carpeted his room, and because of the force of his rocking, the whole crib is falling apart. We have cable ties on the railings of the crib, which have to be replaced every other month or so, because they wear out quickly. We are very concerned about both children and hope that soon there will be some answers or cures for them, and for others who suffer from childhood sleep disorders.

This letter is exceptional in that the woman who wrote it seems to be capable of dividing her attention equally between her husband and two young children, all of whom suffer from major sleep disorders.   This is not always the case. When looking into the area of family sleep and the special concerns faced by parents with siblings, it seems worthwhile to identify three major problems:
     1.   When one of the children is ill, the sibling is, as a rule, ignored for the meantime. The child is left very much alone and his or her needs and problems, including sleep problems, are for the most part disregarded.   The parents' undivided attention goes to their sick sibling.
     2.   It is quite common for siblings to fall ill at the same time or shortly after one another.   This puts additional stress on the family in coping with the situation, especially in cases with working mothers. But this is even more difficult for the children themselves who vie for attention and tend to become more feisty and demanding than usual. Bedtime wars, nightmares, headbanging and sleepwalking intensify at such times.   Having to miss school, in turn, causes academic problems, coping with which can often be impossible without the parents' help and their supportive attitude.
     3.   Parents of siblings often overemphasize early autonomy. They tend to give their young children too much independence and expect them to act maturely at an early age. Such parents want their children to become self-reliant and depend as little as possible both on them and their older siblings.   One example from my practical experience was a case of a hard-working middle class family with four children. After many years, the couple was finally able to buy a four-bedroom house. One of the children, an infant, slept with the parents.   The three others, all boys, each had a separate bedroom. They were 6, 11 and 14 years old. It was the six-year old who had serious sleep problems.   He suffered from terrible nightmares, waking up three or four times during the night, crying, screaming and knocking at the siblings' and

parents' doors for them to let him in. Neither of them allowed him to come in or comfort him. They thought he should be able to resolve the problem on his own. Their concern was for him to develop his autonomy.

This case was very hard to resolve. My final recommendation was for the family to organize sleepover parties, taking turns to invite the six-year-old sibling. Prior to that, he took sleep medication, which did not help. But sleepover parties turned out to be a good solution. It seems that autonomy is not always good and not equally good for everyone. What we should do is focus more on family sleep as a whole. This very important issue opens up new avenues for study and research.

If sleeping with siblings may make havoc of our own sleep and wakefulness, what about twins?

SLEEPING TWINS

There are two major reasons why it is so important for everyone to know about twins and sleep. First of all, making baby twins sleep through the night is the single most difficult task and the biggest concern for parents of twins. The second reason is that sleep in twins is somewhat unusual and conceals many factors which are important for understanding the sleep process and the phenomena of twinning.

The number of twins and the higher order of multiples, such as triplets, quadruplets (four babies), quintuplets (five babies!) in one set is increasing in epidemic progression. According to Dr. Louis Keith, President of the Center for Multiple Births at Northwestern University in Chicago, between 1979 and 1989 the number of triplets and higher multiples increased by 133 percent. In the sixties, the number of triplets was about 500 a year in the U.S.; by 1979 this number rose to 900 sets per year and in 1989 to 1200. In 1989, 229 American women gave birth to four babies at the same time (229 quadruplet sets). If in the sixties, you had never heard about the delivery of five babies, you might be surprised to learn that in 1989 50 quintuplet sets were born!

Twins, triplets and the higher order of multiples are now in the several million and this number is growing fast, producing a big new market for the supply industry (i.e., special cribs, diapers, strollers for twins, triplets, etc.).

Parents of twins are organized into societies, clubs, foundations and other support groups. Every year an International Twins Festival is held in Twinsburg, Ohio. This exciting and fascinating event brings thousands of families of multiples together from all over the world.

There are several causes of the high rate of birth of twins. The mother's age, family history of twins, infertility treatment, etc. are some of the most common. More and more women are going into professional life and delivering their first baby after the age of 30. Those who consider going through infertility treatment should know that infertility agents are a well-known and proven cause of multiple births. For example, among one thousand pregnancies assisted by the use of infertility treatment with clomiphene, there were 84 sets of twins, five sets of triplets, three sets of quadruplets and one set of quintuplets.

Assisted reproductive techniques can result in multiple pregnancies also, because of the practice of transforming more than one fertilized egg during *in vitro* (in tube) fertilization of gamete interfallopian tube transfer. 78 percent of all quadruplets and 100 percent of all quintuplets were born as a result of assisted pregnancies. But the major cause of twins is still natural superovulation, which is when two eggs are released and fertilized simultaneously (so-called fraternal, or dizygotic twins) or a single zygote undergoes one or more cleavages (monozygotic twins).

Those who like scientific hypotheses to have an aura of mystery may admire the appealing theory of "vanishing twins". According to this theory, based on the analysis of placentas, almost all of us were conceived as twins, but our twin sister or brother died early giving to us their food, energy and fortune. As grown ups, we are still searching for our other half.

As you can see, twins and other multiples are many, and problems of raising multiples increase tremendously both for their parents and for the society. Having twins means double pressure and more than double troubles. Parents have to feed, bathe, dress and put to bed two (three or four) babies at the same time.

The real challenge is not the number of children to take care of: twins and other multiples are different from singletons in many ways. On the best side, twins have a greater chance of being gifted and creative than singletons. Having a twin sister or brother creates a unique bond—a feeling of security, strength and joy. Parents of twins are usually ready to have twins, because many of them had twins in their families or went through infertility treatment. Families of twins seldom break up, and are emotionally and financially more stable than those with one or second children.

But there is a price for everything. Two major problems beset multiples: 1) low birth weight and 2) prematurity. The dangerously low birth weight (below 1550g) for twins is ten times and for triplets 33 times more common than for singletons.

50 percent of twins and 95.5 percent of triples are born prematurely before the 37th week with an average of

33 weeks. Very low birth weight and prematurity require very intensive medical involvement, including a prolonged hospital stay in the ICU (Intensive Care Unit). They pose higher risk of significant health and developmental problems and other handicaps. Enormous emotional, physical and financial pressures fall on the family, not to mention the siblings of twins.

Whatever problems baby twins might have, the common denominator is sleeping difficulties. Even if twins are perfectly healthy, it is hard to make them sleep through the night. It is a challenge for parents. Here are some guidelines for how to promote good sleep:

1.   Start thinking about the prevention of sleep and behavioral problems in your children while you are still pregnant. The mother's good nutrition, normal weight gain and sufficient sleep are the best preventive measures. The average weight gain in a pregnancy with multiple babies should be 44 to 70 pounds. Research shows that despite the large weight gain, after delivery weight returns to the pre-pregnancy level as fast as with singletons. The key is enough sleep and food!

2.   After the twins are born and are out of special medical care, the stabilization of their sleep pattern becomes a major issue. At this point, one of the fundamental strategies is to make the twins help each other. Most twins like to sleep together since birth. It would help a lot if they are wrapped in a blanket and put head to head or against soft but firm crib bumper pads. Putting twins to sleep together seems to be a good strategy except when one of the twins has a health problem. By the sixth month they have the capacity to sleep six hours straight through the night, or when waking up, to calm themselves down.

3.   The next strategy is rhythmic, soothing music which may be tape recorded. Rocking, singing, patting, rubbing the back a little during the falling asleep ritual should be more encouraged than in singletons, because twins have an increased need for external rhythmic pacemakers to get them to sleep.

4.   We would like to discourage the common practice of a car ride which is used by some parents as a way to make children fall asleep. This method usually does nothing but add more frustration when children wake up immediately upon arrival after hours of driving.

5.   Even with older twins, parents often found it helpful to leave them alone in the same room if one or both of them had a problem falling asleep. Twins handle this much easier than a single child. They quickly develop their own unique language and calm each other. Many parents of twins reported the unique phenomenon that when alone in a room with their cribs close to one another, they calm each other. If one of them is awake, this does not disturb the other twin.

6.   Regardless of what method you choose to make twins fall asleep, establishing a clear bedtime ritual is the key to success.

7.   Even identical twins are not identical as you will see later. Each baby takes a different amount of time to establish a sleep-wake pattern. Some babies fall into "not quickly waking up" patterns easily, while others continue to wake up every hour and fall back to sleep with greater difficulty. As long as they do not disturb yours or their sibling's sleep and are active during the daytime, the situation should be considered normal. There are many theories of how to make a baby sleep through the night, but my best practical advice is to observe your baby and follow *his* clues as to what makes him sleep.

8.   How long should we let the baby cry before we come in to comfort him? Five minutes? Ten minutes? What should parents do if the issue is very controversial and doctors disagree with each other? Practice is the best test for any theory. As with single babies, until at least four months, you cannot spoil your baby by reacting quickly to crying. After four months, the baby has the ability to sleep 5-6 hours straight and you can start training him to sleep alone. Parents can easily differentiate crying caused by hunger or discomfort from whining. Open doors, lights on, frequent reassurance is a typical start. Some doctors advice the "cold turkey" approach. "Let the baby cry until he falls asleep". For some babies, it works. I personally had more success with a discriminative approach, when parents wait and react only to a cry caused by pain. It is also important to remember that the child's condition can easily change from quiet one night to crabby the following night.

9.   Many children are a little fussy during sleep, making noises and odd movements in the transition between their sleep cycles. Intervening too soon may

interrupt their sleep rather than help. If you wait just a little and delay your response to determine whether it is one of the "transitional" noises or a cry for help, it will be better for you and for your child.

      10.   There is a question about sleeping in the same bed. The concept of a family bed has recently become popular. This issue should be solved individually by each family. The general guidance would be to use the "family bed" (i.e. sleeping with babies) during the first six months and only if the babies are sick or need your help frequently.

      Here is an interesting question to ponder. Do identical twins sleep identically? We found that for many sets of twins, the answer is no. Why not? Actually, twins can be divided roughly into three groups by the similarities in their sleep. One very small group of identical twins has the same sleep pattern. They even change their body positions in sleep at the same time. The second group of twins (identical and fraternal) sleep differently in many ways. The most fascinating and puzzling is the third group, in which monozygotic twins have clearly opposite tendencies in preferred sleep positions, time of morning awakening (lark vs. owl) and, most important, sleep disorders, like bedwetting, sleepwalking, and headbanging. These phenomena are seen in the so-called mirror twins.

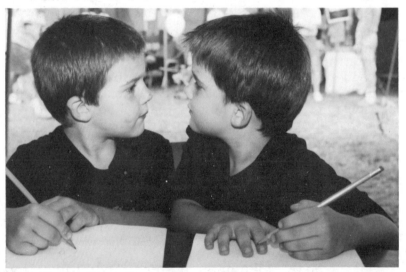

Mirror Twins *Identical in appearance, but if you look closely, you will notice the "mirror" image of the two; including opposite hand dominance. (See text)*

Facial mirroring is a known phenomenon and until recently was associated only with opposite teeth growth or opposite spots on the skin, etc. But mirroring can be not only structural, but also functional (opposite eye, hand, ear dominance) or psychological (opposite temperament, educational, vocational, and even opposite sex orientations). Mirroring also can be medical (opposite dental, dermatological lesions, opposite tendencies in blood pressure, blood sugar level, etc.). In other words, mirror imaging reflects polarization of many biological functions in norm and pathology. Sleep is one of the biological functions. Scientists discovered that bedwetting, injurious sleep and headbanging was found in both identical twins in 60-70 percent of cases. Why not in 100 percent? The reason is that in a subgroup of mirror twins, one twin has a problem, but the other one does not. Another interesting aspect of the mirror phenomenon is co-morbidity. This term is applied when several problems simultaneously develop in the same person. For example, one twin has bedwetting, headbanging, bruxism (teeth grinding) and sleepwalking, but the other twin has none of these symptoms. Mother nature is not fair at times.

It is my strong conviction that we physicians owe it to twins and triplets and the higher order of multiples to develop a special field of medicine devoted primarily to understanding the needs and serving the families of multiples.

"Without a doubt, identical twins, and to a certain extent, their fraternal counterparts, share a unique bond. This bond frequently is stronger and more intense than similar bonds which might unite parents and children or even wives and husbands. This bond cannot be broken even by separation or death."
— Louis Keith, M.D.

SLEEPING WITH PETS

In talking about families with children we are invariably asked to address the issue of home animals and pets. In many cases pets soon become equal members of the household and are treated as such both by children and adults in the family. What about sleeping with pets? How good is it? How healthy?

Whether good or bad, it is known for a fact that a lot of people sleep with pets. Michael Fox, veterinarian and author of a nationally syndicated newspaper column said that probably the majority of pet owners sleep with their pets. Sleeping with pets has a history of its own. Dogs, for instance, were the first animals who became part of the family of man, sleeping by the mouth of the cave to defend its inhabitants. It was a pretty good working relationship and not long after, the dog simply moved in.

So is sleep with animals good or bad? The question should be reformulated to when it is good and when it is bad. Having animals sleep with us—whether in, on, under or near the bed simply depends on our need for company, warmth, touching, security, and on our cultural background. According to Fox, "there is absolutely nothing psychologically unhealthy about it." Chaining the dog in the kitchen or locking it out of the bedroom at night tells the animal that it is an outsider. So why have pets to begin with unless you want a bond with them? Pets give us their love. Michael Cable, Director of the Hamilton Avenue Animal Hospital in Cincinnati stated, "Few things in this world will love you as unconditionally as a dog. Even if you just go to take out the garbage, they act like you have been gone for years when you come back into the house. How can you not like someone like that?" Gregg Levoy, a writer for the *Chicago Tribune*, cited Jeannie Williams, a Washington writer, that for her, pets became an indispensable part of the sleep ritual, like putting on her pajamas or setting the alarm clock. The relationship she has with her two pets, Brazil and Gregg, goes back 10 years, so that their body rhythms have even come to coincide. All three go to bed at the same time. The two cats snuggle up close, one on either side of her. "It can get a little tough to move, though", Williams admits.

There are some extreme animal lovers who allow their pets literally to live in their bed, eating and sleeping with the owner. Gregg Levoy also wrote stories about real love triangles when a new boyfriend or a husband fought with pets for a place in bed. Can you imagine that?

For the unrepentant pet lover, there is even a vacation spot in Wabacha, Minnesota. According to the July 1994 issue of *Cats* Magazine, when you reserve a room at the Anderson house, the oldest continuously operated hotel in the state, you can ask for a cat to sleep with you too or as owner John Halk put it, "A four legged personal, bed warmer."

But companionship has its price. You always risk getting fleas when sleeping with pets. There is an even greater likelihood of catching something like ticks, mites or ringworms when your pet cat or dog climbs into your bed after taking a walk outside. We sometimes also hear hair-raising stories of friendly dogs suddenly getting agitated and killing little children.

How should we act? What is best for our child? For the entire family? For the pet? Based on many experiences with family conflicts about dogs in the bedroom, we would like to give you the following simple advice: think of your pet cat or dog, first, as you would about any human being, and second, as you would think about a medicine. Yes, your cat or dog is a "person", and deal with it as if you were dealing with any other family member. What is its personality? Do you like to be with it all the time or would you rather be alone? Is your dog or cat a troublemaker or a trouble shooter? What about yourself? Are your relationships usually stable or impulsive? Are you getting too close to each other?

Your dog or cat is a medicine. It can really help, especially when you do not feel well. I know a dog who helped a frightened child go to sleep by lying in his bed. I know about another dog who woke up a patient with apnea when he had difficulty breathing. Yes, a dog can help. But the dog might also hurt. Use pets as a medicine. That means—as needed. And as with any medicine, do not abuse it. Too close a contact with pets, and too often, might give unnecessary and unwanted side effects.

It is not good for the animal to over identify with people, either. It is, in fact, quite unhealthy, insists Kathryn Hilker, Coordinator of Education at the Cincinnati Zoo. Her observations show that animals get neurotic and goofy when they are too humanized.

HARM MY CHILD? OH, NO!

"Sure enough, I am not talking about those monsters who abuse babies. Somewhere far away, cruel people on drugs hurt their babies. But I am talking about *us*, good parents, who adore their children, who love them more than anything else in the world. It is not even conceivable that some of *us* hurt our babies. I refuse to even read about it. It makes me sick." I heard this pronouncement from a highly educated mother of three. Just two weeks later, her 18 year old son shook his 19 month old sister to death, because he could not bear her high pitched screaming all night long. He loved his sister. He did not remember doing it. A crazy story? Yes. A unique story? Unfortunately, not.

What I am about to tell you now happened in one of the well-known hospitals in England. Infants, quickly improving after the birth trauma and ready for discharge, suddenly started to have multiple medical problems such as retinal hemorrhages, seizures, weakness, and weight loss. Some of them even died. A medical team began searching for a new bacteria which might have caused such a horrible disease. Investigators found that the majority of infants were under the care of the best nurse in the hospital. During her shift, the ward was in perfect order. Everything was spotlessly clean and the babies were unusually quiet. They just did not cry. Observing this nurse, someone noticed that during the night, as soon as a baby started to cry, she immediately disciplined the infant by shaking him. The baby could not cry ... nor did he live. The source of the problem was the nurse's anger. Dr. Caffey formally described the group of symptoms which resulted from shaking: bilateral brain hematomas, cerebral concussion, bilateral retinal hemorrhages, and all of these in the absence of any external signs of trauma of the head and neck. He called it "whiplash" or simply the "shaken baby syndrome". Blindness, seizures, developmental delay were noticed in 50 percent of these babies.

Infants are at a great risk for damage secondary to shaking. An infant's head is heavier and the neck muscles are weaker. Rotational torque results in excessive tearing and forces the attachment of blood vessels in soft tissues.

Infants might also be at a greater risk to shaking, because they cry more often for no apparent reason, causing quite a serious sleep deprivation for caretakers. Dr. Showers reviewed several studies undertaken between 1980 and 1990 and indicated that between 25 and 50 percent of adults and teens did *not* know that shaking the baby vigorously was dangerous. She began the "Don't Shake the Baby" project in Ohio and reported success in educating parents regarding the dangers of shaking.

However, gentle playful, rhythmical shaking when the caregiver is composed and does not give vent to anger, is very helpful to stimulate the child and develop the central nervous system. It specifically helps develop good balance and improve eye-motor coordination. The difference between good shaking and bad shaking is that in good shaking the caregiver always supports the head and neck.

We do not want to hurt our babies or our family members. But have you experienced the feeling of anger at least once? Just once, the thought that the child screams or wets on purpose? Didn't your friend or relative tell you that you spoil your child and you need to be more firm? Didn't your husband say at 2 A.M., "I have to work tomorrow. Shut him up. I can't stand it anymore?" Nobody ever told you that? Consider yourself fortunate.

I happen to work with child abuse cases. The number of those cases occupy a full team of physicians, psychologists and social workers. Oftentimes I hear the explanation that the abuse was provoked by a sleepless child that was screaming and disturbing the family, forcing a sleep-deprived, short-tempered caretaker to react angrily.

A few months ago, Chicago's newspapers featured a story about a respected engineer who brutally killed his infant son. The reporters did not believe the factual details of that case. The child was crying at the top of his lungs for hours on end. The exhausted father lost his temper and flung the child into the crib. And he missed it. The child died. The father committed suicide.

Another case involved a four and a half year old boy who was wetting the bed and defecating in his sleep. He was placed on the gas stove and was scalded in the boiling water. The mother said that she was too sleepy to check the temperature of the water.

The history of bedwetting is a history of permanent child abuse. (See Part 5). Children with bedwetting problems have been beaten, burned and forced to eat excrements of animals. Their parents put them to sleep upside down, had their penis tied, etc.

On the other hand, child abuse itself causes severe sleep problems. According to researches, children sexually abused by family members, have a dramatic increase of sleep disorders.

Nighttime brings night troubles. We need to be aware of these situations, especially when exhaustion, helplessness and anger grow out of proportion. Self control is the most important and difficult skill to master. This is true for everyone, including doctors. The knowledge of the problem does not prevent mistakes, bad feelings and inappropriate behavior.

We still have a lot to learn by being attentive to our children's needs and to their big and little problems. Sleeping disorders can, unfortunately, be one of them. Our child's sleep can be peaceful and quiet as an ocean in a period of calm, but it can also be turbulent and stormy.

"The beginning of health is sleep."
— Irish proverb

"Sleep is a priceless treasure—the more one has of it, the better it is."
— Chinese proverb

PART
2

NORMAL SLEEP AND ALERTNESS

A Little History About a Big Discovery

What is Normal Sleep

Biological Clocks

Modern Theories of Sleep and its Functions

The Mystery of Dreams

Three Regulators of Alertness

Sleep-Like Conditions

A LITTLE HISTORY ABOUT A BIG DISCOVERY

It was an exceptionally cold night in February of 1926 in St. Petersburg, Russia. Two pediatricians, Figurin and Denisov were trying to do three things at the same time: warm themselves and 20 infants in the ward, stay awake and record physiological parameters of the sleeping children. They worked on a long-term project for the Russian Academy of Sciences researching periodic phenomena in children's sleep. The country was in disarray having gone through a bloody Socialist revolution and a devastating civil war. Millions of infants and children were dying from cold and starvation. The Academy of Sciences made heroic efforts to raise money to organize this first formal pediatric sleep research which revealed that children did not sleep quietly through the night. Several times in the course of the night their chests would suddenly start to move rapidly, their pulse would become irregular and unusually fast, and small muscles have spastic twitches. These strange episodes lasted for about 10-15 minutes every half an hour. The two scientists observed this fact repeatedly and recorded it. As pediatricians, they first thought that the periodic instability of functions was due to chronic starvation and cold. However, the healthier the children were, the more prominent were their "disturbances". In their presentation to the Academy of Sciences in 1926 entitled "Periodic Phenomena in Children's Sleep", the pediatricians concluded, "Even normal sleep is not a state of rest." The Academy of Sciences considered this statement important enough to translate the whole presentation into English and German. But the new government did not have the money to engage in sleep studies.

In the early 20th Century, the dominant view was that sleep is a passivity due to the reduction of general stimulation. Immobility of the body, muscle paralysis was assumed to be due to the inactivity of the brain. This data was obtained through an electroencephalograph analysis (encephalus—Latin word for the brain). In 1930, Berger, a German psychiatrist was able to record brain waves (EEG) for long periods of time during wakefulness and sleep. He noted the significant difference between sleep and wakefulness and reinforced the idea of sleep as rest. In the human electroencephalogram, sleep appeared in the brain as high amplitude, slow waves and active wakefulness as low amplitude, fast activity. The image of the brain "turning off" was associated with the image of high amplitude, slow resting waves. In 1937 Dr. Loomis and his colleagues completed a detailed study of different brain wave patterns, which was a very important step towards sleep medicine. They demonstrated that sleep could be measured continuously and the presence or interruption of sleep at any time could be established objectively without disturbing the sleeping patient. Whether or not a person who *appeared* to be asleep was *really* sleeping could be easily determined.

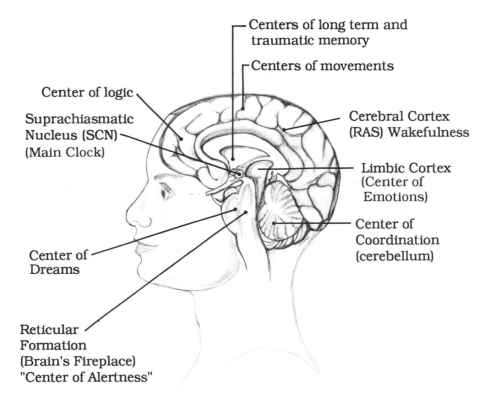

Fig. 2.1   Illustration of the brain with relative areas of function.

After World War II when implantable, insulated electrodes were developed, animal sleep research established sleep as a respected field in science. The most important discovery of this period belonged to two Italian physiologists, Moruzzi and Magoun. In their classic paper of 1949 entitled, "Brain Stem Reticular Formation and Activation of the EEG" they described the "fireplace" on the bottom of the brain. If impulses from this place bombard the cortex, the person is alert and attentive. If the fire of impulses diminishes, the person falls asleep. It is important to mention two major consequences of this discovery. First, sleep and wakefulness could now be considered not only environmental, voluntary phenomena but results of involuntary biological processes. Second, sleep and wakefulness were now seen as a continuum. EEG activation, wakefulness and consciousness are on one end of the continuum, EEG synchronization, sleep and loss of consciousness are on its other end. It is possible to keep the brain alert without any external sensory stimuli, by electrical stimulation of the reticular formation. The imaginary fantastic head amputated from the body and talking to us is conceivable!

In the early 1950s Nathaniel Kleitman, professor of physiology from the University of Chicago, together with his assistant, Eugene Aserinsky, confirmed the concept that sleep was an active periodic process. Kleitman was curious about eye movements in sleep, and with the help of advanced recording equipment, they were able to determine that rapid eye movements were a normal and obligatory phenomenon periodically appearing in sleep. What makes things unusual is the fact that at the time of rapid eye movement other physiological functions also appear paradoxical compared to normal, "orthodoxal" restful sleep. The electrical activity of the brain is increased. Breathing and heart rhythm become autonomic and irregular. Kleitman and Aserinsky identified a new phenomenon—a separate, distinct stage of sleep—very different from orthodoxal quiet sleep or from wakefulness. They recorded this fact on their ink writing oscillograph which is still displayed in Dr. Allan Rechtshaften's lab at the University of Chicago. This machine changed sleep research history. Aserinsky and Kleitman first designed the way to document eye movements by placing electrodes near the corners of the eyes. In the fall of 1952 changes in eye movement were recorded in sleep. Sleep became a scientific field. It was not clear who first had the brilliant idea that dreams related to rapid eye movements. Maybe Kleitman. Maybe Aserinsky. But what is clear is that William Dement, a medical student, was specifically asked by Kleitman to study the relationship between dreams and eye movements. He conducted the test by awakening the subjects (university students) during the rapid eye movement stage of sleep (REM) or during NREM stage (when no movements of the eyes could be detected), asking them to recall their dreams. Dement wanted to be a psychiatrist and was excited by Freud's theory of dreams. Freud considered dreams a safety valve of the mind. He felt that a key to the objective physiological analysis of dreams was in his hand. The concept of active sleep was challenging and promising. Dement contrasted the dream recall within these two distinct stages of sleep, REM and NREM. The relationship between REM periods and dreams was indisputable because every time he woke up the subject from REM sleep, the person gave long and elaborate responses, which were absent when the subject was awakened during the NREM stage.

It was an exciting time, when in sleep medicine, discoveries were made almost daily. One of them was the idea that schizophrenics did not have dreams, and their behavior is bizarre because they "dream" during the day. Dr. Dement tried to connect the number of dreams with the severity of schizophrenia. Unfortunately, it was not so simple. Schizophrenics have the same number of dreams as do medical students. If REM sleep is taken away, very abundant REM sleep will be seen the following night. This phenomenon is now called "REM Rebound Effect". Dr. Dement became a celebrity in psychiatric circles because it was assumed that if REM deprivation persisted, the psychic energy of schizophrenics would eventually erupt during their wakeful hours in the form of hallucinations or psychosis. Unfortunately, it was not the case.

"At what age do people start having dreams?" This question prompted William Dement and Howard Roffwarg to undertake the observation of newborn infants at Columbia-Rush Presbyterian Hospital in New York. Great minds think alike. About 40 years after Figurin and Denisov observed their infants in starving St. Petersburg, history repeated itself. Within one hour of their experiment, Dement and Roffwarg confirmed the abundance of rapid eye movements in infants' sleep.

Does it mean that newborns are dreaming eight hours a day, because REM is connected with dreams? What about a fetus or a newborn kitten, who have a 100 percent REM sleep? What do they dream about? The explanation came six years later. REM sleep reflects an intense neural activity, which is necessary for the proper maturation of the nervous system. One of the primary purposes of REM sleep is to provide organized patterns of genetically determined behavior for the development of the central nervous system. The maturation of the basic programs of the nervous system is completed by the age of one or so. Huge amounts of REM sleep are no longer necessary. The theory emphasized the importance of REM sleep. Later, Howard Roffwarg, demonstrated that even brief periods of REM deprivation in newborn kittens could lead to specific and very serious progressive brain changes.

New names appeared on the scientific horizon. Chicago always played an important role in the history of sleep research.   Dr. Rosalind Cartwright, a prominent psychologist, left her native Toronto for Chicago to study the psychology of dreams. There was no room for dreams at the University of Illinois Medical Center, she was told, except ... next to the men's room! Yes, you read right—the men's room! The beautiful, young, aristocratic Doctor of Psychology, Rosalind Cartwright accepted that. The large storage room on the other side of the men's room was converted overnight to a sleeping room and laboratory. After night fall, interesting scientific experiments took place there. Maybe sometime in the future, there will be a sign there, saying: "This is the place where the meaning of dreams was discovered." Dr. Cartwright is now a leading expert in dream therapy, Head of the Sleep Research Center at Rush-Presbyterian Hospital and teacher of hundreds of researchers and practitioners, including the author of this book. Dr. Cartwright's personal and professional life story proves that romantic dreams are stronger than difficulties of reality.

Another key person in the field of sleep medicine is Dr. Allan Rechtshaften, another Chicagoan. He works mostly behind the closed door of a physiological laboratory, but the results of his work are pivotal for researchers and physicians. Dr. Rechshaften and his colleague, Dr. Kales, did the tremendous and meticulous job of classifying and standardizing sleep stages and came up with the monumental "Manual for standard scoring of sleep stages." Now all doctors and researchers are speaking the same language, using the same terminology.

Dr. Rechtshaften's classical research on uniquely designed animal models (rats) gave tremendous insight into the functions of sleep. In 1975 Dr. Gerry Vogel at Emery University conducted carefully controlled studies on hospitalized patients. Exposing them to selective REM deprivation proved to alleviate severe chronic depression, inducing a very long remission. The results were as good as the most effective pharmacological treatment, and even better. For more than 15 years scientists have been trying to solve this paradoxical dilemma. If REM sleep is such an important stage, why does its partial elimination cure severe depression? If it is not so important, why are "rebound" phenomena so widespread and why is too much REM sleep associated with severe depression? The scientific explanation is the following: REM deprivation enhances drive-oriented and goal-oriented behavior. Depressed patients lose their appetite, their sex drive, and also their motivation. The exciting thing about Gerry Vogel's recent experiment is that it helps to move away from naive and simplistic views about relationships between physiological changes and mental disorders. For example, REM sleep and mental illness are associated closely, but not directly as cause and consequence. REM sleep can create hallucinations. These hallucinations, however, are not identical to those caused by LSD or schizophrenia. Discoveries of active sleep opened the door to new aspects of sleep research.

Sleep was not a major concern for doctors for a long time. They perceived sleep research as a series of academic exercises. Everything in medicine was related to daytime symptomatology, physiology, and pathology. Everyone assumed that the same physiology, symptomatology, and pathology applied to sleep. Stanford researchers under the direction of Dr. Dement were the first to seriously focus on sleep as an object of medical research. This was a conceptual break through. The Stanford School of Medicine opened the first comprehensive, free for service sleep disorder clinic. The

French doctor-neurologist, Christian Guilleminault, joined the clinic and committed himself to studies of sleep disorders. He worked with the disease called in Europe "the Pickwickian Syndrome". The name derives from Charles Dickens' famous *Pickwick Papers* in which fat Joe is described falling asleep even while standing up.   In 1965, two groups of European researchers had recorded the night sleep of such patients and reported periodic apnea (meaning brief cessation of breathing during sleep). One night in 1972 while recording a patient with insomnia, the technician noticed rather alarming periodic, very irregular heartbeats. Dr. Guilleminault later noted that the patient was not breathing. Since that time, recording respiration was added to any traditional sleep study. It was soon discovered that many adult patients who complained of excessive daytime sleepiness actually had a breathing problem, which was later named "sleep apnea". This was the first specific sleep disorder recognized by medicine.

Sleep medicine as a field was born at that time (around 1972). By the way, the first patients formally diagnosed as having sleep apnea were children. One was a 13-year-old girl and the second one an 11-year-old boy. Both were overwhelmingly sleepy in the daytime, even though they slept through the whole night quite well. In those days, physicians believed that excessive daytime sleepiness could be caused only by depression, low blood sugar, thyroid dysfunction or other endocrine problems, or by the illnesses of the central nervous system like encephalitis. These children did not have any of the described medical problems. In desperation, doctors used tracheotomy, the only treatment they had in those days. A surgically produced hole in the throat was kept open during sleep, permitting the patient to breathe and was closed during the daytime when breathing was normal. The results were amazing. An active, vigorous young person emerged. When in another instance a person's heart ceased beating for more than a minute, this recurring a hundred times during the night, doctors finally realized that sleep disorders should be taken seriously. Since then, information about sleep disorders and the possibility of treatment has spread and has gotten the attention of patients and doctors. In 1974, Dr. Elliot Weitszman, opened the world's second sleep clinic in Bronx, New York.

A lot has happened since that time. Researcher Mary Carskadon started a special camp for sleep and conducted tests for daytime sleep. Michael Thorpy, M.D. led the team of specialists who developed the *International Classification of Sleep Disorders*. Richard Ferber, M.D. devoted his medical career to the treatment of pediatric sleep disorders, and wrote the first book for parents on this subject. Stephen Sheldon and other physicians completed the first textbook *Pediatric Sleep Medicine*, intended for physicians. Today, there are about 500 sleep centers around the world. Pediatric sleep medicine is rapidly emerging as a field in its own right.

Many names and discoveries have not been mentioned here, but they will get due respect in the future. Some of them will be mentioned in the discussion on specific topics in the chapters to follow.

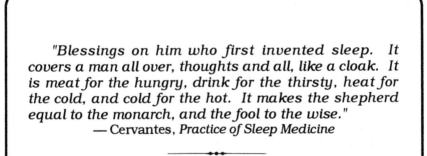

"Blessings on him who first invented sleep. It covers a man all over, thoughts and all, like a cloak. It is meat for the hungry, drink for the thirsty, heat for the cold, and cold for the hot. It makes the shepherd equal to the monarch, and the fool to the wise."
— Cervantes, *Practice of Sleep Medicine*

"Sleep, thou patron of mankind,
Great physician of the mind,
Who does nor pain nor sorrow know,
Sweetest balm of every woe."
— Sophocles

WHAT IS NORMAL SLEEP

Strange things happen to two billion people, when the earth turns one side away from the sun. One billion people on the dark side of the earth cannot stay awake and fall asleep. Another billion people desperately try to fall asleep at any expense. Some internal mechanism forces us to fall asleep even in situations when our lives are in danger. What is it?

Early theories of sleep suggested that sleep was a simple response to the environment. In other words, the enfeebled stimulation of darkness was insufficient to sustain wakefulness. Only strange or supernatural beings like the dark. Normal people can be active only in the sunlight. Now we know that sleep is not merely "time out", our brain is not "shut down", and our body is not "turned off" in sleep. Our brain, our body and our lives are extremely active during sleep, in fact as much as during the day. Sometimes even more active than during wakefulness. But we have not yet answered to our satisfaction the question, "What is sleep?" How can we define sleep?

The best and most recent definition was given by one of the pioneers of modern sleep science, Dr. William Dement, in his new book, *Sleep Watchers.* "The essential difference between normal wakefulness and normal sleep is the *direction of perception.*" In wakefulness we perceive and are conscious of the external world; we are engaged in it, and we respond to it. Wakefulness invigorates us and gives us the ability to find food, to reproduce—in short, to perform external and goal-oriented activity to survive in the real world. The fundamental essence of sleep, in contrast, is a disengagement from the real outer world and an engagement with the inner physical and dream worlds. It is interesting that this disengagement from the outside world is an active and quick process.

Our brain spends enormous amounts of energy to block or modify our sensory input for a complete perceptive shutdown. It is like a "switch" transporting us from the busy street to a dark movie theater, where marvelous or horrible experiences await us. Even if our eyelids are taped open during sleep, we do not see, although all visual signals (and likewise sound signals) are normally processed by our visual and auditory systems.

Furthermore, the central parts of these visual and auditory systems are even *more active* in some stages of sleep than during wakefulness. But the brain "sees and listens" to the inner world, and we are "blind and deaf" to outside stimuli.

Two metaphorical images are important to remember for our journey to the world of sleep.

First, there is the "switch", quickly shifting us from the real world to the kingdom of Morpheus (God of dreams in ancient Rome) and, somewhat slower, returning us back to real time. We have no idea why and how, just seconds before sleep envelops us, we see objects in the real world, are conscious of it, clearly perceive it and ourselves, while seconds afterwards, we are subjectively blind, not seeing at all. Even if we are barely aware of falling asleep, the next thing we realize is that it is morning. A great mystery! How this "switch" works is not merely an academic question; one of the few things we know is that it is not inborn but slowly develops with age. If the development of this "switch" is delayed or deviated, the child's sleep and wakefulness, in fact, his whole life, might be in danger.

Second, let us try keeping in mind the image of the "Magic Glove". Its fingers turn inside out as soon as we fall asleep, sensing our inner world. We have five perceptible organs: vision, hearing, tactile, smell and special deep sensors, receiving signals from our inner organs (so-called propioceptive sensations).

Imagine, that each finger of the "Magic Glove" holds one perceptive organ. During wakefulness this "Magic Glove" on our hand is facing towards the outside world. All the "fingers" are actively moving, like the legs of an octopus, analyzing and reacting to the outside world. At a certain point in sleep, the "Magic Glove" suddenly, but predictably, turns its fingers *inward* toward our body! What do they see, hear, smell, touch and perceive there? What do they react to and what do these magic fingers do? Help us to rest? To forget pain or remember it? To cure us or to make trouble?

As little as we know, we are sure about one fact: contrary to popular belief, our brain needs to rest in sleep no more than our heart needs to stop beating for a few hours every night, or our lungs to stop breathing for a "rest". The definition of sleep as "rest" was dismissed in about 1960, after REM sleep was discovered, which, as we mentioned before, is a completely distinct and extremely active stage of sleep.

The functions of sleep are still a mystery, and scientists spend many sleepless nights uncovering them. Besides general curiosity there are several very important reasons to investigate sleep: to find the answer to why people lose sleep, to clarify the nature of sleep and to find a way to communicate with the sensors of the "Magic Glove". To do this, scientists should find the way to communicate with each other: to have a consensus on the key processes that differentiate sleep from wakefulness, ways of measurement of sleep and its classification.

In order to identify, classify and measure sleep, it is necessary to record the electrical activity of several systems: not only the brain, but the eyes (to analyze the dream stages), the heart beats, the muscle tone and movements, respiration, etc. We can also measure many physiological parameters, including blood pressure, hormone secretion and even erection. For each case, the principle is the same: an instrument called the polygraph allows measurements to be made continuously throughout the night. In a sleep laboratory, tiny electrodes are carefully attached to the subject's scalp and face (they are lightly and painlessly glued on the skin surface). The wires are brought together into a bundle, attached to the scalp in a kind of ponytail, and then plugged into a panel on the headboard of the bed, which connects by a cable to the polygraph. All night the electrodes send signals from the brain and the body to the polygraph, which records them as an EEG (electroencephalogram—records brain activity), EOG (electrooculogram—records eye movements), EMG (electromyogram—records muscle activity), and so on. These waves are meaningless scribbles to the uninformed person, but very meaningful for the specialist. It is very easy to differentiate between the waking and sleeping patterns. Just a glance at the record from any short period allows the observer to know instantly whether or not the subject is asleep and what kind of sleep it is.

What do we know from these records? Sleep stages and their dynamics.

Stage 1: Light sleep. Person can be easily awakened. Eyes are slowly moving under closed eye lids. Heart rate slows down, breathing is calm, some "gross movements" for comfortable positions. Thoughts are still associated with daytime problems. Dream-like visions are very concrete. After 10 minutes in this sleep the person cannot recall what he heard, read, or asked about just prior to falling asleep.

Stage 2: Deeper sleep. Brain waves now have very specific patterns, called "spindles" and "k-complexes". No eye movements. Heart rate is slower but some underlying arrhythmia can be more apparent. In this stage, some forms of disorder may disappear but often they become more prominent, like headbanging, bedwetting, etc. Thoughts are usually absent, and dreams are rare and are not remembered if the person is awakened.

Stage 3-4: Very deep sleep. Because of predominance of special super slow brain waves (delta waves) this stage is called delta stage. No eye movements. Very slow heart rate and breathing. No dreams. Temperature is low.

Stage REM: Gets its name because of **R**apid **E**ye **M**ovements in this stage. Heart rate and breathing become irregular. Body is paralyzed except for jerks of small peripheral muscles. Active emotional complex dreaming. Thoughts are abstract and problem oriented.

Fig. 2.2   **What Happens to the Body in Sleep**
(discussion on next page)

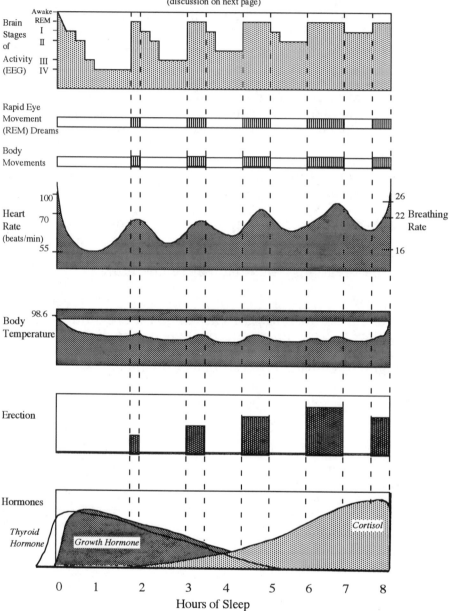

What Happens to the Body in Sleep

1. Brain waves
Very active electric and metabolic processes are sped up. The brain is going through specific stages and these stages are organized in cycles.

2. Eyes
There are two types of eye movements: slow round (stage 1-2) and fast jerky type — REM stage (Rapid Eye Movements).

3. Body movements
There are three types of body movements:
(a) Large, coordinated seemingly purposeful and goal-directed, like changing the position, straightening pajamas, etc. — predominantly in transitional and light stages;
(b) Isolated movements of extremities and head — predominantly in NREM sleep; and
(c) Brisk spasm-like movements of small distal muscles — predominantly in REM stage.

4. Heart rate and respiration
Decrease in NREM and become highly variable, sometimes very vast and arrhythmic in REM; causes nocturnal heart or respiratory problems.

5. Blood pressure
Generally decreases in NREM but is variable in REM. Possible high peaks in transitional stages which might cause strokes or heart attacks in vulnerable patients.

6. Erection
Surprisingly, erection is discovered to be an obligatory phenomenon of REM sleep since infancy with no connection to sexuality. In normal boys erections appear as many times as REM stages. Now researchers are trying to identify equivalent phenomena in girls.

7. Body temperature
A major biological rhythm highly connected with the sleep-wake cycle. As night progresses, the body temperature falls and reaches its lowest point during early morning hours. During REM episodes body temperature slightly increases, *but* meantime our internal regulator turns off, and the body follows outside temperature, sweating and shivering as temperature regulators are not working at that time.

8. Endocrine Variations
Growth hormone is doubled with the onset of sleep and in young children is secreted exclusively in deep sleep. Children literally grow in their sleep. The shift of sleep from night to day results also in the shift of growth hormone secretion. Opposite to the growth hormone, the "stress hormone" cortisol increases toward the morning. The thyroid hormone releases a maximum amount just before sleep. The connection between sleep structure and hormones in young children is quite strong, and large deviations in sleep structure might lead to deviations in endocrine functions.

9. Thought and Memory
The sleeping person is still thinking. At the beginning of the night in NREM sleep, thoughts are concrete and problem oriented. In the morning in REM, thoughts are abstract images, highly emotional and problem solving. We do not remember things just before falling asleep, but if something comes into our long-term memory, it plays back in sleep and stays imprinted forever.

The previous figure shows a typical pattern of the alternating stages of sleep through an eight-hour night. Just after the onset of sleep, a person is in the NREM stage for only about five minutes. Mentally this is a shift from the abstract to the visual imagination. Sleep onset imagery generally does not have the hallucinatory intensity and completeness of REM period dreaming, but it is still very important because the images are quite realistic and superimpose on the real senses. By the way, car accidents often happen when the driver shifts to stage 1 sleep just for a few seconds. After the onset of sleep, a healthy individual progresses rather quickly to stage 2 sleep— somewhat deeper sleep with reduced mental activity. During this stage quite unusual brain activity occurs. After about twenty minutes of stage 2, the sleeping person moves into the deep sleep of stages 3 and 4. This sleep is called the "Kingdom of the Vagal Nerve", because this nerve is slowing the heart beat and decreasing chest movements. The person now looks like a normal deep sleeper—calm, with rare breathing and a slow pulse. Then, in about 60 to 70 minutes the new type of sleep—REM sleep begins. During the first REM period, which lasts for about 10 minutes, dreaming is apparently continuous. Differences between the sleep stages are presented in the Table. There are usually five or six such cycles through the night. It is not uncommon that the last REM period might be as long as one hour.

A healthy adult spends as much as half of the night or more in stage 2 sleep, and another 25 percent of the time in REM sleep.   Unfortunately, real life is more complicated, and it confuses us with multiple dynamics of age development and social crises, individual orders and disorders. What present-day science has definitely established is that sleep is a very complicated, active, organized, and dynamic state of vigilance.

BIOLOGICAL CLOCKS

We live in time, and all our biological functions are organized in time as rhythms. There are many clocks inside us, which carefully monitor the rhythms of every process—be it physical, emotional, or mental. Unlike mechanical clocks, *biological* clocks are separate for each type of rhythm in terms of its period—separate for seconds, hours, days, months, or years. We can see our heart beats as our personal seconds, our breathing as our individual minute, our sleep cycle as our individual hour.

Each biological function has its own clock, and now scientists are working very hard to identify the place and mechanism of each of them, and the reasons why they sometimes break down or "misbehave". If the biological clock is not working properly, the body function of that rhythm can be dangerously accelerated, or delayed, or twisted. Examples would be arrhythmias—like cardioarrhythmia. If the biological clock responsible for the rhythm of some hormones "speeds up", the biological age of this person will change. A broken biological clock is the probable cause of a mysterious disease called progeria, when a small child starts to look like an old person—with symptoms like aging skin, teeth and hair loss.

Who is in charge of putting together so many clocks of hundreds of biological processes? Who is the "chief conductor" organizing our body into a precise orchestra? Among one of the main conductors is a small set of nerve cells just above the place where optical nerves enter the brain, called the *suprachiasmatic nucleus* (*supra* means "above" in Latin, *chiasma* means "crossing together"). This center is responsible for organizing biological functions around the day-night cycle, called the *circadian rhythm* (*circa* —"around", *dias* —"day"), which is 24-26 hours. Biological rhythms with less than 24 hours are called *ultradian* (like pulse or breathing).

Biological rhythms longer than 24 hours are called *infradian*. Examples include menstrual cycles (28-31 days), emotional cycle (28 days), peaks of intellectual activity (every 31 days), seasonal and yearly cycles. Interestingly, the 4 year period between Olympic games is not accidental. The peak of the highest physical performance has a 4 year period. Ancient Greek Olympians knew about that! Today we know how to calculate the peak of performance for each individual. Knowledge about biological clocks is important both for doctors and for patients. Even if people's biological clocks are basically inborn, their mechanisms undergo intensive adjustment in terms of coordination between internal clocks and external environmental stimuli (for example, sunlight, social clues—*zeitgebers*).

Circadian (day/night) rhythm is the basic denominator of all biological rhythms. Its development is associated with joy and pain, like everything in our life. Joy, when the child is peacefully asleep or happily alert in synchrony with the adults. Or else pain, when the adjustment of the clocks is going wrong, and disorders of sleep and alertness appear. There is a special scientific discipline called *chronobiology* which studies biological rhythms and their mechanisms. Many disorders have circadian fluctuations in the severity of their manifestations, with significant deterioration in sleep during the night.

Day-night differences in the manifestation or expression of many diseases, as well as the intensity of their symptoms, are well known. Although asthma has received the most attention as a circadian rhythm-influenced disorder, it is only one of the many common diseases known to differ in intensity or occurrence in cyclic fashion over the 24 hour period due to chronobiologic factors. The following illnesses belong to this group.

Allergic rhinitis with the major symptoms of sneezing, runny noise, and stuffy nose, typically being more severe upon arising than towards the middle of the activity span.

Asthma with the risk of symptoms being more than 100-fold greater during sleep than during alertness for the majority of patients.

Regular angina with chest pains and electrocardiograph abnormalities most commonly found during the first 4 to 6 hours of the daily activity span. Also, *Prinzmetal's angina* with the manifestation of electrocardiograph abnormalities restricted mainly to the sleep span.

The risk of *myocardial infarction* with the occurrence of *heart attack* is the greatest during the initial hours of activity.

Stroke commonly occurs early in the morning.

The highest incidence of *cerebral hemorrhage* is in the evening, about 3 hours or so before bedtime.

In *hypertension*, the peak blood pressure seems to occur at night, commonly during sleep.

Arthritis with the signs and symptoms of rheumatoid arthritis is most intense upon awakening, and those of osteoarthritis are worse around the middle or later portion of daily activity.

Ulcer disease with pain is typically aggravated after gastric emptying following daytime meals, and during very early morning hours when it results in the disruption of nighttime sleep.

Epilepsy with the occurrence of overt seizures is often detected during particular times of the day and night. "Sleep epilepsy" is thought to be different in terms of prognosis and treatment.

The time of a diagnostic evaluation might change the results. For example, allergic response to histamine in the morning is much lower than in the evening, so the results might be misleading.

It was discovered recently that the time of administration of medication might change the intensity and length of good and bad side effects of the medication. A new science—*chronopharmacology* is emerging. Research in chronopharmacology of asthma, for example, demonstrates that the circadian timing of the administration of corticosteroid hormone, prednisone (given in the morning) is crucial for optimizing its effect on asthma and minimizes or even averts its side effects. If taken in the late afternoon or night, prednisone has a high risk of side effects.

In conclusion, our understanding of the biology of human beings is every changing over time. Today, we must ask not just about the type of medications and the dosage, but inquire *when* to administer medications or take diagnostic tests.

MODERN THEORIES OF SLEEP AND ITS FUNCTIONS

Modern theories of sleep agree that all parts of the sleep-wake cycle are active processes. This means that there are special mechanisms that are turning off alertness, pushing us to sleep, switching one stage of sleep to another, and waking us up in the morning. The question is what are and where are those special mechanisms? Are they in the brain? In the blood? Are they big and do they occupy a large part of our brain, or a small and invisible part at the molecular level? The more we learn about sleep, the more we understand that there is not one, but *many* mechanisms on *all* levels. These mechanisms are involved in sleep and work together "orchestrating" them in normal situations.

The different existing theories of sleep emphasize different "conductors"

a) *Genetic theory* emphasizes the inborn genetic mechanisms of biological clocks. Researchers in this field identified a specific protein in one gene. If this gene is defective, the person has several diseases called "I cell" disorders with sleep problems being one of the symptoms.

b) *Molecular biology theory* is very fashionable these days. It emphasizes the regulatory role of chemicals not necessarily connected with genes, but more focused on neurotransmitters. Few chemicals are now believed to be closely connected with sleep, serotonin among them. The *serotonin theory* proposed by Dr. Jouvet was a driving force for many years. Serotonin is a neurotransmitter in the brain. Recent pharmacological data demonstrated that serotonin can induce and also suppress sleep. When serotonin is low in the blood, people's alertness starts to fluctuate, and they become irritable, aggressive, and are apt to act violently toward themselves and others. Now a new chemical, adenosine, is in favor. The *adenosine theory* by Misha Radlovatski suggested that coffee had a stimulating effect because it blocked adenosine. We are alert because our body produces our own endo-caffeine. If we drink too much coffee, it may be because our own endo-caffeine is not produced any more, and we therefore become dependent on coffee drinking.

In any case, now everyone is hunting for a specific sleep chemical. The sleep hypnotic factor was identified in human urine, defect of insulin regulating factors as found in the blood of patients with sleep apnea, etc. We may soon have a blood test identifying all our chemicals related to sleep, and, hopefully, this will help find new cures for our sleepless patients.

c) There is an interesting *immunologic theory* of sleep, based on the fact that some prostaglandins might induce sleep, and sleep increases the amount of prostaglandins. This supports the notion that sleep can treat our immune system. Some sleep disorders such as narcolepsy, bedwetting and others have specific immunologic characteristics.

d) *Anatomical theories* believe that there are special structures in the brain responsible for different aspects of sleep and alertness. This theory has been supported by recent findings of a special nuclei in the brain responsible for REM and for muscles' tonus in sleep. Reticular formation is famous for producing alertness, and so-called suprachiasmatic nucleus is responsible for our circadian biological clock. (See "Biological Clocks").

Historically, physicians have widely recommended sleep for the treatment of many ailments. Yet, the exact function of sleep remains elusive even today. At the same time, it is known that there exists a relationship between sleep and many biological processes, such as the immune system, tissue growth and repair, the function of the body to conserve energy, etc.

The theories presented below focus on the purpose of sleep and explain the numerous effects disordered sleep may have on health.

e) *Restoration theory* focuses on the proposition that sleep is a state required for enhanced tissue growth and repair. This theory also asserts that certain somatic (pertaining to the body) and cerebral (brain) deficits occur as the result of wakefulness, and that sleep either allows or induces physiological processes to repair or restore these deficits. This restoration, in turn, permits normal daytime functioning. As you may remember, there exist two types of sleep: 1) Non-rapid eye movement (NREM) sleep; 2) Rapid eye movement (REM) sleep. According to *Restoration theory*, NREM sleep is thought to function in the reparation of body tissue, and REM sleep in the restoration of brain tissue and the CNS (Central Nervous System) function. REM sleep may have evolved to "reprogram" innate behaviors and to incorporate learned behaviors and knowledge acquired during wakefulness.

f)   *Evolutionary and adaptive theory* emphasizes the development of numerous physiological functions following an orderly progression that mirrors evolutionary process. As we all know, animals sleep in many different ways, which are more often influenced by the environment and life style than by evolution of the species. One type of sleep appropriate for one species, for example, dog, cat or human, or else for the survival of dolphin in its aquatic environment, would be impossible. The lifestyle and environment of the dolphin play a far more significant role in the pattern of sleep development in this species. In some species sleep may enhance survival. Sleep may also be an instinctive behavior, a patterned response to stimuli that conserves energy, prevents maladaptive behavior and promotes survival. According to the *Evolutionary theory of sleep*, REM sleep cortical activation may perform additional survival functions.

g)   *Energy conservation theory* stresses sleep's function to conserve energy. Mammals exhibit a high correlation between metabolic rate and total sleep time. Energy reduction is greater during sleep than during spans of quiet wakefulness. Sleep provides spells of enforced rest, barring the animal from activity for extended periods. However, reduction in metabolism that occurs during sleep in humans is minimal and increase in sleep time does not correlate with increased metabolic rate.

h)   *Learning theory* centers on the role of sleep in memory and in the process of learning. It is known that retention of new information depends on activation of some brain function, which occurs at a critical period after registration of this information. The critical phase of information processing seems to occur during REM sleep. This hypothesis suggests that there are active consolidation mechanisms. Considerable brain activity occurs during REM sleep: brain oxygen consumption increases, as does cerebral blood flow; cortical and reticular neurons are highly active, indicating a vigorous, functional process. Effects of sleep on retention of memories acquired during wakefulness have been documented. REM sleep appears to hold special significance. The activity of REM sleep depends on the influences of vestibular mechanisms. Vestibular nuclei play a major role in the control of eye movements during sleep and wakefulness. If these nuclei are destroyed, eye movements during REM sleep are absent. Owing to many studies, the correlation between vestibular nuclei malfunction, REM sleep, and learning abilities has been determined in children with "Attention Deficit Hyperactivity Disorder" (ADHD), children with learning disabilities.

All this research and different approaches to the nature and functions of sleep assist us in understanding the significance of normal healthy sleep.

The challenge to the medical science is to distinguish the norm from pathology, and, most important, to develop new and successful treatments.

THE MYSTERY OF DREAMS

Dreams.   What can be more absurd, bizarre, unrealistic and illogical?   But for thousands of years, people believed that dreams had their hidden meaning, telling us vitally important things about our past, present and future, about our life and death, about ourselves and our children.

Dreams can be healing and can be killing. People believed this since the days of old. Ancient Greeks had such faith in the healing faculty of dreams that they performed a special ritual to invite dreams to cure them. In their hope for miraculous recovery, they made pilgrimages to sacred temples dedicated to the most popular God of Healing, Aesculapus of Epidaurus. The pilgrims participated in sacrificial and purification rituals, and went to sleep hoping that Aesculapus would visit them in their dreams.

How can we find out what about dreams is fact and what is fiction?   Should we believe or should we be skeptical?

Current science of sleep takes dreams seriously, and it can give us some guidance in distinguishing between facts and fiction.   There is enough data to state that dreams are not always meaningless fragments of our former experience. They are not a sort of byproduct of our brain when it engages in "cleaning closets" during its period of "rest". Dreams may be a result of active, creative, and meaningful reflections of the inner world, with their inner logic and goal. Dreams deserve to be studied seriously.

Dreams should be analyzed as real and unusual, but as comprehensive and cohesive reality with its own rules and principles. The common belief that the sleeping brain is shut down and that dreams are unconnected, fleeting, and disorganized chaotic images of the resting brain proved to be wrong. Dr. William Dement stated that "dreaming is an opportunity to hold a citizenship in two worlds, equally real but with different logic and limitations."

When we watch a movie or are reading a book in which the world has a certain fantastic but clear set of rules, we have no problem following the course of events. We find ourselves fully immersed in this fantastic world, and while we are "in it", we share every experience and every twist of the plot as if it were absolutely real.   From this perspective, the dream world is complete, and the brain is doing exactly what it would be doing in the real world when receiving information. The brain in sleep, specifically in REM sleep, works even harder than when it is awake. It is very interesting that if the person in his dream looks up, the sleep watcher will observe vertical eye movements. If we run in our dreams, researchers will record activity in corresponding muscles. The parallels of dream content and body response are striking. "In sleep, the brain plays God by creating its own world, and eliciting a response to it", observed Dr. William Dement. At the same time, our brain exerts a great deal of energy to conceal this activity from the outside world. To prevent our muscles from moving and our consciousness from interfering, the sleeping brain does indeed have to be more active than the waking brain.

I personally have always wondered, maybe not wakefulness but sleep is the more "basic stage" of the brain's activity. Maybe the waking brain is, in fact, the product of the sleeping brain. The study of animals showed that many survival habits develop first in sleep and only later are transferred to wakefulness. Puppies, for example, first start to bark while dreaming. Kittens make movements as if they are running. The human baby learns to smile and cry first in his sleep.

"Sleep is the mystery of life, a wonderful performance of nature."
— Henri Amiel

Types of Dreams

Dreams can save lives and dreams can kill.   How true is this? Let us judge for ourselves.

Here is an example from a World War II experience:

"He was sound asleep. After many hours of trudging through the forest in the German rear, the group of soldiers he was with found what looked like a safe place, and they went to sleep.

Suddenly, he saw his mother in his dreams. She was talking to him and agitatedly pointing to something. He was too exhausted to move. His mother came closer. She shook him, screamed at him, and ordered him to wake up.   The soldier woke up, bewildered and angry.   He looked around and noticed the Nazis crawling toward them. He was able to alert his companions, and they organized a successful defense."

This dream saved the soldier's life during World War II.   It was described by a prominent sleep physiology professor V.N. Kasatkin in his scientific paper *The Atlas of Dreams*, together with 16,000 other carefully selected dreams.   Professor N.Y. Grott in his book *Dreams as a Subject of Science* described many examples of warning signals coming to a dreamer during life-threatening situations: for example, earthquakes, floods, wars, etc. Dr. Grott cited a life-saving dream of one respected man who in his sleep saw his beloved girlfriend begging him to immediately leave the room. He woke up, frightened and surprised, and left the room. Just a few seconds later, the ceiling collapsed right into the bed where he was sleeping. Dr. Grott wondered if it were not the barely audible sounds of the ceiling cracking during the earthquake that reached the sleeping semi-conscious brain and gave the most powerful signal.

Serious and skeptical scientists accumulated a large number of believable facts about the existence of so-called *predictive dreams*. They are facts, not fiction. How can they be explained? There is what is known as the *statistical theory*. According to this theory, your specific worries produce specific images, and you see the same dreams many times. If your worry really comes through, you remember only this coincidence with the latest dream, forgetting that you saw the same dream many times. Dr. A. Shepovalnikov in his book *How to Order Dreams* offers many examples confirming this theory. A woman who had a dream that her son got killed in the war received a notice the next day informing her of her son's death. One explanation is that she saw the same dream over and over again but remembered only the latest one. Another explanation is that dreams are our connection to the "collective unconscious".

A 48-year-old experienced fireman sent a diary of his dreams written several years before. He described fires confirming his dreams in previous nights. He wrote, "If I see a fire in my sleep, the very next day, there will be a fire." He was offered to continue writing his diary for about one or two months, providing the exact dates of his dreams and dates of fires in his area. After a month and a half he sent this diary back to the sleep center. He described 17 fire dreams, but there were no real fires during that time.

Does this signify the end of the mystery of predictive dreams? Are all the breath-taking stories just a statistical trick? Let us not rush to conclusions. There is another theory, another group of predictive dreams, which are based on *extra sensitivity in sleep*. They confirm that there might be truth in predictive dreams. The father of my young patient asked me one day to decipher his dream: "During his service on a submarine, he fell into the cold water and tried to climb back to the platform. A heavy metal part pushed his chest down, preventing him from getting on board. He tried to scream, but the sound did not come out. He woke up in cold sweat, frightened to death." He saw this dream repeatedly, every night, for a few weeks with increased intensity. He felt normal during the day, working as a truck driver. Our team immediately performed an electrocardiogram, and discovered a large heart attack on the back part of his heart.

Medical journals report the following clinical examples: an old man died from a stroke His only symptom was having repetitive dreams about being scalped by Indians. A child told his mother that he saw a dream about his friend hitting him in the right ear. A few days later, he was diagnosed with *otitis media* (ear infection).

These dreams, with very concrete, focused, and clear repetition can be of important diagnostic value. We call them *diagnostic dreams."* Sub-sensory stimuli are intensified in sleep and reach the central nervous system to produce specific images.

Another medically and socially important type of dream is *suggestive dreams."* They are fascinating dreams which have a specific meaning for us. They influence our mood and force our behavior to change.   They may sometimes result in death.

"The grandmother called her family in the morning and said calmly, 'My children. It's time for me to say good-bye. I saw your father in my dream. He told me to come and join him.' The next morning, the old woman did not wake up". Have you heard this type of story? I heard these same words from my grandfather, and this is exactly how he died. What is this? Just superstition, super-sensitivity or is it a hidden death wish? Or is it the power of self-suggestion which might turn our life off? Animals clearly have the gift to sense their own deaths. Elephants, for example, start the long trip to their place of final rest shortly before they die.

Another documented case: during the morning medical rounds, a young patient told the doctor that in his dream a relative came and awakened him with the words: "Be awake, son. Be awake. You will die on the 19th." Two months later, exactly on the 19th, the patient died in his sleep. Do not underestimate the power of self-suggestion.. During sleep or in an altered state of consciousness, our hidden worries magnify significant emotional images to the level of post-hypnotic suggestions, making a powerful influence on our body, mind, and behavior.   Have you heard the term "anniversary phenomenon"? When a person is afraid that he will die at age 47, on his birthday, just like his father, and this person actually dies on that exact day? There is also the "positive anniversary phenomenon".   My terminally ill grandfather on my mother's side told me that he will not die until he has finished the book of his life. He lived six more years, surprising all doctors, and died a few days after he had finished his work.

Sometimes, a coincidence supports public belief in the power of dreams. A young man from Florence saw one day in his dream that he was maimed and killed by a monument of a lion in front of the nearby church. In the morning he told his dream to his friends, and all of them decided that it was ridiculous to believe in it. To prove that he was not afraid, the young man put his hand into the lion's mouth in front of an assembled crowd and...screamed with pain. He was bitten by a scorpion. The young man died. This tragic coincidence stunned people. The story became a legend and was used by the church to confirm the power of God.

There are many other instances where the impact of dreams on behavior may be less dramatic but equally tragic. Dr. Shepovalnikov cited a number of cases, where emotionally unstable adolescents act upon their dreams. For example, a teenager saw in his dreams that he killed his teacher. He became obsessed with this idea, and did not carry out his plan only because of timely hospitalization. The suggestive effect of dreams is much more common in children who sometimes may not be able to distinguish between dreams and reality.

There are four factors inducing the suggestive effect of dreams:

1. The suggestive effect of dreams comes from their *unclear images*.

2. We always believe in the situation in sleep. *During sleep, everything is real.* What would be absurd for the awakened mind seems real and logical to us when we are sleeping.

3. *Sensations* in sleep coming from our body, our skin, our nose, our mouth and inner organs, make strong "suggestions" in sleep.

4. Reviving a *long term memory* in sleep.

Altogether these factors produce the extremely believable effect of dreams and influence the person's behavior.

You may also know some interesting and convincing examples of how things escaping from your wakened attention come to you as images of dreams. What we failed to pay attention to during the day may suddenly become highlighted in our dreams. One funny example is described by Dr. Grott: French scientist DeLagua had a dream one day that instead of the broken old lamp outside of his apartment, there was an elegant copper lamp. He told his family at breakfast about this strange dream. It turned out, to his embarrassment, that the new lamp had been at the door for the past week. He just did not pay attention to it.

This specific phenomenon of memory being revived in sleep is probably the basis for the secrets of so-called *discovery* and *creative dreams*. Dr. Grott told this story, as an example: one man was in a financial crisis after the death of his father, and he lost several vitally important documents. In his dream, his father came back and clearly indicated the location of the papers.

You might know or have experienced some interesting examples of how problems of real life are solved in sleep. The Russian chemist Mendeleev, author of the famous periodic system of chemical elements, first saw his periodic table in his dreams. He woke up and put his dreams together on paper.

German chemist, Friedrich Kekule, visualized his famous formula of the benzene ring as a dance of six monkeys. The amazing ability of dreams to be a source for creative ideas was emphasized by Dr. Grott. As a striking example, he cited 300 poems written by the poet Kollezidger in his sleep.

Problem solving in sleep is a common experience. Very promising techniques now exist to develop such skills. The present advances in sleep research demonstrated that dreams can be predictive, diagnostic and very creative. Dreams may also be emotionally exciting. In sleep, our emotions are not restricted. We feel blissfully happy or endlessly depressed. We are ecstatic or terrified. In sleep we experience flying and falling, moving and spinning. Scientists have yet much to learn before they can fully understand the mechanism of how this happens, the reasons why our body and mind have these feelings, and how this can be used to our benefit.

Two uses of dreams seem to have the most potential benefit, one using the messages from the dreams to help address crises that we are facing, and the other being the use of lucid dreams.

In *crisis dreaming*, important thoughts, ideas and problems that people are currently facing invade their dreams and alter them. Often, the themes of the dreams are immediately related to the issue at hand. No matter how many dreams the person has during the night, they all seem to be connected in some way. Since the theme in these dreams happen to be identical to those weighing heavily on the dreamer's mind, they can be referred to as *crisis dreams*. There can be many advantages to having such dreams. Dreams involving problems and situations that require people to make decisions can prove to be helpful. They may help a person understand his or her own inner fears and feelings about a particular decision. They may also be important in identifying mental obstacles that may stand in the way of some accomplishment.

In other cases, crisis dreams reflect the recurrence of traumatic experiences. Examples would be kidnapping, rape or certain military experiences. Thinking about these occurrences can create feelings of guilt and blame, leading to recurring dreams that focus on the experiences itself and the events leading up to it or following it. However, if the dreams are analyzed and the problems therein are recognized and properly addressed, these dreams can be a great help in treatment, and assist the person in recovering from a traumatic experience.

Lucid dreaming opens up a whole new world to the human experience. Lucid dreaming occurs when you are conscious and aware of being in a dream state. You are then able to manipulate the content of the dream and its influence upon the body. Often, this occurs when, during a dream, something unusual happens that normally would not have taken place in real life, tipping you off that you are dreaming. This unusual event is called a *dreamsign*. After realizing that you are dreaming, you will have remarkable control of the dream world and your experiences in it. Almost always, realization is accompanied by a heightening of the senses (observing brighter colors, hearing more sounds, etc.). These pleasurable sensations are accompanied by the ability to do anything you want to, literally manipulating the dream world.

In order to induce lucid dreaming, you must first be able to recall your dreams—at least one a night. Then, you need to practice testing what state you are in, whether dreaming or awake. This state test is performed many times a day when you are conscious so that you learn to differentiate between the sleeping state and the dreaming state. Once you have mastered this, you will eventually become used to testing your state in your sleeping hours as well. When you ask yourself during a dream if you are dreaming and realize that you are, you will have achieved lucidity.

One benefit of lucid dreaming is to rehearse a task that you are about to perform. For example, if you are eager to succeed in a basketball game that you have the next day, you can practice all of your moves the night before. When you actually play the next day, you will be surprised to find that you feel comfortable with your game plan and know exactly what you are doing. This usage of mental practice to improve physical skills is being currently researched, and new evidence points to the success of this technique.

Through this dream technique, self-confidence can also be gained. An example would be a speech that is to be performed soon. A speaker can rehearse a speech and imagine a large crowd, thus practicing the speech and getting used to the crowd at the same time. In some cases, healing oneself may be accomplished by willingly being able to control certain body functions. And finally, fears and lack of self-confidence can be fought as one can fight and conquer any force that threatens one's peace of mind.

There are some dreams that seriously threaten one's peace of mind, among them are *nightmares*. According to Calvin Hall's research of 10,000 *"normal"* dreams, two-thirds of them were negative with feelings such as anger, confusion, betrayal and fear being prevalent. Such dreams deserve separate analysis and will be dealt with in detail. (See Part 5.) Other types of dreams, among them *wet dreams* are usually associated with a certain age in a person's life. But before we move to a discussion of how sleep and dreams develop throughout the lifespan, let us try to answer a seemingly easier question: when do we dream?

When Do We Dream?

The scientific answer would be that we dream during both NREM and REM sleep, but the types of dreams are different. It depends on the stage. In *NREM sleep*, it is a very concrete, thought type of dream. After falling asleep, we continue thinking about what happened during the daytime. Our dreams tend to be more rational, related closely to the events of the previous day. Emotional, fantastic, and illogical dreams are associated predominantly with *REM sleep*. Intense dreaming activity and suppression of the muscular activity are the main characteristics of the REM stage. If our muscular activity was not suppressed, we would be moving around in response to any sleep images. This would be extremely dangerous.

People experience several different dreams throughout the night, since there are three or four REM periods each night. We wake up between each part of these cycles, nearly 15 times a night. However, we usually forget most of these awakenings and dreams, and only remember bits and pieces of the last one or two dreams that we have each night. The material for our dreams comes from the same senses that we use in our lives during the day. However, compared to external stimuli, most of the things we experience during sleep are internal sources, such as memories, residue from the day, etc.

We can presently single out five important factors that influence the content and intensity of dreams. First, there are the emotional and physical conditions prior to sleep. Second, the so-called exogenic environmental stimuli during different phases of sleep (stimuli from the environment). Third, the endogenic (inside the body) stimuli coming from different sensors, joins, i.e. inner organs. Fourth, the reviving inner and long term memory associations and fifth, the timing and intensity of our REM sleep.

The combination of different factors and their influence on dreams, as well as what factor is predominant, changes in different periods of life and in certain situations.

The Meaning of Dreams

What do dreams really mean? A recent popular theory called the Activation-Synthesis Theory about the meaning of dreams has been offered by two Harvard psychiatrists and sleep researchers, Allan Hopson and Robert McCarley. Based on the fact that during REM, brain cells in cats have explosive bursts of activity, which disrupt continuity of brain function, Hopson and McCarley suggested that *dreams are an attempt by the brain to make sense of this very intense but basically meaningless activity*. According to their theory, dreams merely have a transparent, not a deep meaning. There is no need, according to them, for "deciphering" dreams. Interpretation of dreams is unnecessary, if only because the same dream image can mean different things to different people. This negative view on the meaning of dreams, especially coming from psychiatrists with psychological training, is to be taken seriously. However, even now, when Freud is no longer in great vogue, we continue feeling that dreams *do* have some profound message for us. So, is it the end of another beautiful tale, that dreams hide our secret destiny?

There are some ways, however, to resolve this controversial question. Are dreams purposeful and meaningful, or are they generated and influenced largely by the random processes in the brain? One way around is to avoid confusing terminology. What is the difference between *meaning* and *purpose*? While dreams cannot be both random and purposeful, they can be both random and meaningful. For example, the random formation of the clouds seems to resemble a face. However, clouds did not purposefully take the shape of the face. The same is true of dreams. Dreams might be like Rorschach's cards with ink blots which uncover different personal meanings. The point is that we should continue searching for the meaning of dreams, because we, parents and children, healthy and sick, doctors and patients, are anxiously attributing some deep meaning to dreams. In these hidden meanings we search for clues which will help us find new cures for disorders of sleep and alertness.

To the honor of science, the random process theory is falling out of grace. More and more facts support our intuitive feelings that dreams are not a product of chance.

Sigmund Freud offered the theory which is impossible to test: in the dream, the subconscious mind works with "forbidden impulses." This is a fascinating hypothesis which is unfortunately very difficult to demonstrate. These impulses can, supposedly, be revealed by a method Freud called "free association" but this method, by its very nature, cannot be tested in a lab.

Freud based his theory on the relationship between dreams and sex. The connection between dreams and sex seems unquestionable to many. More about dreams and sex later. (See Part 4)

The discovery of lucid dreams signaled a positive, active approach to the meaning of dreams and to how they could be used for people's benefit.

A Stanford graduate student in psychology, Stephen LaBerge, asked Dr. Dement to study in the sleep laboratory a phenomenon he himself commonly experienced: knowing that you are dreaming *while* you are dreaming. They recorded Stephen LaBerge in a sleep lab, agreeing that he would give a previously chosen signal as soon as he realized that he was dreaming. This is how the hypothesis that a person can be "awake" in dreams became a scientific fact. It was now also a fact that the dreamer could control his dreams and communicate with the outside world. Dream control became a separate discipline. In 1921 Mary Arnold-Forster published a book called *Studies in Dreams*. It was basically a diary of her dream adventures. She often knew when she was dreaming and had learned to "direct her dreams", going on trips around the world and making conscious decisions about when and where to travel. It sounded very bizarre at that time, but now, in 1994, we do not laugh at her but admire her book. Control of dreams has now become a serious treatment modality. Dr. Stephen LaBerge is now President of the Lucidity Institute. There is even a journal today entitled *Dreaming*.

I believe that lucid dreaming is a gift with a special function. Its purpose is to enable people to use the nighttime world in order to experience alternatives as if they were real. This may be a source of our intuitive wisdom, which is trying to arrive at correct decisions while we are asleep.

Memory in Sleep

In my medical school years, I was fascinated by the idea that in our dreams our genetic memory from our ancestors can be revived. Connection with the past! I read Dr. Kasaneev's papers about genetic memory which is activated in sleep and was fascinated by the idea of being able to talk to my "peers" from previous generations and to look into the future. I studied new techniques of learning in sleep (*Suggestopedia*) developed by Dr. Losanov from Bulgaria. Although scientific data are controversial, I still believe in the idea that somehow, the sleeping mind will reveal its secrets and enable us to retrieve the knowledge accumulated in a thousand years. I believe that the depth of our brain, and its treasures are waiting to be discovered.

This story really happened. The news put the Soviet KGB on the highest level of alert. The cleaning lady in the Turkish Embassy, whom everyone knew to be completely illiterate and who had lived all her life in a poor remote village, suddenly started to talk in the most refined Russian and Turkish languages. She cited famous poems and sophisticated political monologues. It happened when she fell seriously ill and was bedridden with a high fever. Someone sitting at her bedside was able to engage in a conversation with her and was astounded by her knowledge, and the style of her speech. High security was established; it looked like a top secret agent was uncovered. The fever disappeared, and her magical talents with it. The poor woman woke up scared to death from all the unwanted attention. Her incredible talent cost her dearly; she spent the following several years in prison. It was later discovered that when she was a young girl, an exiled Russian poet and diplomat lived in her home for a few years. Without much effort, her brain memorized long speeches and poems cited by this diplomat. Later more reports of a similar nature became known in Germany; for instance, an old woman had a low skill manual job at a metal factory. Suddenly in her sleep, during acute malaria, she started to speak fluent Latin. It was similarly discovered that during her early childhood, a priest from Italy living next door used to sing religious poems in Latin.

Our long term memory retains everything. To find the way to its secrets, is another story and a challenge.

An amazing discovery was made when it was confirmed that the memory of the dreaming brain is as accurate as a waking one. In 1972 William Dement, James Bussell and Terry Pivik asked subjects to recall their dreams and correlated their eye movements with the contents of their dreams. They recorded eye movements at the same time. After awaking, the subject was able to remember the dream that he, for example, dropped a book. His eyes looked down. If the recollection was poor, the connection was generally poor, too. A similar experiment was conducted on an awake person. The team recorded his eye movements and then suddenly asked him what he had been thinking about a few minutes earlier. The corresponding eye movements were even less apparent than during sleep. Memory during wakefulness is not much better than memory during sleep. So, why do we remember during the wakeful times much better than in sleep? Reliable stability of the outside world, that is what helps us. It reminds us every time about things that are not changed. In dreams, everything is changing, and flowing, and flexible. If we had better access to the dream world, we would have learned a great deal.

What is especially important to know is that if one sleeps for more than 10 minutes, one will not remember what happened or what was discussed within about 10 to 15 minutes *prior* to the onset of sleep. This is so-called *retrograde amnesia*, which means loss of memory just prior to the onset of sleep. When the subject is suddenly awakened, about 10 minutes after he has fallen asleep, and is asked to recall what things he remembers, it is almost invariable that he is unable to recall what was being discussed immediately before sleep, but only what occurred 10, 15, or 20 minutes prior to that. As we progress into the dream world, previous information is erased. The rate of decay might vary. Memory of colors, for example, may fade more rapidly than memory of forms. Memory in dreams is very different. Maybe the brain has its own "dream bank" which is locked up for some time. When we recall a dream, it looks bizarre, but why are we not astonished and not skeptical *during* the dream, accepting it as real? Why would the dream the next day start from that place where it "cut off" the night before? Why do dreams, the same dreams, repeat from one night to another? Is it because we know that when we are dreaming, it is not real? Or perhaps for a dreamer, bizarre events and logic are normal?

Interestingly enough, there are individual differences in how much people remember their dreams. It has some relationship with the logical characteristics: people who are introverted, repressed, or very tired have trouble recalling dreams. Those who are less inhibited, more open and extroverted have a better ability to recall their dreams.

Development of Sleep and Dreams
Through The Life Span

Some researchers believe that sleep plays specific roles in specific ages. Perhaps serving as a developmental "trigger" in infancy, as a "stabilizer" in adolescent years, and as a "healer" later on. In any case, the differences in sleep architecture are significant for different age groups throughout the life span. Pathology of sleep is different for different age groups as well. This is probably the right place to mention that the study of sleep in young children is not an easy task for doctors and for parents alike. The process of the study of children in sleep may some day be a topic for a book by itself. There are lots of comic and tragic stories we can tell you. Dr. Dement shared the story of his first sleep recordings of children, when he was a student at the Stanford School of Sleep Medicine. He was able to coax a next door neighbor and her five year old daughter into the sleep study. The girl was obviously very tense but allowed the placement of EEG electrodes to her head and her earlobes. The next morning, he was able to get the little girl's head electrodes off fairly easily with acetone, but the electrodes on her earlobes were another matter. They just would not come off. In the meantime, she kept screaming and crying. Finally, he simply cut off the blue electrode wires, leaving about an inch protruding, and said, "Well, now you have earrings." The girl laughed, and left the lab happy. One week later, he drove by her apartment house and saw this little girl playing outside. The blue wires and electrodes were still there. Dr. Dement said that he had nightmares that the girl grew up, became a mother, and had her own children. She still had blue electrodes attached to her earlobes!

Jokes aside, it is tremendously difficult, technically and emotionally, to evaluate young children in sleep. Tiredness, capriciousness, restlessness, pulling electrodes off are just a few of the problems. Add to them trying the parents' patience. Time pressure: it has to be done before the child falls asleep or gets too agitated. Difficulties of pre-sleep calibration of the equipment; replacing electrodes during the night; awaken the child who might subsequently scream for hours are also factors to cope with. Maybe all of the above are the reasons why many sleep labs had disassociated themselves from pediatric departments. Pediatric sleep medicine still waits for its supporters. And they are coming about, working hard to get solid data about children's sleep.

In 1940, Nathaniel Kleitman established that the total sleep time for newborns was about 16 hours. From this, it was later shown that approximately half (8 hours) consisted of REM sleep. Unlike adults, infants usually drop into REM immediately after wakefulness, bypassing NREM sleep. Newborns do not have stage 4 (very deep sleep), which they develop in the course of the first year of their life. Rapid eye movements in babies are much more active and restless than in adults. They also have no muscle paralysis. Some other features, too, make active sleep of newborns very different from REM stage of adults. REM periods in newborn infants tend to be interrupted every few minutes, usually for four or five seconds. Writhing body movements, simulating wakefulness, occur especially often when their eyelids are semi-open.

Thus, newborn infants sleep about 16 hours daily in short periods of two to four hours. Over the first year, sleep time decreases rapidly, and infants spend more time awake, napping regularly until the age of about two or three. Sleep and napping times have tremendous individual differences! Children 8-10 years old are characterized by very sound sleep (which means it is very difficult to awaken them, especially during the first half of the night). The need for sleep seems to taper off with age. Again, there are tremendous individual differences. In general, adults seem to have a decrease of stage 4 sleep, and in the elderly, stage 4 disappears completely.

How much do we need to sleep? The definition is simple: The need is the amount of sleep required to maintain a reasonable level of alertness in the daytime.

The most predominant feature of a person's sleep is a
special phenomenon overlooked by many: sleep
fragmentation. It is especially important for children and
the elderly. When Drs. Carskadon and Brown carefully
scrutinized the records of four health elderly subjects, the
results were rather astonishing. They found 160-350 brief
prominent transit arousals. It meant that sleep was
interrupted about every minute! It is not surprising that
older people are sleepy during the day. No wonder we
have this common stereotype of the advanced-aged
grandpa nodding off repeatedly in his rocking chair. What
is important for us to consider is that sleep fragmentation
in children is even more crucial than in adults.

Let us talk a little about how dreams develop from
childhood to adulthood. While looking at my sleeping
daughter, my grandmother used to say, "Children grow in
their sleep." For a long time, I perceived this as a
metaphorical saying by the wise old owl. Recent
physiological and biochemical findings have proven one
more time that "old" is by no means synonymous with
"dumb". The old observation became a new fact: children
do grow predominantly in sleep, specifically during NREM,
stage 4 deep sleep. It was known for a long time that
growth is regulated by the so-called *somatotrophic
hormone*, (a growth hormone produced by the anterior
pituitary (the hypophysis)—a gland on the bottom of the
brain). But only recently it was discovered that this
hormone is released only in a certain period of the night.
Specifically, this hormone is released in the blood stream
predominantly during the deepest stage—stage 4 of NREM
sleep—and only during the first couple of cycles (which
means during the first half of the night). The longer this
stage lasts, the more growth hormone is released. If for
some reason NREM sleep is destroyed or disrupted, less
growth hormone will be released. It is a very important
fact, because this may explain the relationship between
sleep problems and endocrine dysfunctions. The
relationship between normal sleep and endocrine functions,
and between sleep problems and endocrine dysfunctions,
might explain another strange notion expressed by
physicians of the past: That very young children with
profound and chronic sleep disorganization had some
typical facial features. Specifically, facial features of

children with adenoids (facia adenoica) and special faces of children with bedwetting and apnea. (See illustration.)

In biochemical laboratories deep inside our brain, under the misleading quietness of a motionless body, highly intensive metabolic activities are taking place. This intensive activity started during our mother's pregnancy, intra-uterus. The notion that during intra-uterus, the baby is oversleeping, is wrong. It is as wrong as the belief that sleep is a state of being "shut down". There is much data telling us that the fetus is receiving many stimuli: sounds, vibrations, pressure, smell, and motions. Electrophysiologic methods allowed differentiation of at least three functional conditions in the fetus: 1) active sleep, 2) quiet sleep and 3) a state similar to wakefulness. Periods of wakefulness are brief, but different in intensity and very interestingly connected with the activity and psychological condition of the mother. It is exciting to know about the relationships between the activity of the inborn baby and the mother's condition in the external world. It is important to remember that a newborn baby is not a *tabula rasa* with zero experience, that he or she has already developed some sleeping structure and some basic biorhythms. After birth, and with age, the sleep and wake cycle undergo may changes. Sleep gets shorter but more complex. As we have mentioned, a one year old baby sleeps up to 16 hours a day. A four year old sleeps for 12 hours. A 12 year old sleeps for 10 hours. When it comes to adolescents, sleep time drops to six hours because their life style is very disrupted. They chronically lack sleep but they do not feel it until they face a problem. This is typical for adolescents.

Sleep is a function of the body system as a whole. Dreams are a function of sleep, and are, therefore, a product and a mirror of the activity of the body. If a person dreams about running, his body feels as if it were really running: breathing and heartbeats quicken, the electrical activity of the muscles in his arms and legs is increased, and it looks like alternating bursts similar to what happens with somebody running. But this is invisible to the outside world due to the paralysis of large muscles. If for some reason the brain forgets to paralyze his legs, the sleeping person might really start running and might hurt himself or others. The same thing happens when a child dreams about movements, or has dreams with an emotional content. The physiological characteristics of anger, fear, and excitement are real when the child feels it in his dreams. Because these reactions are very real, we have to conclude that the world of dreams is real. Moreover, the physiological and emotional reactions are much more intensive in dreams than during wakefulness. In other words, in sleep, children are far more anxious, much more fearful and terrified than during wakefulness.

When does a child start to see dreams? How do they change with age? Some believe that the dream is the product of a mature brain. Others believe that newborns see dreams from a very early age. If we accept the notion that rapid eye movements in sleep are always associated with dreams, then we should admit that dreams occur in newborn babies. Does this mean that the smile of a one month old infant, an emotional grimace on his face, is a reflection of his dreams? The answer should probably be no. It is a reflection of complicated, but more basic activity of the central nervous system. Some enthusiasts of the theory of dreams in newborns go so far that they use these for political goals, such as the anti-abortion movement.

It has been demonstrated that dreams can be seen in other than REM stages. Also, REM is not always associated with dreams. Infant sleep with rapid eye movements, the so-called active sleep, is not equal to the paradoxical REM sleep of adults. In addition, the world of dreams cannot be analyzed without a verbal story. A child can verbally describe his feelings and remember them somewhere around the age of two. The more nervous the child, the earlier he remembers his dreams.   The first reports on dreams are described at about the age of two. Generally, dreams of young children reflect emotionally significant events of the previous days.   An interesting example of a childhood dream was described by the founder of dream psychology, Sigmund Freud in his book *Psychology of Sleep*. A three year old boy gave a gift to a beloved uncle: a box with fresh blueberries. The little boy wanted them so much himself that the next morning he woke up happily screaming, "Hermut (means him) ate blueberries all night long." Freud believed that dreams of young children were free from symbols due to the primitive nature of their psyche structures. His own daughter, Anna Freud, proved that even her famous father could be wrong. Very small children may have symbolic dreams. The more neurotic and nervous the child, the more traumatized emotionally—the earlier his dreams can be documented. The content of dreams changes quite clearly with age. In our research, we have been able to find out the following stages in the development of dreams.

Healthy children, three to five years old, often describe their dreams. We can easily recognize very familiar negative images introduced to the child at one time or another. It is a big gray wolf. It is a policeman. A big bear. They look exactly like illustrations from a book or like television cartoons. These images are aggressive towards the child. "This big wolf wanted to eat me," said one child.

In dreams of five-year olds, not one but many images appear. This many images sometimes construct quite complicated situations, symbolically reflecting a real one, for example, a recent family conflict. What is new is that the child becomes an *active* participant in his dream: trying to run away, escape, or defend himself.

In dreams of seven or eight year olds, concrete images become very rich. They may be a group of peers or school teachers. The situations in their dreams become more fantastic at the same time. The world of dreams acquires a new fascination. Secret planets, mysterious happenings, imaginary friends. The child is not a victim anymore, but a hero and a superman. His awakenings are happy from sensations of flying and singing. I am now in what is euphemistically called a mature age, but I still remember these happy mornings when I would wake up after flying and feeling so omnipotent in my dreams. In my meditation, these are the feelings I try to reproduce. But not all children are so fortunate. My profession gives me too many examples where happy dreams end with a rude awakening into a disruptive, abusive, and frightening daytime world. In this case, the child does not want to *really* wake up. He wants to stay in his dreams where he has imaginary but true friends. For such children, the dream world is better than reality. The healthy, natural defense may, in many situations, unfortunately, bring about an unhealthy chain of events: children may become inattentive, acquire learning problems, become insensitive to others, or develop multiple personalities.

Adults, please do not destroy your children's happy dreams.

Ten- or 12-year-old children experience movements and other sensations in their dreams. They are sometimes so powerful, clear and real that they are indistinguishable from hallucinations. In dreams children can now smell, feel, touch and see colors, etc. Very often these sensations get temporarily disorganized. In this case, time and space relations become distorted, giving another dimension to the strange world of dreams. For example, "Oh, the skeleton grew and grew and grew all the way!" Even the perception of their own body can change: "Doctor, help me! My hands grew in sleep. They became so enormous that I am afraid of them!"

In adolescents, dreams become multi-serial, which might continue from one night to another. In cases of sleep disorder, dreams (See Part 6 on "Nightmares") become repetitive with intensive frightening experiences. Even with healthy children, repetitive dreams are quite common. Interestingly enough, children often see themselves from a distance: "I saw myself today in a dream." "I saw a film about myself." Now is the appropriate time to emphasize once again that dreams are real to the child. A dream may have a profound impact on the child's daytime reaction and behavior, especially if it becomes repetitive. Dreams from this period may be used for diagnostic purposes. Used as signals for common medical, behavior or emotional problems. Dreams of adolescents are a very interesting, controversial and unresearched topic. Many adolescents are so sleep-deprived that they do not report dreams at all, but two most significant types of adolescent dreams deserve very serious attention from parents and doctors. One of them is so-called *wet dreams* and another, *creative dreaming.*

Wet dreams. Who does not know about this strange phenomenon that boys have in their sleep? They wake up with ejaculations and sexual dreams. What is surprising from our interviews of such awakenings after wet dreams, is that the children could not describe the details of the sexual content. It was visually vague, but very strong emotionally. Did sexual dreams induce an orgasm with ejaculation, or did physiological orgasm and ejaculation induce sexual dreams? We still do not know the final answer. Research shows that the second option is the most likely one. In any case, we know for a fact that wet dreams are normal. Adolescents with sexual variations dc not ordinarily report having wet dreams, but let us not jump to conclusions. More extended research is needed (See Part 4 on *Sleep Problems in Adolescents*). It is interesting that sexual dreams in girls at this age are sometimes associated with a sensation of pain in the pubic area.

Creative dreams. Nowadays, when the main focus is placed on pathology, normality, gift and creativity are modestly waiting for the attention of parents, teachers, physicians, and researchers. Adolescents are very creative people. Do not let the violence, drug abuse and destructive behavior of some adolescents overshadow their most important traits: creativity, flexibility, and the inexhaustible resources of their body and mind. This is a brief period of our life when we feel truly omnipotent. Society is responsible in which way (on the right or wrong side of the law) this omnipotence is going. How this omnipotence will be used—for productive or disruptive actions—depends on us: parents and society. One adolescent described a new construction of bridges he saw in his dreams. His sketches were later used. My daughter told me one morning that after many hours of futile attempts, she solved the homework problem in her sleep. The well-known expression "sleep on it" has some truth. The adolescent can see his life ahead of him. All my life I am trying to prove an idea which I saw in my adolescent dreams.

The different content of dreams also have different physiological representations. For example, the brighter, the more interesting and creative the dreams, the more stable and healthy are the physiological processes. The increase in creative dream activity can improve health!

A significant decrease in dream activity may lead to a so-called "vegetative storm" with very serious consequences. Movements are another interesting and important evidence of dreams. The general rule here is as follows: the more dynamic the body has in dreams, the less our emotional problems; the less movements, the more exciting and emotionally charged are the dreams.

THREE REGULATORS OF ALERTNESS

*(SECRETS OF MARATHON HIGHS,
THE MYSTERY OF TEARS, AND
WHAT DO WE NEED A NOSE FOR?)*

Alertness and sleep are two sides of our biological rhythm. What do we know about the distinctive features of alertness, what keeps us alert? How they support sleep, and how sleep and alertness can be confused, even within the norm? Later, we will focus in greater detail on pathology of alertness.

Regulations of alertness go both ways between the brain and the body. It means that our body is actively pushing the brain to be in charge. Among the many body regulators of alertness, movements, tears, and nasal breathing are especially interesting. Movements are not only a response to brain commands, but they themselves act as regulators of the brain. We learned from physiology, that if an infant animal is paralyzed, even for a short time, this will cause irreversible damage to the developing brain. At the same time, if a baby is hyper-active, swaddling will be the best way to calm him down. Movements produce enormous amounts of biofeedback stimuli to the brain. Rhythmical, alternating movements such as in jogging or walking, are particularly important in this respect. It is interesting that marathon runners become "addicted" to jogging, if they jog for a long time. It was discovered that during jogging our skin released chemicals called endorphins which induce a high level of excitement and the feeling of well-being. This might be the cause of what people refer to as the "marathon high". If you want to be alert, exercise more!

The nose was mentioned as a regulator of alertness. How is our nose related to our being alert? What do we need a nose for? The answer is not simple. Incidentally, the structure of the nose in humans is different from animals. Very few animals have a complicated structure of nasal bones similar to humans. We need a nose for nasal breathing. The importance of nasal breathing for health, and the significance of the inability to breathe through the nose for pathology is just now starting to be appreciated. Why do we need nasal breathing? In order to clean the incoming air and modify its temperature? The answer is yes, but not only for cleaning. The significance of nasal breathing is much deeper. Recently, scientists rediscovered nasal cyclicity—we breathe predominantly through one nostril and then our breathing switches to the other. These cycle periods last for seconds, minutes or hours.

Ancient science, such as Indian Yoga or Japan's system of Dzen or Tibet medicine strongly suggest that normal nasal breathing is the key to our health. They designed their elaborate techniques of healthy breathing. During my training at the Tibet Medicine Institute near Baikal, the deepest freshwater lake in the world, I discovered something else: techniques of nasal breathing can powerfully alter the level of alertness from coma-like sleep to active attention. How is this possible? The answer was found at the Pavlovian Institute of Experimental Medicine, in St. Petersburg. Professor Michael Chananashvilli—Chairman of the renowned Pavlov's laboratories where conditioned reflexes were discovered—designed a unique electronic system: the isolated brain. Indeed, it is the isolated cortex with implanted electrodes. His remarkable experiments with stimulations of different parts of the split brain brought him to the concept of the so-called "tonus" brain, similar to the tonus of muscles or turgor of skin. High tonus means high level of activity. Low brain tonus means sleep.

The cyclic nasal breathing is one of the most powerful stimulators for brain tonus. Ancient yoga techniques of nasal breathing were based on correct assumptions that good nasal breathing means good health. Ancient scientists did not have the proper equipment but they were attentive observers and learned from the experience of many generations.

What happens when nasal breathing is blocked and the person starts breathing through the mouth? Allergies, or any other causes of nasal obstruction, breed many problems, especially sleep disorders, bedwetting, different somatic symptoms, including headaches and severe daytime problems of alertness. (See more in Part 6.) It is very important to keep your nose clean, metaphorically and literally, to prevent sleep disorders and problems with alertness.

Tears are another regulator of alertness and brain tonus. We know that tears moisten our eyes, protect from infection, and wash away irritants, but we leave to poets and song-writers to explain the mystery of emotional tears. What is the function of crying? Why do we cry? When we are upset? To get attention or aid? Or to prevent the irritation of mucous membranes during rapid breathing that accompanies sobbing? To rid the body of bad "humors?" Dr. William Frey, biochemist and Director of the Dry Eye and Tear Research Center in Minneapolis, found that the phrase "to cry it out" is more than an idiomatic expression. When people cry, they literally get rid of some chemicals that build up during emotional stress. Dr. Frey determined that the lacrimal gland, which regulates tear secretion, concentrates and removes magnesium from the body. The concentration of magnesium, a mineral that has been implicated in mood alteration, is 30 times greater in tears than in blood. In his book *Crying: The Mystery of Tears*, he described his research on the difference between tears induced by a fresh-cut onion versus emotional tears induced by tear jerkers, like the movies *Brian's Song, The Champ* and *All Mine to Give*. He found that emotional tears have a different chemical make-up than "onion tears", containing a 24 percent higher protein concentration. Emotional tears are controlled from a different brain structure called the limbic system—the same system that is responsible for memory, emotions, alertness, and sleep.

Do you remember Dr. Chananashvilli's experiments with brain "tonus?" Tears are another important mediator and regulator of brain tonus, physiological tonus, and emotional tonus as well. When we are under stress, our emotional and physiological tonus increase. Stress chemicals build up. Emotional tears go through the nose-eye channel which exists only in humans. And together with nasal fluid during nasal breathing, they irritate nasal mucous. When the person cries, this decreases the emotional and physiological tonus, and he feels better. An extra amount of tears go through the corners of the eyes. However, if we cry too much, we feel exhausted. If we are unable to cry at all, we may be in "trouble". Or, perhaps we are "too strong", so we do not need to cry. By the way, the inability to cry in a depressed woman is a sign of a possible suicide risk.

Dr. Frey suggests that we might feel worse, physiologically and psychologically, if we suppress our tears. In a study of 137 men and women conducted at the University of Pittsburgh School of Nursing, psychiatric nurse Margaret Crepeau found that healthy people were more likely to cry and have a positive attitude to tears than those with ulcers and colitis (two conditions thought to be stress related).

Interestingly enough, Dr. Frey found that children who suffered from inherited disease called familial dysautonomia had two things in common: they could not cry with tears, and they had an extremely low tolerance for emotional stress.

Thus, emotional tears are a human gift and a very important mechanism for regulating and balancing our physiological and emotional tonus. So maybe it is not so terrible to be a "cry baby", and you are welcome to have a good cry over this book to improve your spirits.

SLEEP-LIKE CONDITIONS

We mentioned earlier on, that sleep and alertness are intimately connected as parts of the sleep-wake cycle. Normally, they help each other as good "partners", but their "behavior" can become confused, as a result of natural or artificial means of suggestion, hypnosis being one of them.

The 14-year-old girl was screaming day and night. The team of the burn unit tried everything to relieve her pain. The burns were not too deep, but they covered a large surface. The problem was the child's unusual allergic reaction to almost all pain killers. To keep this girl under general or spinal anesthesia would have been quite dangerous. This problem was solved by the use of hypnosis as sole anesthetic administered during the skin transplantation and to keep her in comfort later on.

A robust, tall army officer was jumping on one foot around the large theater stage. All his movements suggested that he was a little boy playing happily with his toys. He was acting under hypnosis. There are many stories like this. Who has not been fascinated by the facts of hypnosis? What is it? Just a psychological trick, an agreement between two people playing certain roles? Is it a kind of sleep? What is the nature of hypnosis, and how is it related to a child's sleep and behavior problems? These questions are commonly asked during any presentation about sleep and hypnosis, or at treatment sessions.

Current science accepts hypnotic phenomena as scientific fact, having a profound significance in medical practice. The American Medical Association recognized the field called "Medical Hypnosis" by establishing a special professional board and a set of rules. The author of this book went through comprehensive training to receive the respectful title of Diplomat of the American Board of Medical Hypnosis. Over 300 such diplomats are currently practicing medical hypnosis in hospitals and throughout the USA. The National and International Societies for Clinical Hypnosis attract hundreds of practitioners and researchers. Hypnotic conditions elicited by a special procedure called "induction" are carefully studied in physiological and psychological laboratories. Phenomena like hallucinations, long-term memory, the possibility to retrieve minute details from the past, have received special attention. Curiously, a scenario suggested by a hypnotist, if not properly directed, may start to unfold in its own way and by its own logic, very similar to that of dreams. A general situation induced by a hypnotist can be easily and with minute details enacted by a subject. If an adult in a hypnotic state is asked to play with toys as he did when he was five years old, he will tell you all the details about his toys, including their names, color and clothes. He will mention the now forgotten teddy bear he used to go to bed with as a child. Hypnosis can elicit not just hallucinatory effects but any mental and somatic phenomena. Hypnosis can activate creativity. The child can easily draw, sing, remember foreign languages, play chess, etc. Some leading experts in psychology of creativity and hypnosis are developing different ways of using hypnosis for creativity training.

Hypnosis is not sleep or a part of sleep. The electroencephalogram registered during hypnosis shows alpha rhythms: a typical picture of the "working brain". Sometimes alpha rhythms are interrupted by an intrusion of delta waves—large, slow waves, typical of deep sleep. Hypnotic sleep, natural sleep, and wakefulness are three quantitatively and qualitatively different conditions. In a hypnotic condition, it is uniquely possible to change deep physiological functions, such as, for instance, the level of blood sugar, urinary excretion, production of some chemicals, etc. Hypnosis may be used to help patients with chronic disorders, such as asthma or diabetes.

An interesting experiment was performed at one of the pediatric oncology and hematology units in the Children's Hospital in St. Petersburg, Russia. A number of children with leukemia were hypnotized by a team of specialists who kept them in a deep hypnotic state for several days with positive suggestions. The patients were closely observed for signs of any change in their condition. To the surprise of many, they were symptom free for a few months.

Another unique hypnotic phenomenon is the effect of post-hypnotic suggestions. Major concerns about the medical aspect of using hypnosis are related to these post-hypnotic suggestions, which can be very serious and sometimes have criminalistic consequences.

This is a real story known as the "Onion Case." An unlicensed hypnotist demonstrated hypnotic phenomena to high school and college students. One young man was asked to come on stage, among a few others. This young man happened to be an extremely hypnotizable subject, who easily achieved the deepest somnambulic level of the hypnotic state. The hypnotist suggested to him that he will eat onions, having learned from a previous discussion that this man hates onions. The public was excited to see him hungrily biting into onions. When the show was over, the poor man continued feeling a strange urge to eat onions, because the hypnotist forgot to make the posthypnotic suggestion that he should stop eating onions. Six months later, the young man was forced to seek medical help for stomach aches, and psychiatric counseling for depression. He was later hospitalized several times due to neurological and psychiatric consequences from medications. During one of the hospitalizations, he was asked to participate in hypnotherapy sessions, in which the story of the previous hypnotic suggestions was uncovered and proper post-hypnotic suggestions (to stop eating onions) were performed.

Unfortunately, the initial inappropriate suggestions induced a chain of illnesses, which the man had prior to the show, and he died. A malpractice suit was initiated against the hypnotist. Such dramatic cases are rare, but we need to know about them to remember that anything and everything should be used properly and professionally. Hypnosis is a real and strong medicine. It is used for medical, educational and scientific reasons, and it should be enthusiastically supported.

The precise physiological nature of the hypnotic state is presently unclear. Sophisticated electrophysiologic methods provide sufficient data to believe that the hypnotic state is a distinct physiological condition, separate from NREM, REM or wakefulness. Within two worlds, wakefulness and sleep, there is another realm called the Transitional State. If you look carefully, you will see multiple phenomena of transitional states of consciousness around us in normal and in pathological cases. In the normal condition, it is hypnosis, meditation, out-of-body experiences, automatic behavior, creative withdrawals, etc. Such states occur much more often in clinical situations. There are so-called disassociations, multiple personalities and parasomnias. The realm of transitional states is around us. We just do not see it, because we live in it.

It is important to know that to get into the hypnotic state, we do not necessarily need words. Anything significant for our stimuli can turn us off reality. Even subsensory stimuli, such as certain types of silence, smell, touch, can put us in this hypnotic world. Some people are more sensitive to such stimuli than others and more prone to get into the hypnotic state right away. For example, children with asthma hear more high pitched sounds and are more sensitive to them than healthy children. People with hysteria are especially sensitive to intonations of speech, much more so than to its content. Patients with some form of epilepsy are more sensitive to smells and odors. Sensitivity to sub-sensory stimuli is the secret of telepathy.

Transitional conditions are the predominant stage of alertness in small children, tapering with age. Look at the child's play when he talks to himself, withdrawn from reality, engaged in his own world. It is amazing. But if the child lives in an abusive, frightening environment, he will develop his own world different from the real one, with no sensitivity to pain, and he will stay there. Transitional states of alertness, both in norm and pathology, need specific attention from doctors, researchers, and teachers. Transitional states deserve a special discussion, and we will talk about this later. Our main reason in mentioning transitional stages is to remind you that a large number of disorders of sleep and alertness occur in transitional states of consciousness.

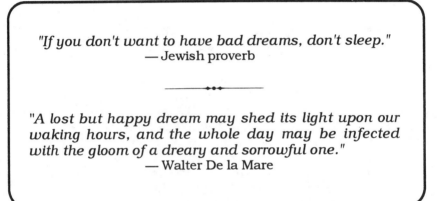

"If you don't want to have bad dreams, don't sleep."
— Jewish proverb

"A lost but happy dream may shed its light upon our waking hours, and the whole day may be infected with the gloom of a dreary and sorrowful one."
— Walter De la Mare

PART
3

THE NATURE OF ABNORMAL SLEEP AND ALERTNESS

What Is Abnormal Sleep?

What Is Abnormal Alertness?

Causes of Abnormal Sleep and Alertness
Why Disorders Can Hurt. Can Disorders Help?

Do Animals Have Sleep Disorders?

Traditional and Alternative Treatments of Sleep and Alertness Disorders

WHAT IS ABNORMAL SLEEP?

Sleep is a highly active and organized process, which has very complex dynamics in the course of the night and through life. It is not surprising that there can be many disruptions, impairments and developmental deviations in its mechanisms and functions. When sleep researchers finally began to pay attention to people's complaints about their sleep, or their inability to stay awake, or about strange things happening to them or their children in sleep, they found many unknown sleep disorders in surprising abundance. Besides commonly known quantitative difficulties in sleep known as insomnia, there are scores of more serious qualitative deviations of sleep. The field of sleep medicine started with a disorder called *narcolepsy*, and later sleep apnea. Narcolepsy is an illness expressed in sudden attacks of sleepiness, muscle paralysis, and frightening hallucinations. Sleep apnea syndrome is manifested in sudden cessation of breathing during sleep. The three giants of disordered sleep: insomnia, narcolepsy and sleep apnea were soon accompanied by a multitude of other disorders identified by specialists.

Sleep medicine is a clinical specialty which deals with the diagnosis and treatment of patients who complain about disturbed nocturnal sleep, excessive daytime sleepiness, or some other sleep related problems. The spectrum of disorders and problems is extremely broad, ranging from the merely troublesome, such as a mild jet lag, to the catastrophic, such as sudden death during sleep. The nature of dysfunctional sleep may be primary, involving the central neural mechanisms of sleep and arousal, or secondary, when it is related to other medical, psychiatric, or neurological illnesses.

Sleep medicine is similar to other specialties dealing with disorders of a specific organ or system in that it studies the manifestations and pathologies of the sleeping brain. At the same time, sleep medicine is different from other specialties, because the manifestations and pathologies of the sleeping brain are as a rule caused by dysfunctional relationships between the brain, heart, respiration and some other systems during sleep and alertness. In this sense, sleep medicine is a holistic medicine, dealing with the organism as a whole. The practice of sleep medicine involves comprehensive diagnostic evaluation of seemingly unrelated symptoms, like snoring, obesity, or bedwetting to uncover hidden and life-threatening problems, such as obstructive apnea.

The first question that patients, and especially parents, ask a doctor is "What is abnormal sleep?" Should a child who wets the bed once a week be diagnosed with enuresis? Are such common symptoms as snoring, teeth-grinding or sleep talking abnormal? For 20 years we have been taught that a child who wets his bed will grow out of it, and we should not be too concerned. Generally speaking, this permissive approach introduced by Dr. Spock a few decades ago is good, because it emphasizes wide individual differences and relates to parental attitude. But the question remains: *when* does the mild and benign childhood situation grow into frightening symptomology? When does normality end and pathology begin? How can we define normality? How can we define pathology? Behavioral science has struggled with this task for many years. It is so important that a new, special field, *"normatology"* has emerged This field integrated the few perspectives, encompassing the definitions of normality and pathology found in literature.

So, what is abnormal sleep? What is abnormal alertness? Based on research, and for many practical reasons, we define a child's sleep and behavior abnormal and in need of serious attention if:

- The child displays unusual symptoms or the usual common features, typical of a certain developmental age, that last far beyond the appropriate age;

- Unusual symptoms or features disrupt the usual course of the child's sleep or wakefulness;

- These symptoms or features disrupt the functioning of the child's (physical or school) activities, appropriate for his stage of development;

- The symptoms control the child, rather than the child controls his habits. (For example, the child can no longer fall asleep without rocking, and if the adult discontinues rocking);

- The child's symptoms disrupt the family's life.

Use of these guidelines helps to screen childhood sleep and behavior disorders at an early stage. At the same time, do not draw any far-reaching conclusions based on these guidelines alone. Their purpose is simply to let you know what to look for during home observations.

Now it is time to look into the classification of sleep disorders. In the International Classification of Sleep Disorders, all sleep disorders (actually, sleep *and* wakefulness disorders) are divided into four groups:

(1) *Dissomnias:* Disorders that produce difficulty sleeping, or decrease adolescent sleep and produce excessive daytime sleepiness. This group includes *intrinsic*, or primary medical sleep disorders, and *extrinsic*, or secondary environmental sleep disorders.

(2) *Parasomnias:* A wide range of undesirable physical phenomena that occur mainly during sleep. The predominant feature of parasomnias is a sudden activation of movements and somatic symptoms which disrupt sleep and cause arousals. Parasomnias are subdivided into arousal disorders, sleep-wake transitional disorders, those associated specifically with REM sleep, and others. The majority of childhood sleep disorders belong to this group.

(3) Sleep disorders associated with *medical*, neurological and psychiatric problems: The majority of psychiatric disorders are associated with dysfunction of sleep. As one known sleep researcher and psychiatrist said, "There are sleep disorders without psychiatry, but there is no psychiatry without sleep disorders." Sleep deviations are more specific for some psychiatric problems (such as depression), than for others (such as anxiety). Many medical disorders have sleep deviations as their first symptom.

(4) *Proposed sleep disorders:* This is the only known medical classification in which "proposed" and "new disorders" have a designated place. It happens because the field is growing very fast. Many new syndromes are being discovered. For example, sleep-related choking syndrome, hyperhidrosis (excessive sweating) in sleep, etc. Their "right" to be singled out as separate disorders is being investigated.

As you can see, sleep disorders are many. Not all of them are related to the classification of *childhood* sleep disorders. This is a separate topic which we will specifically address in another chapter (see Part 5).

If untreated, childhood sleep disorders frequently continue into adulthood. They sometimes change their nature, or build the ground for the specific "adult" disorders of sleep and alertness.

WHAT IS ABNORMAL ALERTNESS?

We take for granted the fact that we wake up in the morning and stay alert all day, running around in an attempt to solve endless problems. You will probably be surprised to hear that disorders of alertness are even more common than disorders of sleep.

There are a great number of brain mechanisms, which work in conjunction with peripheral systems and muscles, and are responsible for keeping us awake. Wakefulness, like sleep, has many stages and levels. Psychologically, wakefulness can be interpreted as stages of attention, and physiologically as levels of arousal. As we have already mentioned, sleep and wakefulness are closely connected as two stages of a biological cycle called circadian. Any serious disruption of sleep leads to compensatory deviations of wakefulness, and vice versa. At some point these compensatory changes may become pathological. Psychological symptoms such as inattention, daydreaming, hyperactivity, and dissociation reflect underlying physiological changes of the level of alertness and the level of arousal.

The most common daytime behavior disorder in children is what is known as the hyperactivity disorder (ADHD), now formally defined as a disorder of arousal and alertness. Instability of alertness leads to instability in behavior—inadequate motor reactions, hyperactivity or passivity, instability of attention, lapses of attention, quick shifts to insignificant details, missing central points. This breeds comprehension difficulties and learning problems.

As we said before, sleep and alertness are two integrated, inseparable states of consciousness. However, sleep developmentally is the foundation for wakefulness, which means that mechanisms responsible for sleep develop first, and the mechanisms of wakefulness develop later. If, in childhood years, the mechanisms of sleep are not developed or deviated—wakefulness will not be properly developed. A perfect example of this is the tragic effect of sleep deprivation.

A man was driving behind a large truck carrying steel girders. He suddenly remembered that he wanted to stop for a cup of coffee. The next thing he knew was that his car slammed into the rear of the truck when it stopped at a crossroads. His wife next to him was killed on the spot, decapitated by a girder that smashed through the car's windshield. Another case from a newspaper. She was on the car phone with her girlfriend while driving on the highway. She was talking about the two week mid-term break from college, shopping, taking her younger sister to the movies. As she steered into a curve, she noticed a set of bright headlights approaching from the opposite direction. A semi was coming. It was the last thing she ever saw. During the investigation that followed this head-on collision, police determined that the driver of the semi had fallen asleep at the wheel, throwing several tons of steel under the wheels of the tiny Volkswagen. These are tragic accidents for people who happened to be in the wrong place at the wrong time. But from the sleep medicine point of view, they are not accidents and can be predicted as an inevitable result of sleep deprivation which might and should be prevented.

To doctors who work with sleep disorders, America looks like a sleep-deprived society. According to the Highway Safety Commission, 40,000 are killed and another 250,000 people are injured each year due to falling asleep at the wheel. Reportedly, about 20 percent of all truck drivers have fallen asleep behind the wheel at least once a year, nearly escaping collisions. The National Transportation Safety Board says that fatigue and sleepiness are the primary causes of truck accidents. Eighty percent of victims are passengers or other motorists and pedestrians. There is a long list of tragic consequences of excessive daytime sleeping at sea, in factories and even in space. The results of excessive sleepiness due to sleep deprivation among medical residents and surgeons may also be tragic. Recently, there was a big scandal revealing that several 911 emergency employees were found asleep at their desks. Media talks about responsibility, but the employees complain about exhaustion and grave sleep deprivation.

Sleep deprivation with consequent deviations of alertness may be caused by a person's work schedule, social stress, or else by medical disorders of sleep. It may be a severe, specific sleep disorder like obstructive sleep apnea, but it also may be a relatively mild problem like pain, arthritis, high blood pressure or frequent urination. Changes of alertness may take different forms. They come in the form of deviated emotions like deep depression or thought or memory lapses, behavior problems such as agitation or dissociation when a person forgets things, not knowing how they got to different places. Our habits, good and bad, are our instruments for stabilizing our sleep and alertness. People invent many rituals to put themselves to sleep or keep themselves awake. Our habits are our natural regulators of sleep and wakefulness.

The level of alertness, just like sleep, has many stages. Some of us achieve great levels of exciting activity. Some of us are even and clear-headed all the time. Some are very unstable. The question is, at what price does the system stay alert? If one stays alert at the price of sleep deprivation, the cost might be too high. Sleep is a primary state in the course of human development, and it is the foundation for wakefulness. The child is born in sleep, and stays in sleep. Arousals and awakenings start as brief intermissions and then get longer. If sleep mechanisms are not developed or deviated, then wakefulness and attention can also become fragmented or deviated. To rephrase, "Tell me how someone slept as a child, and I will tell you how this person will behave in the future." This statement made by one doctor in his lecture is, of course, an exaggeration, but it makes a lot of sense. One of the greatest aspects of pediatric medicine is the possibility and responsibility of preventing behavioral, emotional and learning problems in children. This prevention can be achieved by improving the child's sleep.

CAUSES OF ABNORMAL SLEEP AND ALERTNESS
(Why Disorders Can Hurt. Can Disorders Help?)

There are multiple causes of abnormal sleep and alertness. Some of them come from the past. Some of them exist in the present. Some of these factors we cannot change. Others we can correct. This is determined by two important factors:

1. Never blame anyone for a problem, neither yourself, nor your spouse, nor your child. This seemingly trivial statement is almost totally ignored. Suppose we are discussing possible causes of a child's sleep problems: complications caused in pregnancy, father's irregular work shift disrupting the family's sleep schedule, siblings fighting before sleep. All of these are potential causes of the young patient's serious sleep problems. It is almost inevitable that when I mention all potential causes, family members identify with them, and more often than not, engage in fault-finding.

2. Disorders of sleep and alertness are a process. This means that multiple aspects of those disorders have their own complicated, nonlinear dynamics, influenced by many internal and external factors, including treatment. Some symptoms can get better by themselves. Some need an urgent interference. The purpose of the treatment is to change the course of the problem, and we need to know about previous causes to improve the future. Among internal objective causes, the most important are: genetic predisposition, oxygen deficiency during pregnancy, prematurity and postmaturity, early childhood chronic medical problems, such as frequent ear infections, physical immobilization, chronic pain, etc.

Among external physical and psychological factors, the most important include: prolonged hospitalization during the early childhood, disruption of the family's sleep-wake schedule, neglect and emotional deprivation.

Each of these causes may induce sleep-wake disorders. But the real genesis and maintenance of the problem is much more complex. There are usually multiple reasons, some by predisposition, others by complicated developmental dynamics, creating a unique cause of disorder in each particular case.

And yet, despite the apparent singularity of each case, a similar pattern of symptoms and a similarity of stages or phases can be established in the course of many such disorders.

Surprisingly, many of them, such as nocturnal asthma, bedwetting, hair pulling, headbanging, and sleepwalking, have a lot in common. All of these disorders manifest themselves in a similar manner. In each of these disorders:

1) There are clear and dramatic symptoms.
2) There is no underlying pathology to fully explain the symptoms.
3) These symptoms are typical for children.
4) The symptoms are extremely resistant to treatment.
5) These symptoms are prone to self cure and often disappear by themselves.

No less surprising is that common specific stages or phases can be identified in the development of these disorders. These stages are:

1) The period of undifferentiated irritability.
2) Crystallization when the symptoms appear.
3) A prolonged monosymptomatic period which ends by one of the following: 4) Self-cure or 5) Deterioration.

Any theory striving to synthesize this information should explain these commonalities, analyze why sleep disorders find ways to resist treatment (therapeutic resistance), and show ways of preventing deterioration of symptoms. It seems that our body *needs* adaptive and compensatory phenomena and prevents them from being destroyed through treatment. When our bodies no longer need these adaptive phenomena, they disappear by themselves in what is termed self cure.

Are then sleep disorders created by the body for its own good? Can these disorders be helpful? Definitely! Support for the idea about the compensatory, adaptive role of sleep phenomena is found in different fields of science and put together as the Stabilizing Equilibrium Theory, or "SET".

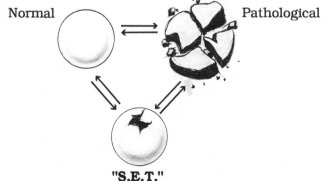

Normal   Pathological

"S.E.T."

The idea that disorders can be helpful is not new. And it is one of the first ideas that was found in organized medicine. Look at the design of the original logo of medicine, and you will find a snake coiled around a glass. The snake is spitting its poison into the glass. The meaning of this logo may read as "even poison can be medication." Ancient doctors used this saying when searching for new cures. Since early ages, medicine men, shamans and organized medics in Persia, India and Egypt, and later on in Europe, have used mild infections to treat patients with mortal illnesses. For example, as treatment for chronic life-threatening infections and diseases like tuberculosis and cancer, patients were infected with malaria, because malaria fever spikes were found to help or even cure those diseases. "Fever therapy" proved to be scientifically sound for the treatment of severe psychiatric disorders. It was observed that convulsions can be used to treat severe depression and psychoses which lead to the development of shock therapy. Electroconvulsive therapy is still considered one of the most effective treatments in psychiatry today. Vaccinations induce mild forms of disorders preventing serious diseases, such as polymyositis, tuberculosis, contagious childhood disease and, in the future, possibly even AIDS.

**TURN
POISONS
INTO
MEDICINES**

So, the idea of helpful disorders induced by doctors as a type of treatment is not new. The body "SETS" a mild form of disorder by itself. Temperature crisis and fever convulsions are not necessarily harmful—they could be a course to recovery! We may soon discover that fever spikes, blisters on our lips or nocturnal leg spasms may help to treat a common cold.

In psychiatry we know that our habits are mild disorders that prevent us from becoming victims of larger disorders. Sigmund Freud said that habits are tools of prevention and protection from mental disorders. Such habits are actively "SET" by our minds as stabilizers of alertness, keeping a balance between different stages of vigilance. We know the expression "mind set", which means a certain fixed attitude to a social situation. A mind set can help or kill (See: Anniversary phenomena).

There is also a "physiological set" which means a certain body reaction to a biological situation. If "stress" phenomena are non-specific reactions, set phenomena represent specific adaptive or maladaptive body reactions. Nocturnal sleep phenomena are actively "SET" by our bodies as starters, initiators, stabilizers and switches in order to keep different stages of sleep in equilibrium.

Another confirmation of helping "disorders" came from the field of physics. Physics has a great influence on our state of thinking. Mechanics in Newton's time and Relativism in Einstein's era induced major changes in medicine. Understanding the human organism as a complicated mechanism has changed since the 18th century: now the organism is viewed as a dynamic, relatively open system. The behavior of complicated, seemingly chaotic and unpredictable systems like the human organism can be explained and predicted. The effects of epidemics, times of convulsions and heart attacks, and any other events inexplicable by conventional, linear logic can now be understood based on new, non-linear principles. Recent experiments identified the inner principles of heart arrhythmias and other disrhythmias called "desynchronosis". (See the Chapter on biological clocks). One of the principles of deterministic chaos as it relates to medicine is that in order to keep a large, complicate system in equilibrium, a certain smaller part of this system should be out of equilibrium.

The simplest example of this logic is *Landau's* experiment. If you are trying to balance a stick in the vertical position on your finger, you can do this only if you are constantly moving your hand. As soon as you stop, the stick will fall down. A more complicated example would be a residential building in which the electricity is kept unstable. A lamp in one of the rooms would be used as a stabilizer, and the unstable electricity would cause the lamp alternately to increase in brightness, decrease in brightness, blink or turn off. To an observer, a lamp may look "infected". But, this "infected" lamp will regulate the electrical current, and all the other rooms will, thanks to it, have "normal" lamps with stable intensity. The same logic applies to our body. The blood pressure in our arms fluctuates in order to keep an equilibrium of blood pressure in the internal organs. A little change or deviation from the norm in one part of the body may help to keep the rest of the body stable. New physics points to what we knew before—do not rush with a treatment before you fully understand the cause of imbalance.

Let us consider sleeping disorders in children from this perspective. Rhythmic rocking, rhythmic sucking, etc. help a newborn baby to go to sleep. These rhythms produce "sleep waves" in the brain which are the same frequency as rocking and sucking. If, for whatever reasons, these natural external stimuli are not sufficient to produce sleep, the infant's body "SETS" up its own internal "starter". The baby starts to rock or sucks his finger, habits which force his brain to fall asleep. Brain science demonstrates the brain's ability to synchronize its waves with rhythmical movements. The phenomenon of synchronization is being studied very carefully today, and it was found that sucking, chewing, walking, running and other rhythmic movements are picked up by the corresponding parts of the brain. Dr. Voino-Jasenecki demonstrated on rabbits that during their development, their muscles produced several different patterns. Their brain developed later by producing the same patterns of electrical activity. The theory is that motor activity acts as a brain pacemaker. During scratching, for instance, the rabbit's brain produced a frequency pattern called a spindle, which is correlated with the central nervous system and the IQ in humans. As we can see, not only does the brain control the body, but the body also controls the brain. Thus, finger sucking and head rocking are the infant's internal "starters", which play the role of physiological switches from wakefulness to sleep.

The role of paroxysmal (sudden) phenomena can be seen in the example of bedwetting. Some bedwetters have a deep sleep. Sometimes, they sleep too deeply showing no movements, and breathing slowly. They have what is called "dead sleep" (see Part 5). Usual stimuli are not enough for their arousal. The body "SETS" up its own mechanism for active arousal. The first level is a jerking type of leg movement, producing brief "starts". If this fails to wake the child up, the next level builds up. This second level is bedwetting—a stream of impulses from the bladder rushes to the brain, "switching" it to the REM stage or wakefulness. Thus, bedwetting serves as a "switch" or "transmission." If it is still not sufficient to wake the child up, the third level develops, called the vegetative storm, during which multiple symptoms come forth, such as asthma, heart arrhythmia, spasms, etc.

Thus, at the early stage, sleep phenomena named parasomnias have a positive function. But if these sleep phenomena increase in frequency and intensity, the body may lose control over them. Nighttime parasomnias will eventually take control over the body. Before we know it, a "good disease" then becomes a "bad disease", or "pathology". Our daytime habits can even be deadly. In a mild form, these habits help us to stay alert and be productive, but if they become part of our behavior, they begin to control all of our actions, making us their slaves.

"A little disorder might be the key to the big order."
From: Physics of the Chaos

"Life sucks order from the sea of disorder."
— Ervin Schrodinger
(Pioneer of Quantum Physics)

DO ANIMALS HAVE SLEEP DISORDERS?

This chapter is dedicated to animals. There are many questions usually raised by parents during discussions about animals. One of the first questions commonly asked, "Is it okay to sleep with pets?" has already been answered in Part 1 of this book. Do animals have sleep disorders? Another hot issue is whether animals can be used in research of sleep mechanisms and for new drug testing. Are you an animal rights activist? Or are you a scientist experimenting with animal models of a human disorder? Or maybe you are just parents of a sick child? In this case you basically have little choice but to consent to the use of drugs on animals, if you do not wish your child to be treated with untested medications.

Most of us love animals. They save our lives. They help us to understand ourselves, our physiology, psychology, and our sleep. Studies of the mechanism of sleep were done on animals, predominantly cats and dogs. Almost everything we know about sleep today is due to animal research, including the usual drug testing.

Sleep disorders are found not only in humans or do they occur in animals as well. We have to answer this intriguing question in the affirmative. Animals are very much like humans, especially children. And like our children, they wet in their sleep, they sleeptalk and sleepwalk, and they often have bad dreams. They have rhythmic head movements and many other symptoms that we find in children.

Dr. John Hedricks and Adrian Morrison from the School of Veterinary Medicine, University of Pennsylvania in Philadelphia, determined that certain diseases were primarily associated with the sleep state. They emphasized that because so much in this are a still remained unclear, animal models were very important for studies of sleep disorders. The physiology of sleep in animals is extremely similar to that of humans. For example, the so-called phasic phenomena (sudden periods or sudden changes) in REM sleep, are the same as in humans. Twitching of muscles, inducing eye movements and facial grimaces are much more prominent in animals. Episodic muscle twitches of distal parts are also much more apparent in animals; in fact, they are so intensive that animals move in their sleep. Every veterinary that was asked whether dogs or cats dream confirmed twitching of limbs and facial muscles, and vocalization which periodically interrupts the animal's peaceful sleep, suggesting that it is actually dreaming. Researchers and doctors who work with animals state that the effect of dreams on animals' behavior during daytime is similar to the same effect in humans. Observations suggest that REM sleep is characterized by a highly activated brain. Visual activity. Movement activity. Metabolic activity. All are on the rise. Eye movements in sleep have a striking resemblance to eye movements in wakefulness. For example, when the cat is confronted with another stimuli, its eyes move exactly the same way as in dreams, which suggests that it is actually seeing something in its dreams.

Patterns of sleep in animals are different in each species, but they are cyclical and have the same stages of development by age. Predators spend a great percentage of the 24 hour period sleeping. Animals with secure sleeping places sleep more than species which sleep in the open. Some animals, like horses, have been commended for their ability to sleep standing up due to their skeletal adaptation. But this does not apply to REM. To sleep in REM, they must change their position and lie down. Birds also have REM stages. Some animals, like dolphins, have unique sleep. They are able to sleep only with one part of the brain turned off, while the other part of the brain is alert.

It is fascinating that large domestic animals spend more time in the state of drowsiness, half awake and half asleep, especially if they are partially immobilized. During that period, their EEG is also mixed, containing waves of both alertness and sleep. It is important to know this, because some behaviors, like rumination and rhythmic head movements are very similar to thumb sucking and head rocking behavior in children.

Abnormal sleep patterns were discovered only in domestic animals. Does it mean that freedom is healthier, and animals in the wild do not get sick? (If that were true, animal enthusiasts would have another strong argument in their favor.) More likely it simply means that animals with sleep disorders cannot survive in the wild but can survive in captivity. There is now evidence that the latter might be true. Animal sleep medicine started with the discovery of a disease in domestic animals, specifically in dogs. This disease is called narcolepsy and all symptoms of it were identical to humans. (See Part 6).

Just as in humans, sleep disorders in animals may be either primary or secondary. A secondary disease is caused by medical problems, such as brain tumor, encephalitis, drug treatment, heart problems, etc. The most serious recognized primary sleep disorders fall into two categories: narcolepsy and sleep apnea. Narcolepsy is a disease which includes a syndrome consisting of four symptoms: excessive daytime sleepiness, sudden sleep attacks, sudden paralysis, and hypnogogic hallucinations (hallucinations preceding sleep). It is a very bad disease, and if not treated, the consequences may be quite serious, as was proved by studies on dogs and Welsh ponies. This research provided invaluable information on the physiology of this life-threatening disease and the role of genetic predisposition. Narcolepsy often develops very early in life but it is difficult to diagnose at the beginning stage.

The second class of primary disorders is called apnea, which means cessation of breathing during sleep. During normal sleep, there are regular respiratory pauses in slow wave sleep, and very irregular and short stops during REM sleep. Animals, as well as humans, experience apnea for several seconds and usually with no ill effects. But later, prolonged and frequent apnea might cause excessive daytime sleepiness and even death during sleep. Usually the disease has a progressive course, and a sleep pattern might develop. Breathing becomes interrupted for long periods of time, followed by spasms of diaphragm muscles, loud, unpleasant snoring and gasping in sleep. Obesity is one of the serious predisposing factors and leads to upper airway obstruction. This apnea syndrome with upper airway obstruction during sleep was found in Persian cats and bulldogs. There were also several episodes of sudden death of young dogs and cats in their sleep, similar to the sudden infant death syndrome in humans.

It is also of interest to us that domestic animals have problems in sleep similar to parasomnias in children such as bedwetting, screaming, etc. Another important factor is that domestic animals, if they do not move a lot, can develop dissociated conditions similar to children's daydreaming. Domestic animals, such as horses, stay awake for approximately 85 percent of the night if they are kept in a stable. It means that they suffer from quite severe insomnia and a strong drowsiness during the daytime. They also have symptoms such as sleep rocking, sleepwalking and night terrors. Enuresis (wetting in sleep) was of special interest in domestic dogs. Owners of small animals often complain to veterinarians that their pets are well-trained and otherwise healthy but consistently make a pool of urine when they sleep. When observed, the dogs seem to begin to urinate while sleeping and then arouse in the middle of this act. Upon awaking, they look guilty and surprised. The problem was detected in dogs of all ages, but is predominant in young dogs. There was no related anatomical or medical problem which might cause urination. Unfortunately, no physiological investigation of sleep was done on these animals.

Sleep related movements were studied in cats. During sleep cats have violent limb movements. Sometimes cats move even around the cage. Observations of this pattern, coupled with EEG and dorsal neck EMG recording, indicated that as a result of such activity, cats, like children, have no sign of epilepsy and otherwise seem to be completely healthy. Head rocking behavior is also common in animals but is considered normal. Horses and especially cows have a lot of body movements. They also have head rocking and movements similar to headbanging.

Disorders of alertness, similar to disturbances in children, can also be observed in animals. Behavior disorders, such as violent behavior toward each other and towards themselves, especially during the transitional stage of alertness, can be seen in almost all animals, with two exceptions. Dr. Rappaport described a repetitive paw licking syndrome in responding to medication, clomipramine. This is a very good example of studying a model from biological and psychosocial perspectives. Such behavior is found as a rule in certain genetic breeds and is usually associated with an inhibited and introverted type of personality. These animals usually have neglectful or overattentive owners who restrict them to confined places. Inadequate care was the core of the problem.

Another interesting phenomenon is the closeness of biorhythms of animals with their owners. We are all aware of a strange fact that many animals look like their owners. It happens because after living together for a long time, their biorhythms might become similar. This phenomenon might be of interest for future research.

In conclusion, animal sleep is a good model for the study of different sleep habits and sleep disorders in children. Animals are with us and around us. Studying animals in sleep helps us develop appropriate treatments for similar human disorders.

TRADITIONAL AND ALTERNATIVE TREATMENTS
OF SLEEP AND ALERTNESS DISORDERS

The treatment process reminds me of mountain climbing and hiking. We need to be sure that we choose the right mountain to climb and have proper equipment to do it. It is very difficult to climb up, and even more dangerous to descend. The most important questions to ask the doctor are what the problem is, when to start the treatment, and how to treat it without falling into the clefts of side effects.

There are three types of treatment strategy: *crisis-oriented, planned maintenance*, and *prophylactic* (preventive). These types are not mutually exclusive and should be viewed as steps. If a three year old child is waking up multiple times crying, screaming with apparent night terrors, this is a crisis situation, and the treatment should be oriented to a fast relief. Only then can maintenance and preventive treatment be considered.

It is important to know about different treatment strategies because parents coming to see the doctor for crisis treatment, often tend to overlook that treatment of a crisis does not cure the underlying problem. Underlying problems might not be very visible and need longer efforts. Treatment of sleep disorders usually includes several modalities. Knowing them will prepare you for a discussion with the doctor.

I. Hygiene (Daily Routine)

This includes age appropriate or specially designated times of going to sleep, waking up, nap times, times for play, meals and study, times and sequence of taking medication or doing exercises, etc. Properly timing events is a major key to develop and stabilize the child's immature and unstable biological rhythms. We wrote in greater detail about biological clocks responsible for our inner rhythms, and their synchronization between each other in Part 2 of this book. Depending on the time of the day the medication is taken, it can have a different effect on the patient (the so-called chronopharmacologic effect.)

One should be aware of the fact that wake up time in the morning or after a nap is more important than the time the child goes to bed. This is a critical time when external social events interfere and reset our biological inner clocks. We call them social *zeitgebers*. The reset, corrections by social events may be positive, or disruptive. For an adult, it is very important to know when to follow the child's biorhythm and when to interfere. For example, in newborns to 4 months old inner biological rhythms are dominant. A sleeping infant wakes up crying to be fed by his own schedule. At that age, the baby is in charge, and "trains" parents or caregivers. On the other hand, an overly permissive approach to sleep-wake-meal time for a two and a half year old might lead to serious problems. This is a time when social *zeitgebers* should be incorporated and synchronized with inner biological clocks. "Is it good or bad to feed the baby in the middle of the night?" The answer would depend on the age of the child and the reason for midnight awakening. It is best to observe the child's response to feeding time for a period of time before coming up with an answer.

Time of exercising for older children might also be used as a regulator, a "pacemaker" for some sleep disorders. For example, bedwetters and children with headbanging symptoms might benefit from exercises (especially rhythmic movements like bicycling, jogging, aerobics, and jumping rope that take place in the evening close to bedtime. In such cases, exercises serve as "a borderline" between daytime and bedtime. After exercises it is good to have the child take a warm shower with a progressive increase of water temperature. Sweet tea (even with caffeine) will help him to fall into deep sleep. In the morning when the child needs to get up but is still sleepy, it is good to have him take a shower with progressively decreasing temperature.

II. Medication

Medication is like food in that it may be healthy and may be poisonous. Even sugar can kill, and snake's poison can bring one back to life! Everything depends on when, how much, and what for. Medication and weapons should be used by professionals for a good reason. Always contact a physician to determine the exact cause of the problem and if medication will be helpful. When treating problems of sleep and alertness, several guidelines need to be observed:

1. The majority of medication, not necessarily sleeping pills, have an influence on sleep and/or alertness. Anti-allergic (so-called antihistaminic) medicines, anti-hypertensives, pain killers (stimulants), antidepressants, anti-inflammatories, steroids, and non-steroidals — all of these drugs increase or decrease sleepiness during the day or night. This is important to know not only to avoid side effects, but also to use these side effects on sleep for the patient's benefit.

2. Drug interactions. There is a complicated interdependency between two or more drugs given at the same time for different reasons or reactions between medications and the amount and type of food, etc.

3. The effect of medication can be changed depending on the time of its intake (chronopharmacologic effect). Intensive sugar intake in the morning increases activity (or hyperactivity) but slightly sweetened tea or milk at bedtime helps to fall asleep easier.

4. Sometimes children react to medication differently than adults. For example, if a healthy adult takes Ritalin® or Cylert® (which are mild CNS stimulants), he becomes excited. For children, Ritalin® or Cylert® have a *calming* effect. Pain killers like benzodiazepines are very good for adults. Small children, however, become sedated and confused but still feel the pain.

5. The most important principle is that medication should be used for the main underlying problem, not for superficial symptoms appearing on and off.

III. *Psychotherapy and Behavior Modification*

These two are still the main methods for treatment of many psychosomatic, sleep, and behavior disorders in children. Through play, hygiene, by reacting to the child's crying, his demands or temper in a special way, we can shape and reshape desired behavior and often eliminate the problem. Psychotherapy has developed new, highly sophisticated, and powerful specific techniques of approach to different problems. For example, behavior desensitization for anxiety, charting for bedwetting, play therapy for children with post-traumatic stress are as helpful as medication.

The good thing is that parents can learn many techniques and use them without too much extra time. Bedtime, wake-up time, and meal time are pivotal for interactions as well as for setting mature biological clocks. Bedtime stories might be not only for fun or education purposes, but for therapeutic purposes as well. (See examples of *Preschool Sleep Stories* in Part 4)

Relaxation techniques and hypnosis are very well-known and powerful techniques. In some countries, like Germany, Russia, Japan, China, and Korea, these techniques are offered at school. Students learn how to regulate their heart beat, blood pressure, sleep and attention, how to handle stress. Those who have mastered these techniques can control their temper, not allowing impulsive or rage outbursts. In our clinics, we treat children who are prone to rage outbursts using "mental karate" to help them stay cool and control their physiological reactions. Parents can easily learn some techniques of hypnotic suggestions useful for specific problems. One of these techniques is as follows: after the child falls asleep, you come into the room and gently touch the child and adjust the pillow like you usually do. Then you gently rub the child's forehead and in a soft voice ask him to get into a more comfortable position. When the child gives some kind of response (ranging from making a face to actually changing his position) it means he is open to hypnotic suggestions. You have just transformed natural sleep into hypnotic sleep in which the body responds to external commands. You may whisper at this point into the child's ear, or continue touching his forehead, saying something like this, "You have a good night's sleep with wonderful dreams, sweetheart. Tomorrow will be another day. You can feel if you want to pee, and you will immediately wake up."

Many parents of children with bedwetting problems use this simple technique successfully as an adjunct to other treatments. Be sure that you do not scare your child in case of his sudden awakening. Talk and move in your usual way, not like a stage hypnotist. For more information on these techniques, contact the *Foundation for Children's Sleep Disorders* or the *Sleep and Behavioral Medicine Institute* (See Appendix for address/phone numbers).

Alternative treatments have become very popular nowadays and rightfully so. First of all, many so-called alternative treatments like herbal therapy, acupuncture, acupressure-massage, etc. have a long history, and are being successfully used in some countries as recognized therapeutic means in conjunction with other accepted medical procedures. For example, such compounds or herbs as Aloe Vera, Ginseng, and Motherwort (*Leounuri cardiaca*), are accepted as very powerful cures for skin disorders, nervous problems, etc. Acupuncture is also formally accepted in the medical community for pain control, treatment of drug dependency, etc.

There are several important principles to be remembered as guidelines when alternative treatment is considered:

1. Alternative treatments should not be considered in opposition to traditional medicine.

2. Alternative medicine should not be "alternative", but considered as an integral component at the beginning stage of treatment or somewhere in the therapeutic plan. It should not be introduced at the end as a reaction to disappointing results.

3. Alternative means are strong medicines, and, as any others, may help or cause harm. We have to remember how dangerous unknown treatments can be if they are used unprofessionally. Exercising caution and not rushing to conclusions would be reliable guides in making good choices for your child's treatment.

"A good laugh and a long sleep are the best cures in the doctor's book."
— Irish proverb

———•••———

"Medicines are nothing in themselves,
if not properly used,
but the very hands of the gods,
if employed with reason and prudence."
— Herophilis, 300 B.C.

PART

4

SLEEP AND ALERTNESS
THROUGH THE LIFE SPAN

PREGNANCY AND SLEEP

With the beginning of a new life, two new people evolve: the child and the mother. Politicians and pro-life supporters talk about the quality of both. For physicians, the primary concern is clear: the mother comes first. She is a changed person now. Psychologically, the whole external world becomes irrelevant to the pregnant woman. Her values and priorities change. So does her body. All metabolic processes in her are changing and, as a result, or maybe due to it, basic biorhythms like the sleep-wake cycle undergo changes, too. At the beginning, she seems to need more sleep.

Why should it matter to us how pregnant women sleep? To answer this, please recall a thalidomide tragedy, when women took sleeping pills, and several thousand babies were born without arms and legs. Why do so many pregnant women have trouble sleeping, to the extent that they need to take hypnotic drugs? How does the sleep-wake cycle of the mother relate to the development of the fetus? Sleep troubles in pregnant women have some influence on the fetus. Is it possible to find appropriate predictors of the future child's health, and can sleep in pregnancy be one of them? And, finally, what would be the best guidelines for the soon-to-be mother?

There are several good studies about the dynamics of sleep in normal pregnancy, including postpartum (after the birth of the child). During the early period, the pregnant woman usually sleeps longer and takes an increasing number of naps. She complains of being sleepy and daydreaming. During the later periods of pregnancy, sleep "latency"—the time from going to bed to falling asleep—increases, as well as the number of awakenings, whereas total sleep time and deeper sleep stages decrease. Why in the later stage of pregnancy does sleep become lighter and more interruptive? It is due to hormonal changes, specifically due to the drop in the thyroid hormone. Within four or five weeks after delivery, the thyroid hormone balance is restored if the pregnancy was normal.

Dr. Cepelak and his associates worked with thousands of women at various stages of pregnancy, and also found that although the average length of sleep increases markedly in the first and second trimesters, with a slight increase in the third trimester, the women's sleep becomes increasingly irregular and shallower. They also noticed that the content of dreams changes, with everyday experiences being replaced by dreams about labor and the baby. Women in later stages of pregnancy often have so-called *prodromal* dreams reflecting their heightened sensitivity to internal changes. *Precognitive dreams* reflect a heightened awareness of details of the external world. Another doctor noticed a very interesting fact, that intrauterine fetal activity appears to follow maternal sleep. These observations were checked with physiological monitoring, including E.K.G. and other physiological parameters during sleep, so-called polysomnography.

Dr. Levis found that healthy, pregnant women subjectively underestimate their amount of total sleep time and overestimate their awakenings. In complicated pregnancies, on the contrary, mothers-to-be underestimate the severity of their sleep disruptions. It is very important that the more deviated the pregnancy, the less the woman understands the severity of her sleep problems. It is also worth mentioning that REM sleep is increased in pregnant women, but it may sometimes be deviated, showing the appearance of rapid eye movements and alpharhythms, which is abnormal for this stage of sleep and characteristic of mixed stages. These changes are observed after four or five weeks of pregnancy and disappear after giving birth. Deep stages of sleep rapidly increase after the birth of the child. This actually means that the quality of sleep improves, which helps the mother to look after her child in spite of multiple awakenings. Pre-pregnant amount of sleep is commonly restored by the first menses.

Sleep disorders in pregnant women are extremely common. Dr. Martin Schweiger from England carefully surveyed a hundred pregnant women, 68 of whom reported significant deviation of sleep, serious enough to complain about to their doctors. Sixty-six of the women slept badly during the third trimester and 10-15 during the first and second trimesters. For 11 of them, sleep was a very serious problem throughout the whole pregnancy. Twelve percent of the mothers-to-be had such disturbed sleep, they took sleeping pills against their doctors' advice. Patients explained their changes in sleep in a variety of ways. The most frequently cited reasons were urination in sleep, discomfort, cramps, uncomfortable body positions in sleep and an uncommonly high rate of itching sensations. Five percent complained about another child disturbing their sleep. Interestingly, these women did not complain of that before pregnancy. This may be explained by the fact that women become much more sensitive during pregnancy. For example, one pregnant woman complained to me that she could not sleep because of the birds singing outside, which never seemed to bother her before.

If a woman had nightmares prior to pregnancy, they tend to occur less frequently during pregnancy, but may reappear afterwards. In emotionally disturbed women, nightmares may get much worse, especially at the end or after pregnancy. This is the reason why some women develop post-delivery blues and depression. The relationship between sleep disturbances, insomnia, and post-delivery psychotic behavior was noted very far back, having been first described by Dr. Savage in 1896. Post-delivery depression was seen as very closely associated with sleep disorders prior and during pregnancy.

Sleep terror was also reported to decrease in pregnant women, but it reappears in the post-delivery stage. Dr. Petre-Quadens, who studied the relationship between the mother-to-be and her fetus, noticed that the latter is much more active during the maternal REM sleep, especially if this sleep is abnormal. Researchers found that smoking destroys the mother's REM sleep. Researchers Formational Center of Health statistics in Maryland analyzed 10,000 normal infants and 600 infants who died later. The mother's smoking increases the chances for Sudden Infant Death Syndrome.

It is most important to notice that the majority of infants grow normally, despite many problems during pregnancy. Infants' resilience is astonishing! But we should not gamble with it.

It is known that triad, endocrine changing in pregnancy, changes and creates mood fluctuations. Emotional and sleep changes, during the menstrual cycle, pregnancy and the post-partum period are well-known.

There is another interesting aspect of pregnancy that seems worthy of consideration. It is the role of superstition during pregnancy. If you see a black cat coming your way, you may take it as bad luck, right? If you look at a disabled child, will your child be disabled? If you really believe that, look only at beautiful children when you are pregnant. This is the advice old folks often give to their pregnant daughters. Should we dismiss it as old wive's tales? When I was a medical student, my teacher, a renowned child psychiatrist, who did research on the relationship between pregnancy and childhood disorders, always advised me to look at the mother's superstitions very seriously. He described the experiments of another physician, who in the early twenties, hypnotized pregnant women, suggesting to them that they see mice jumping on their feet. In that community women strongly believed that if mice jump on your feet shortly after you give birth, the child will have a black spot on its skin, which may later disappear. Curiously, 10 out of 12 children born to those mothers developed this spot which disappeared within two weeks. Another pediatrician convincingly told me the story that when she was pregnant and was traveling to a different state, she met another woman on the train. The new acquaintance was going to the hospital because her newborn child had some kind of intestinal obstruction. The pediatrician was very scared and believed that this was a bad omen. After delivery, she found that her child has incomplete closure of the anal part.

Dear reader, if you happen to be pregnant and are reading this book, you should not panic. The important message of these stories is that self-suggestions are a real influencing factor for you and your child during pregnancy. Positive thinking during pregnancy is not a buzzword. A child who is healthy and talented is born not from a mother who did not have any problems, but from a mother who had a positive attitude and was content with herself. We highly suggest that you work on positive thinking. Focus on the good and positive in life.

In recent years, genetic predisposition became a very important consideration in studying the relationship between the behavior of the mother and that of her infant. Is it possible to predict the behavior of the infant by analyzing the behavior of the mother-to-be? Just 10 years ago this very question would have been considered nonscientific and strange, to say the least. In 1992, however, one of the journals on pediatrics described a study demonstrating that Type A behavior in pregnant women can be a forerunner of future similar behavior in their infants. Psychologists Hoffman and Bune described two characteristics of behavior called Personality A and

Personality B. A Type A person is competitive, and has an urge to master tasks and complete them quickly. This person has a sense of time urgency, and ambition. Type A is prone to have heart problems. Type B people respond to events in a low key manner. The study focused on Type A behavior in 70 pregnant, working, first-time mothers-to-be. They also studied 68 infants, examining them for eight hours after birth and three months later.

Guess what? Children born to mothers with Type A characteristics cried significantly more during their examination than babies born to Type B mothers. When the same infants were observed three months later, the mothers of Type A babies complained more about their infants than mothers of Type B babies. The explanation might be not just in genetics. It might be caused by the different behavior of the mother, and her different reaction to her baby. Type A mothers react very intensely. Their own intense responses increased stress hormones which affected their infant's behavior through the milk or through their body language. The interpretation of this research is not so simple. Yes, we look like our mothers, and we look like our fathers. We might even get our parents' habits. At the same time, our children have their own unique combination of genes and of good and bad genetic lines. We, parents and doctors, should just follow and support the child's own biological type of personality.

Nature should be our guide.

SLEEP IN NEWBORNS

Consolidation of sleep and arousal fragments into circadian biorhythm is a major task for newborns. Disorders of sleep and alertness are among the most frequent complaints of parents in pediatric visits. Sleeping through the night is the early important developmental milestone, which precedes the acquisition of good sleep habits by toddlers. Failure to establish this milestone may cause serious sleep and daytime problems.

There are two connected but different processes: one, regulation and consolidation of sleep and wakefulness and, two, maturation of sleep. Regulation refers to the infant's ability of smooth transition from wakefulness to sleep. Consolidation means the infant's ability to sustain sleep for an appropriate amount of time for his age. Fussiness at bedtime and frequent multiple awakenings represent disruption of regulation and consolidation. The appearance of unusual events in sleep, such as head rocking or apnea, represent deviation of maturation of the sleep state itself.

The human infant is one of the least neurologically mature at birth. Human infants experience the longest delays in both social and biological maturation. It is astonishing that 75 percent of human brain growth occurs after birth. An evolutionary perspective helps us understand why human infants are so immature. This immaturity forces them to rely on external regulation and external support, especially in the first year of life.

Upright locomotion and walking on two extremities (bipedalism) was being favored by natural selection two million years ago. Natural selection also favored two conflicting but equally necessary evolutionary trends:

(1) Smaller birth canal; and (2) larger brain.

The adaptive solution and compromise to this evolutionary dilemma is evident in neurologically immature infants for whom the main brain growth should not be in the womb but after delivery. Even our closest relatives, the chimpanzees, are born with 50 percent of their adult brain, compared to our 25 percent.

The composition of human milk, low in fat and protein, and high in carbohydrates—especially lactose—is a key nutrient needed for brain growth. The concentration of lactose in milk is highest among mothers whose infants are least neurologically developed at birth. (The milk of other mammals, such as lions or deer, unlike human milk, is high in fat and protein, and allows the youngsters to be satiated for longer periods of time.) Human infants need to be fed more frequently and to be in close contact with the caregiver all the time. This will be important to remember when we talk about breast feeding and sleeping.

The evolutionary perspective puts emphasis on the important changes the infant undergoes during the first year of life. Progressively, internal biological clocks that regulate the sleep-wake cycle are synchronized with repeating, internal signals, such as hunger, anxiety, and pain and environmental clues such as the light-dark cycle, ambient temperature, noise and scheduled daytime periods of social interaction. (See Part 2 for more on *Biological Clocks*)

According to a comprehensive study in England, about 50 percent of infants sleep through the night at six months, and about 9 percent are settled by 12 months, which means that they sleep uninterruptedly from midnight to 5 A.M. each night. Nocturnal awakening till 9 months, according to Mark McKenna's theory, is a normal adaptive compensatory mechanism for the prevention of too deep sleep and for training arousal mechanisms. Curiously, 50 percent of all infants who had settled early at 12 months of age began to wake up during the night once again. Night awakening was defined as a "problem" when the child woke up and cried one or many times during the night between midnight and 5 A.M., on at least four out of seven nights, for at least four consecutive weeks. The England study reported transitional awakenings in the nighttime as periods when the child struggles between settling and awakening.

American studies suggest that during the first year of life, infants manifest disruptive sleep seriously enough for parents to seek professional help in about 20 percent of cases. For toddlers, the rate of disturbed interruption increased. Interestingly, infants who became good sleepers early on sometimes had even more problems later. Chronic sleep problems are associated with increasing daytime behavior disorders. Many prospective and retrospective studies in adults emphasized that sleep problems which started in infancy may lead to chronic sleep problems through childhood, adolescence and even adulthood. Symptoms may change, but the underlying sleep pathology may persist.

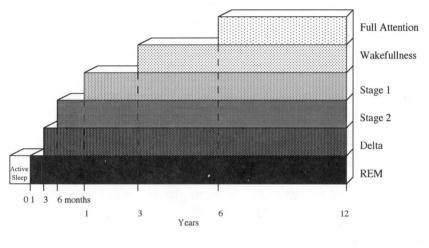

Fig. 4.1 This illustrates that sleep is a primary state in terms of human development. The development of productive attention is based on the development of normal sleep.

Common Sleep Problems and Their Solutions

Sleep-wake problems in infancy may be divided into *sleep onset difficulties, sleep continuity problems* and *a mix of the above.*

Sleep onset problems: problems at bedtime include both problems of going to bed and falling asleep. Sleep interruptions such as feeding, rocking and holding are a cure to sleep onset problems. Even though over 50 percent of infants are able to fall asleep on their own, the pre-sleep ritual is very important for infants' development. Older infants and toddlers will later on resist falling asleep if parents make an attempt to change this ritual. Problems of falling asleep include the procedure of going to bed. The child may demand to lie next to the parents while falling asleep. This particular moment of lying with parents and sleeping with parents elicits much controversial publicity. Co-sleeping — that is what it is called in scientific papers— became a big issue, especially in relationship with SIDS. In a New Zealand study, researchers believed that co-sleeping is bad, that it increases the risk of SIDS. In the program for SIDS prevention, they formally included co-sleeping as the fourth risk factor among the other three: prone positions, maternal smoking and non-breast feeding.

Proponents of co-sleeping base their arguments on the idea of so-called ecological validity introduced by Brunswick in 1955 and developed by McKenna into the anthropological theory of co-sleeping. To put it simply, McKenna's theory said that infant-parent co-sleeping was the prototypical behavior during evolution. That it is normal, natural, and has a lot of benefits. He and his colleagues believed that co-sleeping built up infant-caregiver attachments. Even physiologically, the co-sleeping environment is good. For example, CO_2 concentration from the mother's breath may alter the infant's breathing, inducing more rhythmic breathing. A low rate of SIDS in Hong Kong, Japan, Bangladesh, and the United Kingdom where co-sleeping is commonly used seems to support this idea. Serious consequences of parent-infant separation also became an argument in favor of co-sleeping. It was demonstrated during experiments that if monkey infants were separated from their parents just for three hours, the infants could experience significant detrimental effects, such as decreased body temperature, increased stress hormones, sleep disturbances and a compromised immune system. These experiments, however, were done during the daytime when both the parents and infants were alert.

Based on the idea that the infant and his mother had synchronized breathing, heart and metabolic patterns, McKenna recorded simultaneously several stages in mothers' and infants' sleeping together. It was discovered that the number of nighttime arousals increased greatly as compared to sleeping alone. The sleep stages shifted more frequently. There were more overlapping arousals due to confronting the baby. And most interestingly, both the mother and the infant spent more time at the same stage of sleep. The amount of known REM sleep was decreased due to multiple touching, to reassuring the infant, etc. Nevertheless, the mother reported that subjectively she slept better than at home. There are two other things worth mentioning. One, the mother and infant were asleep face to face, a few inches form each other. Two, infants were responsible for their own positions. If the infant sleeps alone, he spends more time in stages 3 and 4 (deep sleep).

Dr. Abrahan Sadeh compared two methods of calming infants with multiple awakenings: one is "checking" and the other, co-sleeping. He found that both are equally effective in 50 percent of the cases.

How can we interpret all these studies in terms of their practical implications? First of all, we should not overemphasize the practical implications coming from focused research studies. The data obtained shows trends, not concrete details of individual cases. I had several parents coming to me with scraps of paper, saying that we should trust this and this because it is the last word of science. Remember, sleep research focused on premature infants and was done mostly in laboratory situations or based on parents' questionnaires. Even if in the course of evolution, co-sleeping was natural, it does not mean that it is so today. Co-sleeping has its negative and risk factors. Sleep, both for parents and children, is less deep. Parental breathing might not be the best, both in terms of smell and rhythm. Co-sleeping itself might increase sleep problems in children. For example, "reactive co-sleeping" in older children who have frightened or conflicted feelings, tends to exhibit sleep problems.

Parental attitude to co-sleeping is also a crucial factor. One exhausted mother would like to sleep alone, to have enough room for herself during sleep, and feel comfortable. Or, you may have an anxious mother who likes co-sleeping because she feels calmer if she can touch her infant anytime. Do not forget fathers, either. Their point-of-view on this subject is equally important. Do not hesitate to ask yourself: do you feel comfortable with co-sleeping or solitary sleeping? Which is best for the infant? Time lapse video somnography demonstrated that during the first year of life, healthy infants may awake briefly one or a few times during the night without disturbing their parents.   Two thirds of them return to sleep without crying, i.e. "self-soothers".   One third of the infants will stay up for a longer period of time and finally arouse their parents, "signalers."

Self-soothers were found to be more likely to use sleep aids, such as pacifiers, fingers or lulling sounds. Moreover, self-soothers were generally put into their crib awake at bedtime, and they were able to fall asleep on their own. This pattern was repeated after they woke up in the middle of the night. The situation just described usually refers to older infants. One third of infants' "signalers", could be helped if crib rocking and singing were more accepted in our society.

As for co-sleeping, I would suggest, based on my understanding of research and my personal experience of being raised in a culture where co-sleeping was widely accepted, the following guidelines:

1.   Do not mix different sleeping arrangements. If you choose to sleep all night in the same bed, do not bring the infant over while feeding or comforting him.

2.   Use co-sleeping as a temporary measure, not as a rule—unless it is your strong cultural belief or financial necessity.

3.   Sleep alone separately within close proximity of the infant, which is healthy for you and for the infant.

4.   It is okay to sleep all night together with the infant in one bed if the baby is temporarily sick, if you are very anxious and do not want to jump from your bed many times. This arrangement should be clear for both parents, and it would be nice if the mother did not forget to brush her teeth an extra time.

5.   The family bed concept works only if all family members really feel good about it.

Frequent nocturnal awakenings are examples of *sleep continuity* problems. An interesting question arose from McKenna's study of the natural causes of sleep-wake development during the first year of life. It is how to distinguish between the infant's nocturnal awakening as a problem for the *infant* and a problem for the *parents*. It is accepted by many doctors that the first six to nine months of life are a period of rapid changes in sleep-wake patterns, sometimes in opposite directions ("inversions").

Intervention should be considered very carefully during that period. Reducing the number of awakenings at that age reportedly could have adverse effects on the future development of the infants. Nevertheless, very frequent awakenings, with crying or reversal of day and night, sometimes might be a very serious concern. Multiple nocturnal awakenings of infants cause serious problems for the family as a whole, waking up siblings or making parents very exhausted. The reasons for such awakenings may be different, ranging from internal problems to external problems, and medical disorders such as allergy, colic, breathing obstruction, including apnea, etc.

Feeding problems are quite common, and bottle feeding versus breast feeding is another controversial issue. Just a few years ago, many parents considered breast feeding as fashionable. Recently breast feeding became more accepted again. A somewhat controversial study published in a British medical journal found that premature infants who are breast fed scored significantly higher in intellectual tests than those who were breast fed. Out of 300 premature children, 210 were not breast fed. Three months later, they found that breast fed babies had, on average, an IQ eight points higher than equally weighed babies who did not receive breast feeding. There is data that breast milk has some components that enhance future development. Many researchers are now inclined to believe that multiple nocturnal feedings may increase the frequency of nocturnal awakenings, although this has to be researched more thoroughly.

Separation anxiety might be a cause for sleep disorders in young children, but it usually manifests itself a little later, somewhere about 18 months. We will discuss this in the next chapter.

In conclusion, real life presents many variations of normal development, as well as many individual problems. These solutions should not be at the expense of the child's future or the parent's present health.

"Sleep, Silence's child, sweet father of soft rest,
Prince whose approach peace to all mortals brings
Indifferent host to shepherds and kings,
Sole comforter to minds with grief oppressed."

— William Drummond

A Few Words About Non-Nutritive
Sucking and Pacifiers

Non-nutritive sucking is as important as nutrition. There is data that non-nutritive sucking has something to do with physiological states of alertness. In our own research, we investigated nine full term healthy infants, 9-12 weeks old, in sleep, active alertness, and the transitional stage. We recorded frequency, amplitude, duration, and intervals between sucking movements and EEG. We found that non-nutritive sucking and physiological states are connected to each other, and this connection is a process consisting of several phases. First, the children who cannot fall asleep start to have intense, high frequency, and long duration sucking movements with very short intervals. This time on the EEG is connected with large body movements. Movements are formed into clear alternating patterns. One EEG at that time, we see a synchronization with sucking movements while the child behaviorally and electrographically looks sleepy. And then, at that moment, sucking movements stop, and the child looks objectively asleep. During short episodes of arousal, short bursts of sucking movements appear again. Synchronization is EEG, followed by sleep.

This finally suggests that non-nutritive sucking can be an intrinsic isolator, functioning as a pacemaker of physiological states. In other words, sucking is a self-regulator of stages of alertness. Sucking also appears when the infant stops breathing during sleep, which is normal. Sucking movements interrupt this apnea and arouse him, functioning as a mechanism of prevention from deep sleep. This is the reason why we suggest a pacifier in situations when the child has multiple awakenings and also in cases of breathing irregularities.

Guidelines About Feeding

Speaking of breast feeding during the first month, several guidelines should be kept in mind:

1. To support and facilitate successful breast feeding experiences, both for parents and babies, the first guideline is to initiate breast feeding as early as possible within the first hour after delivery. Immediately following delivery, the infant is in a quiet, alert state and up to suckling with a little help. It also helps build the mother's confidence in her ability to nurture the baby. In general, it is good to feed the baby when he is alert, not sleepy.

2. Encourage frequent feeding. Most newborns need 8 to 12 breast feedings per day. Babies have different appetites and suckling styles. Remember that rigid schedules can lead to problems, such as engorgement, milk insufficiency, and slow weight gain in infants. Breast feeding should be comfortable for both the mother and the child.

Non-nutritive sucking with pacifiers should be encouraged during pre-sleep, because it helps sleep initiation and later on, self soothing.

3. The third guideline is to avoid bottles or supplements unless medically prescribed for the first three weeks.

4. For mothers returning to work—breast feeding and working are compatible. It just requires preparation. Breast milk can be frozen up to six months! Milk supply has daily and weekly biorhythms so the quantity of milk may fluctuate; thus, the most important guideline is *flexibility*. This is a major factor for successful breast feeding.

Another simple recommendation to remember— sweetened water quiets a noisy nursery. Grandmas knew about this long ago. A pacifier dipped in sweetened water will quiet crying infants almost every time. A modern study at Cornell University verified this popular belief. The investigators found that a small quantity of sweetened water reduces drying, and even seems to reduce pain for newborns undergoing medical procedures, such as blood collection or circumcision. Remarkably, the dose administered to the infant was no more than the size of a teardrop. The effect of the sugar was immediate, and the babies remained quiet for about five minutes after this.

Babies given just plain water "knew" the difference and kept on crying. Why? First, sugar is one of the natural "medications" with chronopharmacologic effects.   This means its effect depends on the time of intake or the patient's physiological state. (See Biological Clocks in Part 2).   Given upon awakening and in the morning, sugar activates the child.   Remember the notion that candy makes children hyper?   Yes, but only in the morning or upon awakening.   But sugar before sleep is one of the best sleeping pills, making infants calm down.

Nocturnal awakenings may be due to allergy. Allergy is a sort of immaturity in regulation of the immune system. It is hyper-sensitivity to inner or environmental factors, called allergens. Some allergies are caused by milk.

Dr. A. Kann of the Pediatric Sleep Laboratory at the University of Brussels, Belgium studied 33 infants who had difficulty falling asleep and staying asleep and found that almost all of them had allergies to milk. After elimination of milk, sleep improved.   When milk was given again, insomnia returned.   But parents should not rush to conclusions. In reality, allergies to milk are not common.

Allergy may be a cause of babies' colic. Colic may be treated by giving heated milk.

The most common food allergies are those to milk, corn, wheat, chocolate, eggs, nuts, seafood, yeast, red and yellow dyes. The latter is also important to remember for practical reasons. I had several patients who experienced unexplainable fever and deterioration of their sleep and behavior after my treatment with medications. Embarrassed, I searched for any mistakes in my logic, until, by accident, one parent told me that the fever occurred whenever yellow dye was present in the pill coating. When we changed the dose of medication (making it stronger), and eliminated these colors, all side effects disappeared. I recommend that you and your doctor check this possibility to eliminate unwanted side effects.

Childhood Colics

Colic is defined as intermittent, inexplicable crying during the first three months of life. This crying is not due to physical pain. A colicky baby is usually well fed, healthy, and happy between crying spells. Usually colics start in the first week of life with a peak at the end of the first month. The main symptom is a very disruptive screaming for a long time—between 30 minutes and 2 1/2 hours. Colic might happen at any time but the frequent and the longest periods are during the nighttime. Premature infants also have the same frequency of colics except that the onset occurs a little later—delayed until 39-49 weeks of gestational age. Boys and girls both may have this problem. Colics may disappear spontaneously after about three months of age.

Why do some babies cry so much? The majority of cases have at least two groups of factors: 1) inner, biological reasons making the child cry excessively; 2) external environmental reasons such as parents' responsiveness. The current view on colics, expressed by Dr. Marc Weissbluth is that colics are psychological problems, not caretaker's mistakes. Clear association with a certain time in the sleep-wake cycle, disappearance of colics after three months, and the delay in the onset of colics in premature babies support a biological cause of colics. In terms of psychosocial environment—the families of infants with colics are predominantly stable with good parenting skills. The mothers of these babies tend to be more anxious. What is cause and what is effect? Do the babies have colics because their mothers are anxious or are they anxious because the baby has colics? The latter is more probable. Colics happen independently of mother's reactions, although mother's reaction can prolong the episode. The nerve wrecking crying, especially during nighttime, can lead to significant emotional and psychological distress and sleep deprivation in all family members up to the point of irrational and injurious reactions.

Conceptually, colics are considered to be a symptom of disorganized sleep-wake cycles. Their treatment should be among the methods and means of stabilizing and developing good sleep habits with stable biorhythms.

Recommendations

1.   Colicky babies need to be held; never let the baby cry too long. Touching is the best treatment. Dr. Barton Schmith said that "there is no way to spoil a baby during the first 3-4 months of life".

2.   Gentle motions are very helpful to calm a baby, especially important rhythmical motions in different axes—rock, side to side, up and down, forward and backward. Of course, vigorous motions are not good, neither is shaking the baby. We found that one technique used to "hypnotize" animals is helpful in calming down a crying baby; put one hand on the baby's chest-abdomen, another on his back and head, and gently turn the baby over and back a few times. You will be surprised how infants like this motion.

3.   During the day it is important to carry the baby—carry him in a vertical position facing your breast; the baby will hear your heart beat and your breathing.

4.   During nighttime when crying is especially unbearable, rocking and pacifiers are extremely helpful.

5.   During the day, do not let the baby oversleep or overeat!

6.   Avoid bottle feeding. If it is not possible, check the formula.

7.   Co-sleeping for a few days with parents can be helpful in some cases.

YOUNG CHILDREN

With a newborn baby parents become quite busy, but they are still lucky, because the infant sleeps quite often and hopefully for a long time. But when the child turns into a toddler and then starts walking and running, parents can forget about time for themselves. Running all day after a tireless child, parents have fewer chances to get a restful sleep, because their sleep-wake cycle has lots its inner rhythm, and a new biorhythm connected with the external world is just starting to develop, but is not yet completed.

Multiple awakenings, whether disruptive or not, are typical and do not deviate from the norm as long as they produce no bad consequences due to extreme behavior of the child or extreme reactions from caregivers.

Why is good sleep so important? Because sleep is a fundamental biological metabolic state.

Sleep in small children is their release of growth hormones such as thyroid and cortisol. This release is strongly related to different stages of sleep. Sleep is the foundation for stable alertness and attention. Fragmented sleep leads to fragmented alertness with lows and highs, irritability, and colics. Aroused, irritable babies get exhausted and "crash" to sleep at the wrong time and in the wrong place, which further disrupts sleep and interferes with normal development. To develop good habits of hygiene is also important, because these habits have a tendency to be fixed. If bad habits get fixed, we have a problem. At this age parents can prevent or create problems. It is nice when visitors can play with the baby, but if it is too late in the day and happens too often, the child will become agitated and have difficulties falling asleep.

At the same time it is clear that some children cry less and sleep more, while others are just opposite. There are many individual traits and many cultural differences in the rearing process. There are no right or wrong ways. And there are no easy ways, either. In correcting bad sleep habits, some people believe in a "cold turkey" approach claiming that overreacting to the problem tends to spoil the child. Others support the method of gradually teaching the child proper sleep habits. Either can produce good results. Between 12 and 24 months, children usually nap once a day. A 1-2 hour nap is good and restorative, but napping after 3 P.M. might actually increase the child's irritability.

It is interesting that night sleep cannot make up for a nap. Nocturnal awakenings in ages 1-3 are considered by many to be a protection against sleep that is too deep. In other words, some arousals are the active brain's response to prevent obstructed breathing or to shift from deep to light sleep. In older children, bedwetting or other parasomnias will have preventive functions. At this age, it does not make any difference in what position the child falls asleep. Spontaneous periodic changes of body position develop in healthy children. However, strange sleep positions should be considered a warning signal. Abnormal positions differ from healthy ones by 1) strange appearance, and 2) resistance to a forceful change of a visibly uncomfortable position. (If you try, for example, to put the child's head from being upside down back on the pillow, he immediately slides back with his head down. If you continue to try, it ends in awakening or agitating.

Cry-babies become crabby kids, but well-rested children will have more chances to have a pleasant disposition during the day and to develop an optimistic, adaptive, and flexible personality.

PRESCHOOL SLEEP STORIES

The period between 3 and 6 years of age is extremely important in a child's life. It is a time of increasing social interactions when children's games transform from playing *near* each other to playing *with* each other. It is a time of joy and pain in relationships. It is a time of increased mobility and language comprehension. Daytime and nighttime become extremely rich and turbulent.

It is a time when major biological rhythms should be basically set. But at this time many sleep problems occur: nightmares, sleep talking, teeth grinding, multiple awakenings with and without agitation, bedwetting, numerous medical problems such as stomach aches, headaches, not to mention behavior problems related to alterations in alertness.

Preschool time is an age when external regulations of the biorhythm by parents or other caregivers are crucial. Children of this age should go to sleep no later than 9 P.M. and should be awakened between 6:30 and 8 A.M. Few children take naps after the age of 5. If they do, their nap time should be moved to between 11:30 A.M. and 2:30 P.M., and no later. If children have nighttime sleep problems, naps may be a good tool to correct them. Children at this age often have difficulties falling asleep, get agitated, or anxious. They often get out of bed, wander about, or go into their parents' room. The issue of sleeping with parents is extremely serious at this time. Parents' attitudes range from strict "NO" to the enthusiastic support of the concept of the "family bed".

Parent-child-sibling interaction becomes sensitive and fluctuating at this time. The whole world looks unstable: parents' own issues, such as their job, marriage, and finances, are reflected in their moods and behaviors. The child's increasing demands and disruptive sleep, add frustration and decrease parental patience.

The message is that during preschool age, more than ever, the WORD can stimulate peaceful sleep and happy alertness, but can also destroy both.

Any stories are real for children, because the fantasy world is their real world. Some people, psychologists among them, think that it is not good to tell children fairy tales, because in a way we are lying to them. Mother

Goose, Snow White, and Cinderella are not real. We have to teach kids reality.   Irena Nemchonok and Victor Peppard, who organized the Center for Healing Fairy Tales (see Appendix), believe just the opposite. Fairy tales are not only important for the normal development of a child's personality, but can treat some problems including sleep disorders.   According to them, children are especially sensitive to words. It is exactly their perception of words that helps us educate children, and acquaint them with the laws of nature and the rules of adult life.   Frequent repetition of "life's truths" at an early age is the cornerstone for the development of a child's common sense and moral values. And the more expressive that word is, the less moralistic and overbearing it seems to the child, the better the results we achieve. It is not surprising that we remember for the rest of our lives, the songs, verses, rhymes, and fairy tales we learn in childhood.

Fairy tales occupy a special place in the lives of children. The struggle between good and evil with the triumph of good, are especially captivating to the child. Children try to imitate fairy tale heroes in their dreams and fantasies. Fairy tales not only capture the child's imagination, they stimulate the child's ability to fantasize, promote the child's intellectual growth, and teach the rules of "life's game" in an unobtrusive way. Fairy tales teach us how to act in life's different situations and what consequences our mistakes can have.   Fairy tales encourage creativity. After all, it is our little dreamers who grow up to be inventors, artists, and creative people in all fields.

The great power of fairy tales may also be used *for the purpose of healing.* A fairy tale may act to enhance the healing process initiated by the doctor and by medicine. These are a few examples of how fairy tales are designed to help children of preschool age who suffer from bad dreams and bedwetting.

Examples of Presleep Stories

Fairy Tales from Irena Nemchonok and Victor Peppard
Story #1

"SWEET DREAMS"

Once upon a time, there was a Mama Turtle and a Papa Turtle who had a Little Daughter Turtle. The Mama and the Papa loved their Little Daughter Turtle very much, and they were always happy together.

But once misfortune struck: Little Daughter Turtle couldn't get to sleep at night. Every night at bed time Mama and Papa Turtle would make a nice comfy bed under a bush by the lake, and the best place in that bed was the one for Little Daughter Turtle. Little Daughter Turtle would lie awake for a long time with her eyes wide open, and when Mama and Papa Turtle closed their eyes and hid their little heads inside their shell-houses, she would get up and walk around the lake. She would walk and walk. She really wanted to go to sleep, but she was afraid to even close her eyes, because she had terrible dreams.

Soon Mama and Papa Turtle noticed that their Little Daughter Turtle was growing thinner by the day, and that she did not feel well and had a bad appetite. She even began to walk slower than the other turtles. So Mama and Papa decided to go to see the Wise Old Turtle. "Bring me your Little Daughter Turtle," said the Wise Old Turtle, "and I will have a little chat with her."

So Mama and Papa Turtle brought their Little Daughter to the Wise Old Turtle.

"What's the matter with you?" the Wise Old Turtle asked Little Daughter Turtle. "Why are you so sad? Why do you look so tired?"

"I can't sleep at all at night," answered Little Daughter Turtle.

"Why is that?" asked the Wise Old Turtle.

"I'm afraid to go to sleep, because I have terrible dreams," said Little Daughter Turtle sadly.

"And whose dreams do you see?" asked the Wise Old Turtle.

"I see my own dreams, of course," said Little Daughter Turtle.

"If they are *your own* dreams, then make them good and sweet."

"But I don't know how to do that," said Little Daughter Turtle.

"Here's what you do then," said the Wise Old Turtle. "As soon as you have a bad dream, wake up and tell it to your Mama."

That night the whole family lay down to sleep. Suddenly, in the middle of the night, Little Daughter Turtle woke up her mama. In a trembling voice she said, "I'm scared, Mama. I'm so scared. A Great Big Worm crawled inside my shell and wanted to eat me up!"

"Don't be frightened," said Mama calmly, "just keep seeing your dream. Tell the Worm to crawl out of your shell. Just look at how long and funny he is. He doesn't look at all like us, and he's not even a little bit frightening. And anyway, worms don't ever eat turtles. Go to sleep and don't be afraid. It's your dream. Make it a sweet one. Play with the worm. Make friends with him..."

Little Daughter Turtle went to sleep and saw in a dream that she was running a race with her new friend the Worm and all the time she kept coming in first...

In the morning Little Daughter Turtle woke up rested and happy. She ate a tasty breakfast and had a marvelous day...

Every night Little Daughter Turtle would go to sleep happy in her little bed. She knew that she could make any dream a sweet one, because it was *her very own* dream!

Story #2
"DRY WINGS"

Once upon a time, there was a Little Butterfly who felt very unhappy. She felt unhappy, because in the morning when all her Little Butterfly girl friends were having fun flying around from flower to flower, she had to sit in the sun and dry out her little wings. Every night she wet her little wings, and she didn't know how to put an end to this misfortune.

She told her parents about her problem, and they told her to talk to the Flower Fairy.

When Little Butterfly came to the Flower Fairy, she said to her, "Please help me, Kind Flower Fairy. Every night I wet my little wings, and in the morning I can't fly around with my Little Butterfly girl friends."

"What do you see in your dreams?" asked the Flower Fairy.

"I don't see anything," answered the Little Butterfly.

"That's your problem," said the Flower Fairy. "Try to see yourself in your dreams flying around from flower to flower with your Little Butterfly girl friends, gathering delicious pollen and drinking sweet nectar. You'll wake up in the morning dry as a bone, and you'll turn your dream into reality."

That night at bed time when Little Butterfly was getting into her bed, she recalled the words of the Flower Fairy, "You'll be flying around from flower to flower with your Little Butterfly girl friends..."

Little Butterfly went to sleep, and she had a dream. In her dream she was gathering delicious pollen, drinking sweet nectar, and happily flapping her little wings, and flying around from flower to flower with her Little Butterfly girl friends.

In the morning she woke up and saw that her little wings were dry as a bone, and she could go out to play and fly just like all the other Little Butterflies.

Every night Little Butterfly saw only sweet dreams, and from early morning to late in the evening she would fly all around on her dry little wings.

SCHOOL YEARS (6-12 YEARS)

School puts a lot of pressures on the child.   These pressures develop mature ways of learning and social interactions, setting the structural circadian rhythm of sleep and work.   The majority of children go through this period adequately.   Late studying, difficulties of awakening, daydreaming, and overactivity during breaks—are all normal, as long as these patterns are not fixed.   Many factors can cause deviations from the normal biorhythm—sickness, family stress, conflict with peers, etc.   Children do not usually complain about their sleep and have difficulties in verbalizing sleepiness.   They might be hyperactive, significantly dissociated from school situations, feel tired, and have learning problems.   If parasomnias appear, they may cause significant difficulties. (See Part 5)

At this age girls present different symptoms from boys.   Girls' symptoms are less apparent but they are more severe.

SLEEP PROBLEMS IN ADOLESCENTS

It is clear that adolescence is a unique period of life with its own problems and achievements. For the second time after infancy, there is such striking physical growth, hormonal restructuring and major psychological, cognitive and social changes. It appears that adolescents sleep like adults in terms of REM sleep or stage 3-4 deep sleep. Total sleep time is decreased from 10 hours during middle childhood to 8 1/2 hours. Current studies started by pioneers in pediatric sleep research, Mary Carskadon, William Dement and their colleagues revealed several interesting patterns.

The significant difference between school and non-school nights was manifested in very little sleep during school nights and oversleeping on non-school nights. This means that during non-school nights, teens are recovering from sleep deprivation. The following observations revealed a continuing decrease in total sleep time through the middle and late adolescence by approximately two hours. *Sleep deficiency has a tendency to accumulate.* The brain keeps complete records of the sleep "budget", and teens have to pay for sleep deficiency. A special test measuring daytime sleepiness, called MSLT (Multiple Sleep Latency Test), developed in 1987 in Stanford by Mary Carskadon, dramatically demonstrated that adolescents, even if they do not complain about lack of sleep, almost invariably go to sleep if they are given the opportunity.

The usual assumption that adolescents have a reduced need for sleep as they mature is *wrong*. The adolescent's need for sleep is even *greater*. Sleep requirements do not decrease. On the contrary, they *increase*. Teens have no dreams, or their dream life is extremely rich. One type of dreams is wet dreams, which include sexual contact, and we will talk about this a little later.

Several studies are devoted to sleep problems in adolescents. Results show that a significant number of adolescents complain of sleeping difficulties. A major study of adolescent sleep involving 900 teenagers from New Zealand, demonstrated that 33 percent of adolescents spoke of severe sleeping problems. Specifically, the most frequent concern was sleep deprivation. The need for daytime sleep was reported in 25 percent, and 10 percent of adolescents developed difficulties in falling asleep. About 7 percent had numerous severe sleep problems.

The quality of sleep changes in about 15 percent. These include parasomnias, such as severe nightmares, in about 12 percent; sleepwalking more than four times a week in 19 percent; headaches and other medical problems also appear to be excessively high. At the same time, we have to mention that most adolescents have no major problems, so we cannot say that adolescence in general is a bad age.

A very important fact was confirmed by different studies. Adolescents who suffer from sleep disorders are more than twice as likely to have daytime physical behavioral, or emotional problems. Physical problems include excessive daytime sleepiness and fatigue; also headaches and weakness. Emotional problems include anxiety and angry outbursts. Behavior problems include impulse control and attention deficit disorders. Sometimes there might be psychiatric problems, such as depression, including suicidal thoughts. Multiple sleep problems very clearly are associated with a higher level of psycho pathology, including depression, obsessive depression, violent and homicidal activity, obsessive thoughts, anti-social acts, and personality problems.

New findings suggest that adolescents' insomnia and multiple sleep problems should be used as biological markers, as red flags for mental health and other public organizations.

Surprisingly, research showed that the difference between girls and boys at that age was not as significant as expected. This means that social pressure, not biological pressure, is more responsible for sleep deprivation and other sleep disorders. The same conclusion is reached in analyzing the prevalence of sleep disorders, which show an increase of sleep disorders from 25 percent at the age of 13 to 33 percent at the age of 15 and then a slow decrease later on. It also speaks of the problem being chronic. Sleep problems are early signs of possible behavioral, emotional, and psychiatric deviations. As one doctor put it, "There are sleep problems without psychiatry, but there is no psychiatry without sleep problems."

Good sleep habits are important skills for adolescents to learn.

Adolescents like night. The put off going to sleep until early morning hours and then sleep until noon. Is this normal? After having read numerous articles, observing my own adolescent child, talking to many parents and trying to find the best answers, I came to the simple conclusion: "This is a period when your body is trying everything, but your mind should find what is the best for you." Given the adolescent age, social pressure, social clocks, are the most powerful regulators of biological rhythms. Biological needs and social pressure are competing. It is generally good if an adolescent tries his limits up to a certain point.

As much as parents like to stay away from their rebellious adolescents who fight about everything, the issue of enough sleep should be one of the most important things that parents should be concerned about. There is a simple rule for parents: within two weeks adolescents should balance their sleep checking account. The best way would be by taking a nap or going to sleep early. The worst way is to oversleep until 1 P.M. This is also the way to get a headache, depression, feelings of anger, and behavior outbursts.

Significant deprivation of sleep in quality and quantity causes major fluctuations in daytime alertness, the quality and quantity of wakefulness. As a result, many biological, psychological, and social stabilizers are developed, good and bad. To put it simply, multiple internal and external daytime "social habits" are created to calm oneself down or to wake up to focus attention or get rid of unpleasant feelings. Our habits are our pacemakers or switches. Habits are special functions that regulate, maintain and switch our levels of alertness. Many habits that are developed during adolescence are precisely such regulators of alertness. Loud sounds, dancing in discos with loud music, blinking lights, darkness and fogginess. If you look at the adolescent's facial expression, you will often see that he is in an altered state of consciousness. The message for parents is this: the deviation of the sleep schedule, unknown daytime habits of adolescents, are not bad by themselves. In fact, this may be a basis for creativity, a state of consciousness helping the person to find his or her own meaning in life. What makes the difference is *how* the teen and his peers, get into these altered states of alertness and *how* they *get out of them.*

Those pacemakers and peacemakers may be productive. They may be in the form of a small cup of coffee to awaken the person, exercises, excitement during a sports competition or before a tough exam. Or else it may be dancing to relax, or going to a friend for a good cry.

But it might also be a bad habit. It may be drugs, or alcohol to calm oneself down, self-cutting to release tension and angry outbursts to display depression. The question of why a beautiful little girl grew up to be a bitch, how a compliant boy became a raper later on, or why a very kind, good-natured child developed into a sadistic deviant is a question of the development of biological rhythms. Our personalities grew out of sleep. We, parents, have to encourage certain personality features, or some habits which may later play a more important role. Good habits of sleep and alertness are keys to making the difference between a good person and a bad one.

WHAT ABOUT LOVE AND SEX?

Love and sex are important for everyone, especially for adolescents. Sex, love, and sleep are connected. Even the expression "sleep with someone" means sex, but the connection between sleep, love and sex is much deeper.

Many vital habits which demand the coordination of body and behavior reactions, started in sleep. The sexual function is one of them. We have learned in Part 2 of this book that all physiological functions are channeled to different stages of sleep. In NREM sleep, physiological processes of rest and physical growth, including the growth hormone, are concentrated. In REM sleep a different type of reactivity and strong emotions are developing. We know, for example, that erection is present since the early days of life and active later in REM sleep. It has nothing to do with sex yet, but it has something to do with the coordination of all other bodily functions and dreams around the time of erection. One renowned sleep researcher, during an emotionally tense discussion about functions of REM sleep, exclaimed: "I don't know, but I feel that the erected penis is a conductor, orchestrating physiological rhythms, and it is an antenna to catch the dreams!"

He was essentially right. Experiments in sleep with measuring erection, so-called NPT (Nocturnal Penile Tumescence), clearly demonstrated that during erections rapid eye movements appear, breathing and heartbeat, electric skin response and other parameters are changed. If a person is awakened, he recalls vivid, emotionally charged dreams.

Adolescence is a period when this orchestra starts to play sexual symphonies. In 30 percent of dreams, adolescents reported sexual content with intensive, emotional feelings, including orgasms. In boys, ejaculation (so-called "wet dreams) is normal and serves some functions:

Physiologically, the body is ready for sexual activity and already has another serious function: discharge of energy. Boys after wet dreams and girls after sexual dreams wake up much earlier with a deep sense of rest, happier, and emotionally much more stable, during the day.

Real sexual activity is *not* vitally necessary for adolescents. Wet dreams in boys and something equivalent in girls are complete mechanisms to discharge sexual energy. Moreover, we are now accumulating data based on clinical practice with sexual deviants that very early, real sexual activity suppresses mechanisms of wet dreams. Some sexual deviants reported early sexual activity. The decrease or the absence of wet dreams decreased the vividness and emotional excitement of dreams in general, and during the day the adolescents had an increased sense of worrying. They developed an urge to do something unusual to elicit excitement.

One boy with sexual, sadistic habits told me his story. He grew up as a sensitive boy with a very rich dream life, including wet dreams. In his dreams he had created a new world where he and his friends were strong and all-powerful. He was coerced to have sex at the age of 12 with some older girls. He was excited at the beginning but felt increasingly tired and emotionally burned out after that. He found himself getting bored very easily. He had no dreams. On one occasion when he was tired and could not perform a sexual act, he angrily struck himself with a sharp pen and suddenly felt a rush, as if he had recaptured his previous level of excitement and alertness. Since that time he found that he needed to hurt himself to get aroused. His self-injurious behavior got more and more complicated. He inflicted pain to himself and later on to others. He developed a daytime confusional state. Fortunately, this case had a happy ending. He was successfully treated and became a good student. He went to college and he is soon going to be an architect.

Dear teens, do not rush into early sex!

Our habits, including sexual habits, have roots in our sleep. Good sleep is a foundation for good habits, and bad sleep is a foundation for bad ones. In this case, the REM orchestra might play something other than symphonies.

The sex drive and love are strong emotions. There are neurological structures and chemicals responsible for producing strong emotions. Cortisol, the hormone for strong emotions, is released in the morning during REM sleep. Research on violence discovered that persons, especially adolescents, who are prone to have rage outbursts and violent behavior, have a deficiency of central neurotransmitters. Studies from the Institute for Juvenile Research and the University of Illinois, confirmed that violent adolescence has a deficiency of a neurotransmitter called serotonin. Serotonin is a major transmitter for sleep mechanisms.

Our brain has centers for strong emotions, including "love" and "hate" centers. The search for brain mechanisms associated with emotions was started in the last century by Ivan Sechenov. His book, *An Attempt to Introduce Physiological Foundations into Psychological Processes* encouraged many to follow his lead. The renowned American neurophysiologist Carl Pribram demonstrated the existence of such centers by using electrical stimulations. You can observe the touching picture of a monkey who is gently holding her baby, feeding, scratching, and petting her gently. There is an expression of love and tenderness on her face. Suddenly the mother throws the baby on the floor and heartlessly watches her cry and suffer, an expression of hate and anger on her face. The next second, as if waking up, she jumps to the baby, grabs her, holding her and crying together with the baby with an expression of anxiety and guilt. What is that?! This is an experiment with implanted electrodes into different parts of the brain. Short electrical stimuli convert love into rage by blocking the centers of love and turning on the centers of hate. If you say that these experiments are cruel, you might be right, but you should also know how many people, suffering from epilepsy or brain tumors, have been saved by these experiments in which centers of dangerous emotions and behavior have been found and treated by being blocked with electrical stimuli.

There are also centers for the sexual urge in the human brain. Dr. Shepovalnikov, in his book, *How to Order Dreams*, presents a documented case when during an electro stimulated therapy session with implanted electrodes, a young patient suddenly fell in love with the physician performing the procedure. These feelings disappeared after the session. She ironically called it "electrical love." This is a good story for film makers, moralists, and politicians. But for us, parents and doctors, the moral of the story is that sex, strong emotions, and sleep mechanisms are strongly connected.

Allow me a small deviation from the topic. I read that if pigs were permitted to have copulation at any time, this activity would always result in pregnancy. Only 60 percent of unrestricted sexual activity will result in pregnancy in dogs, and only 25 percent of such sexual activity will end up in pregnancy in humans. (Sorry, if your experience was different). So, why do we need sex in the other 75 percent of times? Just for fun? It was generally assumed before, that during ejaculation, only one spermatozoon produced conjugation, and the rest were just a waste. New hi-tech methods demonstrated that the rest of the spermatozoan are not the best quality, but a huge hormonal pool which is sucked into the wall of the vagina, giving the body an enormous hormonal boost. This hormonal fluid contains material regulating biorhythms. Many lovers have closely synchronized their biological rhythms.

From a physiological point of view, love is a unique symbiosis of two people who develop synchronized biological and psychological rhythms. These fortunate couples develop not just common habits, but synchronized, deep biological metabolic rhythms, including sleep time, sleep positions, movements, breathing and heartbeats. Literally and metaphorically.

Many lovers are intuitively aware of this.

True love is monogamous.

Have you seen older couples who look alike after living together for many years? They also live longer than the rest of us.

They live together. They die together. God bless them!

Science agrees that love does exist. It is a real thing. It is born in sleep as "wet dreams" and continues to develop in daytime as mental creativity and physical strength. It makes our lives longer. Love is happiness. Love is a gift. If you have this gift, use it. Do not abuse it!

> *"The secret of genius is to carry the spirit of childhood into maturity."*
> *— Thomas H. Huxley*

PART
5

WHEN SLEEP PROBLEMS
BECOME A DISORDER

Types of Sleep Disorders

Static Phenomena in Sleep
(*"Quiet" Pathology*)

> Strange Sleeping Positions
> Sleeping with Open Eyes

Sleep Related Rhythmic Movements
(*"The Sleeping Pendulum"*)

> Headbanging, Head & Body Rocking,
> Shuttling, Folding, Periodic Leg Movements
> and Other Disorders

Paroxysmal Phenomena in Sleep
(*The Sleeping "Hurricane Andrew"*)

> Sleepwalking, Night terrors, Nightmares,
> Sleep Panic Attacks, and Bedwetting

TYPES OF SLEEP DISORDERS

When a sleep problem becomes a disorder, it can present itself with many "faces". Sleep medicine knows about fifty undesirable phenomena in sleep which can grow to severe, sometimes life-threatening proportions. These disorders are known under the umbrella name of parasomnias (*para* means around and *somnia* means sleep). It is important to note that the majority of parasomnias occur in children. At first sight, these disorders differ from each other immensely but upon closer scrutiny, it becomes clear that they have a great deal in common (see Part 2).

Scientists tried to classify these parasomnias into *primary* (caused by a deviation in the brain sleep mechanism) and *secondary* (those affiliated with other medical disorders, like heart, lung, or abdominal diseases).

In another scientific classification, parasomnias are divided depending on the stage of sleep with which it is primarily associated. For example, NREM parasomnias (bedwetting, sleepwalking, night terrors) and REM parasomnias (nightmares, REM behavior, disorders, etc.). All these classifications serve a good purpose because they help doctors, researchers and other people in the medical profession to establish a common language. The problem with existing classifications is that not all parasomnias are either primary or secondary, or else belong to certain stages of sleep. Another drawback, is that satisfying such classifications requires a great deal of expensive scientific equipment and this is not practically possible in many cases.

Based on many years of work as a practitioner, as well as a scientist, I found that the following clinical classification is best suited for purposes of parents' understanding of the issue and utilization of known scientific information.

Three easily identifiable features of parasomnias strike both parents and professionals—their suddenness, appearance, and duration. Accordingly, three basic types of parasomnias can be distinguished for practical purposes: *static, rhythmic, and paroxysmal.*

Static phenomena are the most misleading of them, because despite their "quiet" look, they might be signs of future serious problems. We can take as an example strange body positions in sleep which are, for the most part, within the norm but may sometimes verge on pathology.

Rhythmic phenomena bring to mind the pendulum of a clock. Children move their heads or their entire bodies in sleep for long periods of time. Just as static parasomnias, they are normal in most cases, but can also trigger medical problems.

Paroxysmal phenomena are sudden inner, vegetative, or mental outbursts of activity. Like the notorious Hurricane Andrew, they can destroy the family's peaceful sleep. Among them we find night terrors, nightmares, sleepwalking, etc.

These phenomena may develop to such severe proportions as to become injurious and life-threatening (see more in Part 7).

STATIC PHENOMENA IN SLEEP
("QUIET" PATHOLOGY)

The child sleeps deeply and quietly without moving and without disturbing anyone. Still his sleep might be considered deviated. Among the peculiarities of children's sleep, it is important to mention the static phenomenon. An example of this phenomenon could be a strange body position and sleeping with open eyes. These phenomena have escaped the attention of research but are quite important for practicing physicians and parents. It is very helpful to have some information to recognize deviations from normal sleep features.

Strange body positions. Old medical books seem to emphasize the strange way some people sleep. In recent years we have had a chance to rediscover the importance of body positions in sleep, especially for treatment of obstructive sleep apnea syndrome in adults. Unusual and peculiar positions in sleep are common in children as well. They are part of normal development. When and what kinds of positions can be considered abnormal?

All parents know that body position is a short-lived feature. If a child sleeps with his head hanging off the bed or his arms twisted in a peculiar way, then he is perceived as being uncomfortable. We know that the child will soon change it, and if not, we can easily move his head back onto the pillow, and his arms back into a more comfortable position. Many unusual positions might be especially favored by the child and may look "cute" to us. It is perfectly okay to have many and varied sleep positions.

But the situation might be different. The peculiar, unusual and strange positions can last too long. Most importantly, you may not be able to change them. If you try to put the child's head, for example, back on the pillow, he immediately slides down back into the same position. If you do this another time, it will have the same effect. If you forcefully prevent him from going back to the same position, the child may wake up, get irritated or exhibit some somatic symptoms. He might urinate, have an asthma attack, or start coughing. Observation convinced us that such positions are forced by some kind of inner physiological process. They are *internally set*. What is important, is that the children who have strange positions later on may develop some different sleep deviations, or some somatic problems. These strange positions may be early symptoms of future problems. It has become apparent that such specific, strange positions reflect some changes in the integrated activity of the sleeping brain. The following types of sleep positions, in our experience, may predict the appearance of psychosomatic problems:

1. There is a group of so-called *get-ready* positions which increase tones of muscles. They have what we call *hyper-tonus*. For example, the child looks as if he is stretching his arms or legs, and his muscles are very firm. The child pushes or butts his head and arms against the headboard of his bed. The tonus of his muscles is increased. Some of the children that we observed developed compulsive hair pulling later on. This position is usually associated with stage 2 of the first two cycles of his sleep.

2.   The so-called *upside-down* position. As in other forced positions, such as the first one described, the tones of muscles increase. In this case the child stayed for a long period of time with his head down and did not change his position. If you tried to put his head back, the child slid down to the same position. Several children with similar sleep patterns were found on the trauma unit having experienced a concussion from head trauma. We also saw such children developing body rocking.

3.   *Arched positions*. These are really strange variants of hypertonus. The whole body is over-extended. It looks like the child is standing on his head and feet. The body seems to be arched in an odd fashion. There was a

case when a doctor saw a child in this strange position in the hospital. He perceived these positions as a symptom called *opisthotonos*. This is a symptom of increased intracranial pressure. Lumbar puncture showed no abnormality nor did a thorough neurological examination. These types of positions were also observed in children who later developed nocturnal asthma attacks. This position, just as the upside-down position is usually common for stage 2 sleep.

   4.   These body positions are almost entirely opposite to the previous ones. All muscles of the body are completely relaxed, and even the chest is not visibly moving. To the observer, it looks like the child is "dead". Many mothers, in fact, call them *dead positions*. They often check if the child is breathing. Sleep recording shows stage 2 sleep. Such positions are typical of bedwetters before they actually urinate and of patients with sleep apnea before apnea develops. This position can also be seen in headbangers.

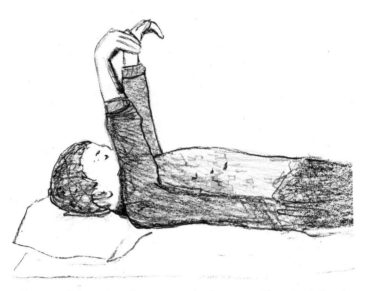

5.   Parents also report sleep with *stretched arms*. The arms are stretched in front of the child when he is sleeping on his back, and in some cases the child waves them in front of him. Sleep recording shows stage 3 sleep. These children are also prone to having sleepwalking, and/or sleeptalking episodes.

6.   *Sleep with open eyes*. Sleep with open eyes is quite common and normal for newborns and infants, and sometimes perhaps for older children. During the first stages of sleep, the child's eyelids are not closed

completely, and you can see the eyes between the eyelids. However, sometimes in older children and adolescents the space between the eyelids is large enough to leave an impression that the person is looking at you. Sometimes the eyes are turned up and toward each other, and you can see them clearly. This has quite a threatening appearance, and it is called "rabbit eyes." The view might be quite disturbing for parents. It happens during the 2nd and 3d stages. This phenomenon is not seen during naps, nor is it observed in REM sleep. The significance of open eyes for diagnosis or the prediction of different disorders is not clear, and it should be investigated much more carefully. We know that open eyes may be one of the first symptoms of neurological disorders. In many cases, the prognosis for treatment is quite favorable.

These are just a few of the positions that we believe to have clinical significance. There are many variants of positions which need to be studied more intensively.

Analysis of the dynamics of normal positions developing with age shows that the positions are maturing parallel to the age of the child. The fact of "maturation" is important to know, because different ages are associated with different types of dominant positions in sleep. With every year the general characteristics of basic positions are also changed. And it is fascinating that often the position changes to the opposite type. We call it "inversion" of positions. For example, newborns have predominantly hypertonus types of positions, but after six months the child's positions become hypotonic when his muscles are very soft and look like they are paralyzed. During the second year of life one position quickly changes into several different positions. At age 8, again we can see predominantly one position. When the child gets sick, sleep positions change, often to the most recent previous ones, or to the position favored by the child when he was an infant. Position changes are very sensitive to internal (somatic) and external (psychological) factors. In older children, we have seen regression to the position of young children, especially if the person got sick or depressed. Strange positions in sleep are, in fact, the exaggeration of positions seen in normal situations. In 1962 Dr. A. Peiper described the position similar to the arched or so-called opisthotonos position in children who were suffering from Vitamin D deficiency.

There are so many different positions, some of them very elaborate, whose significance is not clear. Some have the same characteristics as those described above. For example, the child covers his head with a blanket or when touching a cold surface with his feet.

If the position is forced, changing it can cause irritability or some somatic and related symptoms, including breathing or heart problems. Strange positions might have clinical significance if you cannot easily change them, and you become aware of changes in the quality of awakening, next day alertness, hyper activity at bedtime, and other negative symptoms of the quality and quantity of sleep. If these positions are associated with problems in sleep and awakening, maybe we should consider addressing this issue.

SLEEP RELATED RHYTHMIC MOVEMENTS ("THE SLEEPING PENDULUM")

Headbanging, Body Rocking, and
Other Rhythmic Related Activities

Headbanging, head and body rocking, and other similar rhythmic movements around sleep time are fascinating, puzzling, and sometimes frightening phenomena. It is fascinating to the observer because it is a very dramatic picture of the child rhythmically banging his head against the pillow, his fists on the corner of the bed, rocking side-to-side, or otherwise thrashing his body in the bed for a long period of time. It is puzzling because these phenomena are unusual and contradict the common logic that sleep is a restful state. Besides they are unexplainable by traditional medical theories. It is frightening for parents because they feel helpless against the prolonged and sometimes injurious behavior of their children. The parents often forcibly try to stop these movements. The child stops such sleep behaviors for a short period of time, only to resume them more intensely. In severe cases, the child can hurt himself, which results in bruises on the face and head, or he may have associated breathing and pulse arrhythmias. The family will experience sleepless nights due to loud, annoying and dreadful rhythmical noises from the shaking bed, or they may endure complaints about noise from neighbors or even accusations of child abuse. To further complicate the issue, the child often has difficulty waking up in the morning, experiences daydreaming, attention and learning problems at school, and the parents, too, show a decline in their own performance during the day.

There are several misconceptions about headbanging, head and body rocking, and other similar rhythmic movement disorders. The common notion that head banging and rocking are benign is the *first misconception*, causing denial by parents until the habit starts to control the child's and the family's life. The *second misconception* is that these phenomena are rare. Dr. Sullivan found 500 cases of rocking and banging in just one California school district. The Sleep and Behavioral Medicine Institute of Chicago, without advertising, has 115 patients with severe rhythmic movement disorders. The Institute was featured on a television show, and after that single program we received 250 calls during several following weeks. The *third misconception* is that bizarre activity such as headbanging is the result of brain damage, and as such would be seen only in mental institutions for severely handicapped and neglected children.

It is true that brain damaged and severely neglected children are involved in self-injurious repetitive behavior, but in such cases the activities are not sleep related and occur in the daytime. Sleep related rhythmic movement disorders occur predominantly in intellectually normal or even gifted children who have been raised in caring and loving families. The *fourth misconception* is that head rocking, banging, finger sucking, and playing with one's hair is a "cute" phenomenon of infancy. When the older child or an adult bangs and rocks his head, or sucks his thumb, it is not cute anymore. It becomes an annoying problem that persists through adolescence, into young adulthood, and on into old age. Our oldest patient is a 61 year old woman. Dr. Felicia Cohen of the University of Illinois surveyed sleep habits of patients with narcolepsy (a disorder causing sudden sleep attacks and muscle weakness) was surprised to find that 7 percent of these patients, whose mean age was 61 years, exhibited body rocking. The *fifth misconception* is that nothing can be done to control this habit. Hopeless and helpless parents and older patients often give up, explaining the problem as "just a bad habit". Others get "sucked into" the short-lived pleasant dissociative component of this "habit".

Now with the emerging field of sleep medicine and the new discoveries in the physiology of biorhythms, we are getting closer to understanding the nature of these problems and are developing effective methods of treatment. Keeping this in mind, let us look at this problem step by step.

Terminology and Classifications

The International Classification of Sleep Disorders recognized the association between sleep and headbanging, rocking, and similar stereotyped repetitive movements involving a large group of muscles, by creating a category of "rhythmic movement disorders" separate from other repetitive activities such as bruxism (teeth grinding).

These types of motor activity can be seen in humans and in animals; young and old, in normal and pathological, in natural and experimental conditions. To treat clinical forms of sleep related rhythmical movements we should select human sleep related rhythmic motor activities from other stereotyped behaviors as a separate clinical entity to investigate the specific subtypes. To name this distinct clinical entity we use the Latin term *jactatio nocturna* as an umbrella term. This term reflects movements appearing around sleep time in identical cycles with frequency closely related to the heart rate. It may be rhythmical swinging of the head (jactatio capitis nocturna), the body (corpora), or the extremities (arms). The term jactatio is an abbreviation of the noun *jactation* derived from *jactare* which literally means "rhythmical swinging of the body and limbs to and fro"; "to toss about"; "to throw back and forth". Since 1680, French and German literature has commonly used the word *jactation* to mean rocking. In 1731 in Temple Ess it was noted that "Jactation... help or occasion sleep, as we find by cradles or dandling them in their nurses arms." In "Enthus Methodists" (1754) by Levington, there is a chapter entitled "Various Tumults of Mind and Jactation of Body".

Because of its original meaning of rhythmicity, cyclicity, and relation to sleep, the term "jactatio nocturna" was formally used in European medical literature since Zappert (1905) and Cruchet (1906). Jactatio nocturna is close to other parasomnias such as enuresis nocturna.

Clinical Forms (Subtypes of Jactatio Nocturna)

There are differences between patterns of rhythmical movements which seem to be clinically and therapeutically significant: direction (axis) of movement; monotony versus bouts of rhythm; asymmetry; relation to the stage of sleep or level of alertness; age of onset; severity; transformation from one form to another; and progression into adulthood. These parameters seem to be different for each pattern. At least five groups of clinically significant sleep related rhythmic movement activities can be identified. (The following figures illustrate these groups)

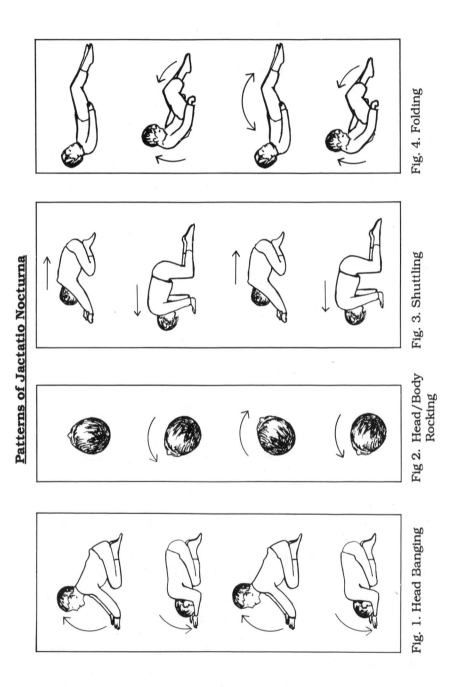

Patterns of Jactatio Nocturna

Fig. 4. Folding

Fig. 3. Shuttling

Fig 2. Head/Body Rocking

Fig. 1. Head Banging

1. *Headbanging.* (See Figure 1) In the prone position the person repeatedly lifts his head or upper body with outstretched arms and forcibly bangs his forehead or cheeks against the pillow, his fists, or against the hard edge of the bed. Parents and older patients label this pattern as headbanging and easily identify it when presented graphically.

In infants or in mild cases of older children, the child moves only his head. In more severe cases the whole upper body is involved. The movements are up and down. The force and speed increase on the way down, giving the strong impression of "beating" the forehead, cheeks, or temporal parts against the hard surface. In mild cases or at the beginning, the banging lasts 5-10 minutes without interruptions with a frequency of 60-65 per minute then increases to 82-89 per minute and appears in clusters. Clusters start and end abruptly as if turned "on" and "off". Several clusters of banging compose an episode, lasting from one minute to two hours. Episodes may occur through the night and later shift to the day during sleepy or drowsy conditions. External stimuli usually stop movements for a short period of time but the movements soon resume with greater intensity. Turned to the supine position, the patient either turns back on his stomach or begins to rock his head so vigorously and asymmetrically that it appears as if he is still beating his cheek against the pillow.

2. *Head rocking.* (See Figure 2) In the *mild degree*, the patient is supine, eyes closed, and performs pendulum-like movements of the head in a sideways fashion. The movements are rhythmic, smooth, stereotyped, with a frequency of 60 to 80 per minute. The length of an episode varies from a singular movement to 5-10 minutes. The general pattern of movement (the length and frequency) is individually constant. An episode starts and ends smoothly. The extremities and the whole body are relaxed and immobile, or with some slight movements in the same rhythm as the rocking of the head. Movements occur when falling asleep or waking up. There is no rocking during the daytime. The patient is always aware of the rocking and reports feelings of pleasure and peace from them. In the presence of other people or sounds, these movements stop immediately but resume shortly thereafter. In the morning, the children have full recollection of the

behavior and willingly demonstrate rocking. In the daytime, such children are cheerful, active, and creative. Emotional instability with exaggerated affective reactions is usually the reason why their parents seek medical help.

In the *moderate degree* of rocking there is greater motor involvement of the extremities and the whole body. An episode occurs with movements that are more intense, and appear in clusters (as in banging). The duration of an episode increases, and there is an increase in the number of episodes per night. Movements occur in the daytime when the child becomes excited. The child no longer appears to be relaxed; on the contrary, he is tense while performing the stereotype. Sharp movements of the head are followed by sharp movements of the body in the same direction. An important feature of the moderate form is involvement of the upper extremities and asymmetry of the movements. A movement of the head is followed by that of the arms, with the elbows bent. The movements are more intense on one side than on the other. The duration of clusters is greater (up to 30 minutes) with the frequency remaining at 60-90 per minute. The clusters start and end abruptly as if "plugged in" and then abruptly "unplugged". In the presence of another person, the movements stop. This is the reason why parents do not try to stop the child. During the daytime children do not appear to be suffering. Sixty-one percent of patients in this group have a tendency toward other stereotypes such as thumb sucking or nail-biting.

In its *severe degree* rocking can be so intense that it looks like a seizure;
sharp throws of the head, the arms and the entire body are flung in a sideways fashion. The arms may be outstretched with fists clenched, or the arms may be bent at the elbows and pressed to the body. The movements are always asymmetrical. The asymmetry does not significantly coincide with right- or left-handedness. The duration of a single episode of rocking may be up to several hours, and as many as two thousand movements may be made without stopping. In two cases, the episodes lasted for five hours with some pauses (about a minute in length). During pauses, EEG readings showed transitional sleep between stage 2 and 3. In severe rocking, dizziness and vomiting sometimes occur. It is not always possible to forcibly stop the movements. Children with *mild* rocking wake up

cheerful, active, and showing no signs of sleepiness. But, children with the *severe* form of rocking frequently have difficult awakenings, are late to school, and have learning problems due to a shorter attention span and daydreaming. In general, children who rock have a normal IQ and are creative, but may have difficulty in conformity and discipline required to perform well in school. Their involvement in rhythm may at times assume exaggerated forms.

3. *Shuttling.* Rhythmic movements of the body at the elbow and knee position, moving forward and backward along the horizontal body line. 50 percent of patients describe it as "shuttle-like"; 12 percent call it rocking; 7 percent use the term banging; 31 percent are unable to name it. We prefer to keep the term "shuttling" which was readily accepted by the patients and are identified in the illustration. (See Figure 3)

Like other non-epileptic forms of movement in sleep, shuttling stops for a short time only to resume with increased intensity. This form is usually seen in infants. Later, it may transform into headbanging, but may continue in the original shuttle-like way. We have observed six children (5 males and 1 female), ages 6-10 weeks old with this problem. (All of the boys were referred to the doctor's office with a chief complaint of masturbation. Video documentation of the children in sleep demonstrated that the movements had nothing to do with masturbation.) The forward component of the shuttling is faster than the backward component. The head is always set against the pillow or the wall. The child actively swivels the head with increased pressure on the head. Children do not express pleasure from this activity. They vaguely remember this, and they sometimes attempt this activity to get rid of drowsiness, anxiety, and shaking sensations.

4. *Folding.* (Figure 4) Six patients described "folding up" movements similar to a jackknife, while in a supine position with sudden rhythmical movements forward to sit up, back to lie down, and then forward to sit up again. The force and speed increased on the way up and forward, so the child might actually hit his forehead against his knees.

Other rhythmic phenomena may form a part of the above described types as their prelude or else may entail leg/hand waving, kicking, extensive finger or tongue sucking, rhythmic vocalizations, or rhythmic hair pulling.

The Natural Course of Jactatio Nocturna

Despite many differences between different types of jactatio nocturna, there are common stages or periods in their course.

1. *Undifferentiated period.*   This is a period of unspecified deviations of the sleep-wake pattern, and it is usually related to newborns or infants.   It reflects instability of the development of the sleep-wake cycles. The child is irritable, hyperalert, has "colics", and a reversal of night and day is apparent. This period usually ends with the appearance of jactatio. The symptoms may also be seen during the course of treatment.

2. *Period of crystallization.*   This term reflects the critical period of the appearance of jactatio. Many parents report this interesting phenomenon: appearance of rhythmic activity with "normalization" (disappearing) of symptoms of instability of sleep.   Children sleep better after and between episodes of movement and are more alert during the day.   The age of onset for jactatio nocturna in otherwise normal children ranges from one month to two years of age, depending on the type of behavior.   Overall mean onset is 5-6 months.

3. *Monosymptomatic period.*   This term reflects a long period of predominantly one form of jactatio in children and adults who are generally normal medically, neurologically, and intellectually. This period may last for years and end by self cure. It may become transformed into other symptoms (substitutions), disappearing under or during treatment, or else move into a period of deterioration. There were cases when a patient with headbanging, after a head trauma developed leg kicking of the same frequency.

4. *Period of self-cure or deterioration.*   This term reflects a period of a dramatic increase in the intensity and amplitude of movements; the appearance of additional types of movements; and often medical and psychological symptoms.   For example, previous mild head rocking may dramatically increase in amplitude of movements with involvement of the arms and the entire body. Additionally, headbanging, bedwetting, and breathing or pulse arrhythmia might appear.   This is a period when problems that once occurred only in sleep and were hidden from others by the cover of night begin to appear in the light of day as emotional, learning, and behavioral disabilities.

Psychological Profile of Children, Adolescents and Adults with Jactatio Nocturna

As it was mentioned earlier, the majority of the children, adolescents, and adults are intellectually normal with a wide range of intellectual abilities from "below average" to "superior". The general impression is that this is a group of nice looking, likable, emotionally warm, and active children. Often they are gifted in humanitarian subjects and may have difficulty in structural settings and boring tasks. They seem to fancy activities connected with rhythm such as dancing, or music (especially drumming); they like swinging and rotating. Adults also enjoy clear rhythm, like jazz music.

It is possible under the close scrutiny of treatment, to differentiate between "bangers", "rockers", etc. Generally, "headbangers" are more hyperactive during the day, have more problems in early development, and have a more turbulent course of the affliction. "Headbangers" remember their movements less and report more unpleasant sensations, while "rockers" have a tendency to like the feelings produced by rocking and often "do it" voluntarily which quickly makes jactatio into a daytime habit.

Objective Evaluation of Patients with Jactatio

Evaluation of patients with jactatio nocturna is somewhat difficult because it is unclear what to look for. The children are generally healthy, without apparent medical problems. However, ear infections, difficult nasal breathing, and morning headaches seem to be more commonly encountered than in the general population. Neurological and neurophysiologic examinations usually reveal a frequency of so-called soft neurological signs. These include sensory-motor disintegration; right-left confusion; increased sensitivity to one stimuli and a decreased sensitivity to another; decreased sense of danger, and increased anxiety to benign situations. Examinations of bioelectrical brain activity (EEG) show an increase in maturational deviations compared with age matched normal controls (especially in headbangers). All changes are soft and diffuse. There are almost no cases with epileptic activity.

Most significant findings come during the recording of sleep using all night registration of multiple physiological parameters: EEG, eye movements, heart rate, breathing, muscle activity, etc. The sleep architecture of patients with advanced forms of the affliction is disorganized. The "switch" from one state of vigilance to another is difficult. For example, from restfulness to sleep, from slow sleep to REM, from deep REM sleep to awakening, etc. It is important to mention that episodes of head banging and rocking might be in any stage of sleep, but predominantly between stages. During jactatio heart beats, breathing, and brainwaves slowly start to synchronize with the rhythm of the movements. In other words, the movements induce a similar rhythm of brainwaves. Movements stop when the child falls asleep. This fact made researchers conclude that jactatio has some function as a "transmission" or "pacemaker" switching or stabilizing different states of vigilance. Started as a compensatory phenomenon, rocking and banging may bring many problems later on.

Where is this natural "transmission" switch mechanism of our states of vigilance? We do not know many details but it is a complex of central brain circuits including the so-called central vestibular system. Vestibular tests show that although the peripheral parts of the vestibular system are intact, their central circuits are undeveloped in those with rocking and banging. This is evident by functional asymmetry (superstability of movements in one direction and significant reactions in another direction of movement). Rhythmic movement disorders can be conceptualized as sensory-motor disintegration. Simply stated, immaturity of the central coordinating system might be the basis for self-induced (physiological and psychological) rhythmic movements in specific instances.

Periodic Leg Movements

Periodic leg movements and restless legs syndrome (PLMS) was described in adults, but was thought to be rare during childhood. Recently, Dr. Sheldon from Chicago discovered that this phenomenon is actually not so rare. Symptoms are typically characterized either by a complaint of difficulty initiating and/or maintaining sleep or excessive daytime sleepiness.

During the polysomnographic evaluation in a sleep lab, periodic episodes of repetitive and highly stereotypical leg movements in sleep were recorded. Muscle contraction lasted 0.5 to 5 seconds with more than five consecutive movements. The interval between the clusters of such movements ranged from six seconds to 90 seconds. Sometimes movements persisted during awakenings. Little is known about the character, etiology or clinical significance of these periodic leg cramps. They are different from the slow rhythmic movements of the legs as a part of jactatio where the whole limb is involved. In PLMS only separate groups of muscles are involved in the fast spasm-type of jerks. PLMS is seen during the sleep-wake transition. Daytime symptoms of these children ranged from behavior problems, hyperactivity and school learning difficulties and excessive daytime sleepiness.

Treatment of Rhythmic Disorders

The treatment of stereotyped behavior is rather challenging. It is recommended to begin the treatment with paying more attention to the child. Attention especially before sleep might be quite helpful for children growing in unstable families, or having chronic illnesses. The value of the attention factor in healing stereotyped movements during sleep, especially in case of rocking, is shown in the next example.

Jane is six years old. When she was two months old, she was hospitalized with pneumonia. Right after that, it was noticed that the girl was rocking for a long time before falling asleep. She was raised by her grandparents until she was five years old. Then she went to live with adopted parents and soon won their love. In this new family, the rocking symptoms eventually stopped.

Besides attention, the child needs physical exercises (skiing, running, jumping rope, etc.) In all of these activities, participation of fathers is important.

Rhythm and music therapy occupies an important place among treatment methods. Children often ask to sleep to the sound of music with a clear rhythm like drums and metronome. Music with a distinct rhythm promotes the process of synchronization in the brain and sleep (for example, a lullaby with rocking). Some families successfully use a metronome. It is known that imagining oneself rocking can cause the same effects of synchronization in the brain as actual rocking. Children with rocking are distinguished often by their vivid imagination. They can easily imagine rocking before sleep. This produces, in the brain, an appearance of EEG waves which synchronize in rhythm with such imaginary ramming and rocking. That is why the image of rhythmic movements (swinging, watching an imaginary clock pendulum) might be helpful. It is not recommended to stop rhythmic movements in sleep by forcefully waking up the child, or punish him for "bad habits". Also, it is not good to limit children's freedom of movements during the daytime, and especially during bedtime when they get overexcited. In this case, parents have to change these movement activities or social activities by organizing something like "nighttime exercises" with a maximum number of rhythmic movements (dancing, jumping rope, etc.)

In moderate or severe cases there may be a need of pharmacological supplements to psychotherapy. Again, this must be discussed with your doctor.

Sleeping medicine like Phenobarbital is not recommended because this group of drugs may cause movement cycle disorganization in sleep. Moreover, it slows activities during the day.

We received promising results using medications which regulate and stabilize functions of the vestibular system. One of them is Antivert®, an antihistamine widely used for the treatment of "sea sickness" or motion sickness.

There is no data for the use of Antivert® in the treatment of children's movements associated with sleep, but we have positive responses for headbangers. Antivert® was somewhat less effective for headrockers.

In cases of stereotyped movements in sleep, we found the internal use of Hydrocarbonate Na to be highly effective.

This method was originally suggested by Hasegawa (1949) for patients who are easy to lull.

In 1960 the same author informed the reading audience about the effect of this solution for the treatment of Meniere's disease (a fairly common problem presenting with vertigo, nausea, and hearing problems). At the same time, antidepressants, which were so good for many childhood sleep disorders such as bedwetting and bedtime fears, did not demonstrate high efficiency for stereotyped activity. Imipramine was better than placebo for headbangers but less effective than a mild tranquilizer.

Mild tranquilizers such as Xanax 0.25 before sleep for children older than five years bring about some improvement (as well as the long acting benzodiazepine, Klonopin®). Tranquilizers of the non-benzodiazepine group (those that are not addictive) were also mildly effective.

We found that a combination of medications increasing daytime alertness and improving sleep structure usually gave better and faster results. A combination of Ritalin® or Cylert® (mild CNS stimulants) in the morning and Imipramine at bedtime was the most effective. We also found that natural stimulants such as Siberian Ginseng (in pill form) can substitute Ritalin® for some children.

For children with a severe degree of headbanging or rocking, we found it to be a successful treatment, but unfortunately this included intravenous infusion of Hydrocarbonate Na. Because this method is used in Europe and is little known in the USA, let us dwell on it a little more.

As we already mentioned, it was suggested 45 years ago by Japanese doctor, Hasegawa, for patients who often fell down or had functional vestibular problems. He later wrote about the effect of this solution for motion sickness.

According to research, Hydrochloride Na stabilizes metabolic balance, promotes better oxygen utilization, especially in sleep. It also stabilizes blood pressure, and the cardiovascular and respiratory systems.

Hyperactive children with severe headbanging, sleepwalking and enuresis responded well to this treatment, but a word of caution should be said regarding children with acute respiratory problems.

This method can also be used in neurologically compromised children with self-injurious behavior when behavior modification did not work.

Old Rocking Bed   Used in the past for a "rocker", the infants were often placed in the parents' bedroom; used as a *rocking bed*.

The treatment of headrocking and headbanging is still a challenge. We do know that if the child still bangs or rocks at the age of five years, the chance that he or she will outgrow it is very little. The search for a better understanding of the nature of these disorders and their successful treatment should be continued.

At the Sleep and Behavioral Medicine Institute, we have developed a special rocking bed which moves in synchrony with the patient's rhythmic movements. The treatment protocol is in research stages; as of the current response to this treatment, results are promising.

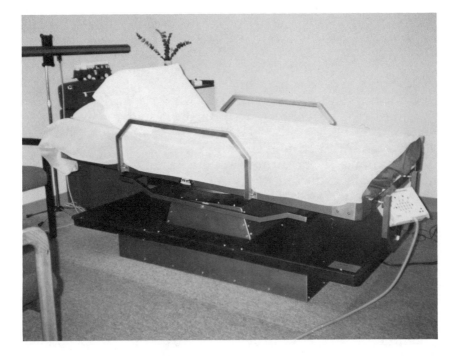

Rocking Bed   The bed mimics movements of a patient; control panels may also change variables such as the frequency and direction.   Applications in treatment of rhythmic movement disorders. *(Source: Sleep and Behavioral Medicine Institute, Chicago)*

In conclusion headrocking and banging are not always benign phenomena. They reflect immaturity of the "switch" mechanism responsible for biological rhythms. The treatment of these afflictions should be based on methods and means of stabilizing or inducing maturation of the sleep-wake cycle.   Further research should be concentrated on more effective and high technological means, on safe medications, and most importantly, on preventive measures.

> *"If you want truly to understand something, try to change it."*
> — Kurt Levin

PAROXYSMAL PHENOMENA IN SLEEP
(THE SLEEPING "HURRICANE ANDREW")

"I can't take it anymore! During the night, in the middle of a restful sleep, suddenly, he starts to scream bloody murder. The entire apartment building is awake. Nothing can calm him down. Nobody can help. He fights, kicks, and screams in a high-pitched voice. He sweats, looks around wildly, and doesn't recognize anyone. In a few minutes, he calms by himself, and can go back to bed. He is okay now. But we cannot go back to sleep. We are lying in bed and waiting for another episode. In the morning, he does not remember anything. And this happens a few times a night and every night. Why? Why doesn't he stop? What are we to do?"

This is a typical story of a seven-year-old boy with what we call night terrors, which are a part of a large group of paroxysmal phenomena. We call him "Hurricane Andrew".

The term originated from the Latin word *paroxismus*, which means "sudden attacks". This is a key word joining very different phenomena into one group. In the course of a seemingly calm sleep, there is the sudden appearance of a symptom with a short-lived but dramatic picture, after which the person returns to quiet sleep or wakes up. The next day, the person deals with the consequences.

Among the most well known problems relating to this group are night terrors, nightmares, sleepwalking, sudden somatic symptoms, such as headaches, stomachaches, bedwetting, nocturnal asthma attacks, and complex activity in which the person is reacting to his dreams. Also belonging to this group are the sudden deaths of infants, children, or adults. Before we go into the graphic description of each group, there are two points that should be remembered: 1) The mild intensity and frequency of many paroxysmal, sudden phenomena are a normal and necessary part of their development. Thus overreactions are not helpful and might actually aggravate the problem. 2) If this phenomenon becomes more frequent and increases in intensity, we should not hesitate to seek immediate help. Paroxysmal phenomena are not as benign as we thought before, but treatment is available.

157

SLEEPWALKING
(SOMNAMBULISM)

Clinical Manifestation

This is a disorder in which the patient suddenly sits or stands up, or walks around clumsily; sometimes avoids obstacles, mumbles, or utters words that are often meaningless or incomprehensible, and responds to questions in an irrelevant way.

Careful evaluation of these patients in sleep laboratories has demonstrated incidents of somnambulism. The patient gets out of bed, eyes open, with a blank or fearful expression, and moves in a clumsy and awkward manner. Somniloquy (sleeptalking) can occur simultaneously. The level of complexity of the motor activity ranges from sitting up in bed or walking about the room to episodes of running and screaming. Sometimes the patient may leave the bedroom or the house in an attempt to escape or avoid something. The patient is awakened with considerable difficulty only to exhibit confusion, disorientation, and complete amnesia of the episode.

During these episodes, children are prone to urinating in inappropriate places, using obscene words that they would never use while awake, and frequently falling and injuring themselves.

Several of our pediatric patients have come to us after fractures or major injuries acquired during a somnambulistic attack. In adults, these episodes can lead to serious harm to themselves or others. (See: Injuries in Sleep.)

Somnambulism is one of the abnormalities of consciousness that in extreme cases can lead to suicide. Frequently, the somnambulistic patient returns to bed and continues to sleep. The patient only learns about the somnambulistic attack if told about it by relatives or upon noticing unusual changes in the bedroom. Analysis of the cases mentioned above prompted the term "sleep drunkenness" to describe this type of behavior.

"Sleep drunkenness" is a normal but inappropriate behavior observed in some individuals. Cases of "sleep drunkenness" reported in medical literature lead us to believe that the distinction between this disorder and somnambulism is not as clear as originally thought. There are many similarities between somnambulism and "sleep drunkenness."   In both disorders:

1. The patient has amnesia of the episodes.
2. The attack can be precipitated by external stimuli that interrupt sleep.
3. There is a personal and family history of other sleep disorders (mainly enuresis and night terrors).
4. Alcohol or drugs may play a contributory role.
5. Episodes occur during the first 2 to 3 hours after the onset of sleep.
6. Episodes include erratic, aimless behavior that occurs during a different level of consciousness than complete wakefulness.
7. There are similar descriptions of automatic behavior.

Both types of patients usually suffer equal embarrassment, shame, guilt, anxiety, and perplexity after being informed of their behavior.

The only feature that clinically differentiates the two disorders is that "sleep drunkenness" usually occurs with an arousal precipitated by external stimuli, whereas somnambulism is usually associated with spontaneous awakening.

It is important to emphasize here that somnambulism can be provoked by external stimuli such as a click, calling the patient's name, or bringing the patient to his feet while he is in deep delta sleep (stages 3 and 4). Obviously, it is difficult to pinpoint the role of external stimuli in precipitating a somnambulistic episode if a patient is sleeping at home.

Dr. Broughton demonstrated that arousal produced by different mechanisms, such as termination of a sleep cycle and mental activity, can also trigger somnambulism. These observations led him to consider parasomnias as disorders of arousal.

Incidence and Family History of Somnambulism

According to medical reports, about 18 percent of the population is subject to sleepwalking. This disorder is more common in children than in adolescents and adults. It also develops more frequently in boys than in girls. The highest prevalence of somnambulism was 16.7 percent at 11 to 12 years of age. This epidemiologic study states that the frequency of sleepwalking episodes varied from once a month to once a year.

Hallstrom published cases from three consecutive generations that had night terrors. He emphasized the need to consider a genetic origin in these parasomnias. On the basis of his observation that these disorders were present in three consecutive generations and in both males and females, Hallstrom created a hypothesis that night terrors as a syndrome are transmitted as a dominant trait. Several authors have established a parent-child transmission of these disorders.

Genetic influence in these disorders received further confirmation with Bakwin's report of the evidence of somnambulism in both monozygotic twins. He found that concordance in monozygotic twins was six times more common than in dizygotic twins. The frequency of night terrors and enuresis is higher in children with somnambulism.

However, Kales demonstrated that the incidence of these parasomnias increases in relation to the number of affected parents: 22 percent when neither parent has the disorder, 45 percent if one is affected, and 60 percent when both are affected.

All of the above mentioned studies add a genetic factor to possible causes of these disorders.

It is important to know that several medications have been reported to provoke somnambulism.

NIGHT TERRORS

In the olden days, night terrors were a source of many frightening legends about the spell known as "incubus". At that time, there existed a book called *Malous Maleficarum* meaning a harmer of witches. It was used by the inquisition to identify and execute devils and witches who were actually merely men and women suffering from night terrors.

Night terrors are incomplete arousals from the deepest stages of sleep. The symptoms are screaming loudly, or in a high-pitched and agitated voice. The child is confused and talks incoherently. When parents attempt to hold the child, it increases the agitation. The child's pulse is very fast; he sweats. His breathing is very quick, shallow, and fast. His eyes are open. The general impression is that the child is terrified. After 10 to 15 minutes, his agitation subsides, and he either falls asleep again or wakes up. After awakening, he vaguely remembers what happened. As one parent put it, "Night terrors are terrors for parents more than for the child, who has no idea what happened to her last night."

In the course of development of sleep medicine, several studies were performed to uncover the nature of this frightening phenomenon. Psychological investigation demonstrated that night terror emerges exclusively from stage 3 or 4 of NREM sleep, predominantly during the first or the second cycle (within the first 90 to 100 minutes.) In an adult, night terrors might occur during stage 2.

It is interesting that before an attack, heart rate can increase or decrease. Normal existing variations between heartbeats are decreased. The longer the child remains in deep sleep, the greater is the probability that he will have such an attack. It is impossible to predict this after 60 minutes of deep sleep. At this point, large, super slow waves are recorded, and there is a possibility of night terrors. It is important to know the physiological symptoms, because night terrors are not psychological problems, but biological disorders. In a classic study by Dr. Gastaut and Dr. Broughton in 1984, night terrors were described as episodes that start with a series of so-called "K complex" attacks, large spike waves followed by small, fast activities in the slow wave sleep. Soon after, circling eye movements become noticeable and repeat at about 15 second intervals. One second after the first K complex, the heart rate suddenly goes up 15 percent, and then doubles in about 20 seconds within four seconds of the first K complex. The skin resistance begins to fall and does so for 30 second periods. Just after the drop in skin resistance, four seconds after the onset, global body movements occur for 25 seconds. One second after global body movements (five seconds after the episode starts), respiration starts to double from 19 to 38 for about 50 seconds, and there are five seconds when breathing stops (apnea). This is the peak of the heart rate. Breathing resumes with large body movements, and then the patient utters a cry which ends the attack.

Later studies of night terrors confirmed this description, giving some variations in terms of time. Thus, this is a sudden highly structured paroxysmal phenomenon, determined by biological rather than psychological factors. Previous speculation about psychological traumas and emotional conflict as the cause of night terrors did not have any objective support.

Night terrors are to be distinguished from the crisis-like conditions of nighttime, which means dreams or anxiety attacks, known as nightmares. We will specifically discuss nightmares and compare the difference between both conditions a little later (See Part 5). These two syndromes are very different in terms of appearance, physiological mechanisms, and personality characteristics. The key is the difference in treatment and prognosis. Nightmares in small children are generally benign. The frequency of nightmares is about three percent in ages 4-12 and one percent in adults. In adults, they are common usually between ages 20 and 30.

Night terrors might go into adulthood, and the longer they stay, the more they start to become associated with medical and psychiatric pathology. They are very important medically, and they are not benign, because they become a symptom of sleep disorders simultaneously with other neurological and organic pathologies. If episodes of night terrors occur less than once a month and do not result in harm to the patient or others, they are considered mild, and if they increase to one per week, there is a need for evaluation before the case becomes any more severe. They are linked to changes in EEG, heart rate, etc. A recent study of sudden adult death in young males, recent immigrants from Asia, discovered that almost 100 percent of SUND victims had a recent or previous history of night terrors.

Night terrors may be precipitated by medications such as neuroleptics and tricyclic antidepressants, which alter neurotransmitters in the central nervous system. Night terrors are not benign, and as stated before, should be addressed quite seriously if episodes increase in frequency and continue into adolescence and adulthood.

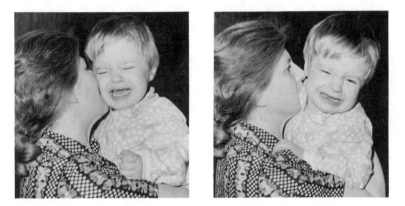

Night Terror Child is confused, screaming loudly and is in "terror". The mother may desperately try to wake the child, but the child is unresponsive.

Natural Course of Somnambulism and Night Terrors

Somnambulism that starts early (age of onset) tends to disappear, whereas if the age of onset was 9.9, the disorder tends to persist into adulthood. For patients that outgrew somnambulism the age of termination of the disorder was 13.8 years old. Stress affected 80 percent of the patients experiencing somnambulism at the time of study but only 38 percent of those with a previous history of the disorder.

Fifty-five percent of patients who were still exhibiting somnambulism had night terrors, as opposed to those with a past history of somnambulism, in whom the incidence of night terrors was only 14 percent. A potential for injury was higher in the patients with current evidence of somnambulism compared to those with a past history. The same was true for incidence of violent behavior.

One of the most important findings in the study by Kales (of patients with somnambulism present after the end of adolescence) was the presence of abnormalities in both the Minnesota Multiphasic Personality Inventory and psychiatric interviews. This did not apply to their patients whose somnambulism disappeared before adulthood.

These findings illustrate the need for psychological interventions in adult patients with somnambulism. There was no major evidence of psychological disturbance in children with somnambulism. In children, the neurological component along with genetic factors seemed to be more important. The findings of Kales' research group are consistent with their hypothesis of a maturational or developmental delay in children with this disorder.

In another study by Kales' group, adults with night terrors also had evidence of psychopathology. According to the authors, adults with night terrors inhibit the expression of aggression, and sleepwalkers show outwardly directed expression of aggression. In both disorders these mechanisms are maladaptive.

Barabas found a high incidence of somnambulism in patients with Gilles de la Tourette's syndrome (GTS) and created a hypothesis that sleepwalking in children with this disorder may be related to disturbed serotonin metabolism. The same authors reported a strong association between migraines in children and somnambulism. Migraines have been associated with abnormalities in serotonin metabolism possibly causing a disturbance in the transition between sleep stages.

Evidence of higher incidence of somnambulism, night terrors, and enuresis in patients with GTS than in children with seizures or a learning disability has been demonstrated by Barabas' group. These authors showed that of 57 patients with GTS, 38.6 percent had at least one of the following disorders: somnambulism, night terrors, or enuresis, and one patient had all three disorders.

Glaze's group described an increase in delta sleep and a decrease in REM sleep in patients with GTS. This increase in delta sleep probably explains higher incidence of these parasomnias. A strong association between migraines and parasomnias as well as between GTS and parasomnias could give us interesting clues in the clarification of the role of neurotransmitters in manifesting abnormal behavior at night.

The observation that these episodes of parasomnias occur during delta sleep explains the patient's amnesia of the episode and the absence of dream recall. Some patients relate only very simple "dream like" episodes, but most of them deny having had a dream.

More studies are yet to be done to clarify why these patients who have a "tendency" for somnambulism by neurophysiological characteristics develop the disorder. On the other hand, it is a well-known fact that somnambulism and night terrors occur much less frequently when the patient is being observed (in a sleep laboratory or during filming for educational purposes).

Studies of more neurophysiological parameters with these disorders are necessary. They will contribute to the understanding of the cortical and subcortical activity during the episodes. We think that evaluation of these patients with the new imaging techniques (primarily brain topographic mapping) may contribute to the clarification of this problem. We are currently performing these studies.

Our hypothesis is that these parasomnias as well as the episodes of "sleep drunkenness" occur during the transitional time between stages of sleep. It is important to mention a few studies that make it necessary to include nocturnal epilepsy in any discussion of these two disorders.

Fuster proved that 94.5 percent of cases with "sleep terrors during which the patient is unconscious" were associated with epileptic discharges.

Other cases of abnormal nocturnal automatism associated with epilepsy were reported a few years later by Guilleminault and Silvestri.   Two of their patients with somnambulism and/or night terrors had clinical and polysomnographic evidence of sleep apnea, the obstructive type.   Children with these parasomnias should also be evaluated clinically to rule out sleep apnea as the precipitating factor in the manifestation of these disorders. The older the patient, the more pathology is associated with somnambulism and night terrors.

Treatment of Somnambulism

It is very fortunate that the great majority of children with somnambulism have only mild manifestation of the disorder and a very low frequency of it. Therefore, in the majority of cases, we can reassure and educate the child as well as the parents. By doing this, we help them disregard other explanations that could generate anxiety or guilt. They are relieved to know that most children will outgrow the disorder with time.

For patients with the frequent and/or the intense disorder leading to the possibility of psychological or physical harm, we should consider other measures recommended by Dr. Nino Marcia:

1. Improving the patterns of sleep-wake cycle thus eliminating the possible role of sleep deprivation as a triggering mechanism.

2. Since Broughton demonstrated that stimuli such as a full bladder could trigger an episode, we recommend reduction in fluid intake prior to bedtime.

3. Parents should remove anything from the bedroom that could be hazardous or harmful to a child.

4. The patient's bedroom should be on the ground floor of the house. The possibility of the patient opening windows or doors should be eliminated.

5. An assessment of the child with this disorder should include a careful review of the current medication so that modifications can be made if necessary.

6. Hypnosis has been found to be helpful for both children and adults.

7. A judicious psychiatric evaluation could help to decide the need for psychiatric intervention.

8. Benzodiazepines have proven to be useful in the treatment of this disorder. A small dose of diazepam or lorazepam eliminates the episodes or considerably reduces them. Other benzodiazepines (alprazolam, for instance) need to be explored as possibilities, all the more so, since diazepam may interfere with the child's normal daytime activities. Imipramine is another alternative. The use of these medications could be limited by the physician to only those times when the patient is considered to be at risk.

Treatment of Night Terrors

We described night terrors in great detail. Be sure that you are able to describe the night terrors to your doctor clearly enough so that he or she can differentiate night terrors from nightmares. The clearer the description, the better the treatment will be, because treatment for nightmares and for night terrors is different. There are several strategies that you and your doctor can consider: (1) Crisis management - what to do if the episode occurs suddenly in the middle of the night ; (2) How to treat the problem, not just trying to avoid specific episodes; and (3) How to prevent night terrors.

(1)   If at a certain time during his night terror you feel that the child is not responding to your verbal reassurance, is pushing you away, yelling and thrashing about, just make sure that he will not hurt himself or others. Try to get a wet towel and wash his face with cold water, gently patting his back. This usually calms him down, ending the episode.

(2)   Treatment of moderate cases in general should focus on the entire problem and not just the immediate incident. The child needs to be evaluated by a pediatrician to rule out different medical causes of the problem, such as ear infection, thyroid dysfunction, or a neurological condition. At this point, you should not be afraid to take medication, if it is advised by the doctor. Taken appropriately, medication might alleviate the condition. Medications may have negative effects, so do not go to extremes. You should not use medication too often, but you should not be afraid of it either. Using it for a short time in small doses might be very beneficial. Such medication as Benadryl® Elixir, one teaspoon before sleep for two weeks, might be helpful. In severe cases, there are specific medications to treat night terrors such as a combination of Klonopin® and Imipramine. As with any medications, these should **not** be used until you have consulted with your doctor on the matter.

Physicians involved in the evaluation and treatment of these two disorders could be faced with serious legal or forensic questions as well as with difficult diagnostic puzzles. Many challenges remain to be solved in the understanding of these disorders. With the clarification of the underlying neurophysiological mechanisms, light may be shed on the mystery of mental activity or its inhibition during sleep.

Nightmares and How They Differ from Night Terrors

If night terrors terrorize family members, because they are behavioral and physiological agitation from deep sleep, nightmares stemming from our dreams, emotional and psychological fears, terrorize the *child* himself infinitely more. He is running to you, describing vividly the frightening picture he just saw. He consciously knows that it was only a dream, but his body and his mind tell him that it might be true. Especially in children fantasy produces a much stronger physiological and psychological effect than reality. Adults have difficulty accepting this fact. Some parents spend an hour looking in closets or outside the window trying to convince the child that there are no monsters around. This method is bound to fail because the child "saw them clearly" and his heart is still pounding from running away from the monsters. Nightmares are part of the normal process of growing up. Almost everyone has experienced nightmares.

Recent research done by Dr. Cartwright on dreaming in crisis situations, demonstrated that nightmares of divorced people and depressed people actually help them to get through their troubles. Nightmares have some compensatory meanings. They can stabilize our inner psychological and physiological storms. The problem begins when nightmares become very frequent and disrupt sleep, changing the child's behavior. Scary dreams are psychologically explainable. The content of night dreams presents a cohesive story reflecting a specific worry about the situation. This context might also depend on the age of the child. Nightmares appear earlier than neutral dreams if the child is in distress. The more nervous the child, the earlier he has scary dreams. A one year old child, for example, can wake up screaming, wave his arms and utter some sounds, as if wanting to get out of bed during the daytime. At age two, the child is able to verbalize what he is worried about, and can say that the monster has just left. At age five, the child can realize that he had a dream, but he is still shaking. He is looking for a snake under the table and believes that he just saw it. He runs to another room to check on his uncle, because he saw him killed in his dreams. Children can live in two worlds at the same time. They know that they dream, but somewhere in the deep recess of their mind, the monsters have not entirely disappeared.

Nightmares, as dreams, psychologically come out of REM sleep. This makes nightmares different from night terrors which come from the slow wave sleep. Therefore nightmares tend to happen in the morning and during naps. Another psychological difference is that during nightmares, the heartbeat increases as in any psychological or emotional arousal, but the pulse does not double and the heart rate is the same as during night terrors. So physiologically in bad dreams, the arousal is not as high as in night terrors. Interestingly enough, there is a correlation between emotions during sleep and the heart rate— pleasant dreams are associated with a high rate. Nonaggressive dreams with a passive attitude of the dreamer are associated with a variable pulse. If the dreamer gets involved in the dream and becomes really active in it, his sleep is deeper. Paradoxically, highly aggressive dreamers have a slow pulse rate.

Nightmare   A child's interpretive drawing of a nightmare.

Nightmares should be treated seriously because they have a tendency to increase in frequency and intensity, and may induce dysfunctional behavior during the daytime. Anxiety caused by dreams inflicts much more serious changes in the body than real anxiety. It might paralyze the spirit, and fix the whole mind and body on the object of the fear. The heart and breathing, as well as all autonomic functions may also be paralyzed. As the famous European teacher, Ushinski, said, "At that moment, we are neither alive nor dead. We're not alive, because all the activity of our spirit has stopped. We are not dead, because we fully sense this terrible torture of the stoppage of life." Based on his research, Dr. Foulkes states that dreams in children, specifically nightmares, reflect directions in which their personality might go. If the child has not adapted well to the external environment, his scary dreams have a lot of symbolism and symbolic characters. They appear just before the child moves or breathes. The neurotic child has a lot of active daytime situations, but at the same time, he is very passive in his dreams. A five year old sees "movies"—multiple figures with situations reflecting the dynamics of his family life, people and animal fights, wars, stories, stones falling on him—a lot of movement. The child is actively participating in his dreams. He is fighting, running away, crying, and telling stories to other people. A seven year old experiencing a nightmare focuses on one figure but includes in his dreams his teachers or his peer groups. Ten- and 12-year-old children with nightmares are very sensitive to different sensations and may have smell hallucinations. They have a lot of feelings dealing with the senses of touch and sight. The child sees a skeleton, for example, growing towards the sky. A lot of changes in space and time are taking place. One child told me, "See how the skeleton is growing, all the way to the sky." Another one said, "Oh, doctor, my hands are growing and growing, and they're slowly moving. I'm afraid of them."

Table 6.1
Differentiation of Sleep Terrors from Nightmares

Characteristic	Sleep Terror	Nightmare
Name	Pavor nocturnus	Anxiety dream
Time of night	First third	Last third
Stage of sleep	Slow-wave sleep	REM sleep
Movements	Somnambulism common	Rare
Severity	Severe	Mild
Vocalizations	Common	Rare
Autonomic discharge	Severe/intense	Mild
Recall	Fragmented	Good
State on waking	Confused/disoriented	Function Well
Injuries	75%	Rare
Violence	55%	Nonviolent
Displacement from bed	18% Run from house	None

During childhood, a lot of repetitive and obsessive dreams may occur. Surprisingly, older children have more color dreams especially if they are diabetics.

Nightmares reflect daytime events, but daytime behavior can also be influenced by the child's condition during sleep. Some smells, some colors may also carry into the daytime. One child said he knew his teacher had red hair, because that was what he saw in his dreams. Similar images might confuse the child and induce some anxiety.

How do you explain and treat nightmares? Nightmares have a connection with different psychiatric diseases and are sometimes very similar to hallucinations. Dr. Rebalsky was the author of the theory of connection between dreams and hallucinations. Hallucinations, at times, can be as frightening as nightmares. The criteria for the differentiation between dreams and hallucinations, especially in children, is the level of consciousness, because when the child is daydreaming, his level of consciousness can be very low depending on the child's emotions and general type of personality. Therefore, attention, obsessiveness, and personal characteristics, are important to analyze dreams. Images in hallucinations are very dynamic. Dreams are less dynamic and more emotionally charged. Recent research shows that there are two types of nightmares. One of them might even be healthy and good for personal growth. Dreams, according to this theory, are the compensation for rejection of a solution during the nighttime. After nightmares, the child might feel better and get much healthier.

Thus, nightmares are a normal phenomenon and are sometimes healthy. Nightmares become a pathology, when they get very intense and serious. There are many ways to treat the pathological aspect of nightmares.

"Bad dreams and nightmares are unavoidable. Welcome them. They are useful. They, like all dreams, stretch your perceptions."
— Eileen Sturanc, *The Dream Worlds of Pregnancy*

———◆◆———

"A miserable night so full of ugly sights, of ghastly dreams ."
— William Shakespeare, *Richard III*

SLEEP PANIC ATTACKS

Panic attacks during the daytime, in the waking state are a known and common disorder. Research demonstrated that in patients suffering from panic disorders, 65 percent of all panic attacks start in sleep. Recently panic attacks were observed during sleep in children and adolescents.

Panic attacks are sudden, unexpected discrete episodes of profound fear. There is also a sudden arousal of all physiological systems with such symptoms as frequent or stopped breathing, tachycardia, profuse sweating, chest pain, abdominal discomfort, and hot flashes. Psychologically, the patient feels that something terrible is coming, and he is going crazy. He feels strange sensations inside his body, and the whole world strikes him as strange and dangerous.

Objective physiological evaluation shows that sleep panic attacks are coming from deep sleep (between stages 2 and 3 NREM). Sleep panic attacks are different from night terrors and nightmares. In nightmares the person sees a bad dream. He knows that it is a dream. During night terrors the child is agitated but is still sleeping. He remembers nothing upon awakening. The person who experiences a panic attack started in sleep, "flies" out of sleep to hyperalertness. The sleeping state of these patients is characterized by cardioarrhythmia, increased amount of movement, and late REM periods.

During the day these children develop a fear of sleep. They do not want to go to bed. Paradoxically, they sleep better in the hospital because they feel safer. Adolescents with these sleep problems are prone to self-injurious habits, such as cutting themselves to decrease tension. If these problems last longer, panic attacks spread from deep sleep to any relaxed state during wakefulness.

Sure enough, the afflicted person becomes depressed. Single episodes of panic attacks in children and adolescents are normal, but if these episodes happen more that once a month, consider a medical evaluation to rule out possible underlying problems.

Treatment of sleep panic attacks is usually successful with behavior modification techniques. If sleep panic attacks are still present do not hesitate to use anti-anxiety medication for some time, if it is suggested by your doctor. The prognosis for this condition is good if treatment is not delayed.

> "...I have seen her rise from her bed, throw her nightgown upon her, unlock her closet, take forth paper, fold it, write upon it, read it, afterwards seal it, and again return to bed; yet all this while in a most fast sleep."
>
> From: Macbeth, Act V, scene I

SECRETS OF BEDWETTING
(NOCTURNAL ENURESIS)

Five paradoxes of bedwetting. Involuntary urination in sleep (bedwetting, or nocturnal enuresis) conceals many secrets and paradoxes. Uncovering those secrets and understanding the paradoxes of bedwetting is a challenge for medicine and for society. The nature and causes of enuresis are not completely understood, and the treatment of this affliction is not simple. A clear and simple syptom (involuntary urination during sleep) contrasts with unclarity of the nature of enuresis and complexity of its treatment. This is the *first paradox.*

This paradox is best illustrated by the long and dramatic history of treatment of enuresis. The term "enuresis" is rooted in the Greek word "enourein", translated as "running urine" in an involuntary act. The child wets in his bed being sound sleep, and his consciousness is completely "sleepy". So, he has no intention to urinate at that time. But the common sense usually refuses to accept it. Our logic usually tells us: "Why do all other kids of my child's age sleep dry through the night, but this kid is always wet? He can hold all day long, so why not during the night? Sure this is bound to aggravate me." It is difficult to find another disorder in which physical and mental abuse was accepted by society as a formal treatment. Here is how doctor Duchanov described his collection of routine "prescriptions" for the treatment of bedwetters in old times, "Wake him up after wetting and give him a hot pepper." "Make him sleep with his head down." "Put him in a tub with cold water." "Make him eat feces of a pigeon." "Do not change his clothes." "Do not allow him to sleep for a few nights." "Tie the penis and glue the vagina". "Make him eat birds' excrements."

Imagine the time or place where there are no diapers or individual bedrooms. Many people crammed together, and one bedwetter. He wets, he smells. Everybody is infuriated. Results: potential abuse. If you think that society had this type of attitude toward bedwetters only in the past, you are gravely mistaken. Not too long ago, we tried to resuscitate a young man who was beaten to death by his campmates. The reason was that he wets "on purpose" to "aggravate". A child was admitted to the hospital with severe burns not so long ago. An angry parent threw the wet child into the bathtub and turned on the hot water. He claimed that he was sleepy and turned the wrong knob. Ostracism and physical punishment are inflicted on bedwetters by their families and the society. Self punishment and suicide as a "way out" will be discussed a little later.

Medical scientists have also been aggravated by this simple, but inexplicable phenomenon. It "defied" the traditional rule: "Each symptom should reflect a broken part in the body". Two centuries of intensive search for the organ responsible for urination during sleep did not lead anywhere. Infections of the urinary bladder, kidney stones, spinal cord splits, and other organic changes in parts of the urinary system could not explain nocturnal bedwetting. There was no organ or endocrine gland which was not blamed for bedwetting only to be acquitted later.

No underlying organic pathology was found to clearly explain bedwetting in sleep. This is the *second paradox* of enuresis. Believers in the organic changes in the urinary or other systems produced "treatments" no less brutal and no more successful than ancient techniques: insertion of tubes into the rectum, intensive X-ray radiation of the head and pelvic areas, surgery, etc. In the middle of this century, the aggressive treatment of bedwetting due to its complete failure, was substituted by overpermissiveness. The pendulum of logic swung to the other extreme. "Now, your seven year old child wets the bed? That's okay. He will grow out of it. Do not make a big deal out of it. Just give him more attention, and everything will be all right". The treatment looked easy. The medical model of enuresis as a disease was substituted by a series of learning exercises in which the bedwetter was promised to be taught how not to urinate. A hundred of papers and books appeared with attractive titles like: "Treatment of bedwetting within one day", or "Relieve bedwetting forever", etc. But as Dr. Glukovich ironically concluded in her brilliant review of literature, "Bedwetting was, is, and will exist." Many clinicians and parents know: whenever a new treatment is initiated bedwetting disappears for a short time just to reappear again to the dismay of parents and doctors.

Nocturnal bedwetting is very resistant to any treatment when direct suppression of urination is the goal. This is the *third paradox* of enuresis. Why? For some reason, our body stubbornly fights back.   Or it quietly gives a message that urination in sleep might have a reason.   This therapeutic resistance should be analyzed and explained by anyone who claims to come forth with a theory of enuresis.   The same is true about the *fourth paradox*.

When doctors cease treatment, bedwetting in many cases spontaneously disappears.   Self cure!   How to explain that?   Well, if enuresis disappears of its own accord in so many cases, why bother to treat it?   Just leave it alone, and sooner or later it will stop.   There are two problems with this logic.   One—the child and family will pay dearly by low self esteem, emotional, and behavioral reactions.   Two—in some instances the child does not "grow out of it".   Moreover, the problem gets worse.

While the majority of children grow out of bedwetting, in some cases the condition deteriorates, and other behavioral and sleep disorders appear.   This is the *fifth paradox* of enuresis.   The theory of enuresis should adequately explain these paradoxes and how to solve them for successful treatment.

Theories of Enuresis

1.   *Anatomical theory:* This is the oldest existing theory.   According to it, bedwetting occurs due to anatomical changes in the urinary system (bladder, kidneys, spinal cord or central nervous system controlling urination).   Such pathology (inborn or due to disease) related to cases with involuntary urination *at any time* of night or day.   This theory can be applied to a very small percentage of bedwetters.   Nevertheless, the possibility of structural changes should be checked routinely before it is ruled out.   All organs and endocrine glands were investigated as a possible cause of bedwetting. The latest version of this theory was the *functional anatomy theory* when the emphasis was shifted to function versus structure.   The small bladder was the most popular "culprit".   There are data that some children have small functional capacity of the bladder.   It means that a child with a normal bladder for some reason needs to urinate more often.   Based on this theory, multiple training programs have been designed to increase the functional

capacity of the urinary bladder. Again, this theory is based on true, but limited cases, and it can be applied to a subset of children with organic problems. The role of doctors and parents is to remember this possibility and rule it out.

2. *Genetic theory:* The role of genetic factors was studied on the models of twins and by so-called genealogical analysis. Among monozygotic (from the same ovum) twins, the frequency of bedwetting is twice as much as in dizygotic ones. The interesting question is why monozygotic twins do not have 100 percent concordance? The answer, accidentally, was found in the secret of so-called mirror twinning. (See: Sleep in Twins.) Genealogical analysis shows that 75 percent of close relatives of bedwetters had enuresis. If both parents had enuresis, the probability of enuresis increased six times. Thus, genetic factors play an important role as a predisposing condition, but it is not the cause of enuresis.

3. *Stress theory:* According to this theory, enuresis might result from psychological stress. Stress factors which might cause bedwetting include: a newborn sibling, parents' divorce, family violence, sudden relocation, hospitalization, or surgery. There are data that the first five years of life are especially important. Assumptions that nocturnal enuresis is a way to attract special attention due to neurotic personality did not get any factual support in research.

4. *Theory of the maturational delay of the central nervous system:* The delay, according to this theory, is based on physical undevelopment. The frequency of enuresis is negatively proportional to the child's birth weight. So, physical maturation and also psychological maturation (toilet training) are believed to be the causes of the problem. This theory, as attractive as it sounds, did not explain nocturnal versus daytime enuresis.

5. *Enuresis and sleep:* It is so natural to think that enuresis and sleep are connected. By definition, nocturnal enuresis is involuntary urination *in sleep*. The paradox is that formal sleep evaluation did not show any specific changes, and bedwetting can occur in all stages. This disappointment almost stopped search in the area of sleep. But slowly several important factors are uncovered. In its clinical course, enuresis is similar to somnambulism, night terror, and sleep talking. All of them predominantly

appear in the first half of the night and are often seen together. The next phenomenon we discovered was that urination in sleep occurs most commonly in the transitional stages. The third group of facts confirmed that bedwetting can appear much earlier than any other problem.   Very interesting correlations were found between EEG and cystometry (when the urologist actually inserts special equipment into the child's urinary bladder). During deep sleep, EEG shows slow (delta) waves and bladder-zero line. When the bladder gets full, it starts to contract. Delta waves disappear for seconds. After 10-13 minutes the child awakes. This happens to children without enuresis. In enuretic children the majority (61 percent) with filled bladder did not wake up (Type I). In Type IIA- EEG did not react at all. In Type IIB neither the bladder nor the EEG reacted. Thus, in Type I there is a partial awakening, in Type IIA no awakening at all, and in Type IIB clear pathology of the urinary bladder.

Dynamics of bedwetting with age. It is generally accepted that enuresis starts in the period between three and eight years of age.   In normal development it is assumed that daytime bladder control will be accompanied by nighttime dryness. There are many data revealing that the daytime wetting rhythm is entirely different from that of nighttime and has a basically different mechanism. We developed some criteria for defining the physiological age at which bedwetting in sleep is pathological and, therefore, the beginning of nocturnal enuresis. These involve: 1) the age at which a fixed biorhythm in sleep appears, and 2) measurements of the ontogenic maturation of sleep stages. Normal reflexes of suppression of urination in sleep might be achieved by one year of age. If, however, a 2 1/2 to 3 year old child wets the bed at night and shows an irregular, age-inappropriate pattern of sleep structure, he should be diagnosed with nocturnal enuresis.   The frequency of his wetting in sleep is a measure of the extent of the affliction.

Bedwetting that occurs up to the age of 2 1/2 years should be considered physiological since this is a period during which there may be delayed biorhythm formation (the so-called "risky period", 1 to 2 1/2 years of age). During this "risky" (or latent) period of enuresis a child may manifest general unrest, drowsiness during the daytime, crying, sobbing, and sleeplessness at night. At about three years of age he may stop being drowsy during the daytime and restless at night, and begin sleeping soundly but wetting at night. We call this period the "crystallization period". This will be followed by the monosymptomatic appearance of enuresis which may go on for years during the "manifestation period". Spontaneous remission occurs abruptly in 23.2 percent of all cases. Gradual recovery takes place in 42.6 percent of cases. In 34.2 percent the sleep mechanisms do not mature, and at a certain period enuresis is joined by other pathological phenomena such as nightmares, night terrors, bruxism, and daytime behavioral disturbances. This we call the "deterioration period".

How enuresis develops. The key to the problem of nocturnal enuresis lies in the integration of already known facts regarding this phenomenon. Urination during sleep and the disturbance of the sleep-wake cycles are central features. The question is, which of the two is primary?

The following facts confirm that bedwetting is primarily a medical problem and should be treated as such:

1. Sleep pattern distortions precede enuresis ontogenically.

2. During the night, behavioral and electro-physiological sleep distortions precede bedwetting.

3. Following bedwetting, behavioral and EEG distortions disappear.

We can add from our experience that drugs that decrease diuresis (antidiuretic hormone) but do not help restructure sleep produce a short-term effect which is followed by deterioration. Methods which normalize sleep structure have a therapeutic effect on nocturnal enuresis.

The physiological development of enuresis in sleep can be modeled as follows: The system of the brain responsible for the smooth transition from wakefulness to sleep is often dysfunctional. There then follows a deep sleep, deeper and longer than normal. In this so-called "dead" sleep, breathing becomes shallow and infrequent, and motor activity is absent. A change of stages normally takes place in 60-80 minutes, but with enuretic children this process is delayed. To compensate, higher levels of stimulation must set in. This involves increased motor activity; the child becomes episodically restless. It appears that only two kinds of motions can activate sleep stage changes: phasic, quick, short paroxysms resembling jerks, or massive thrashing movements with complete changes in body positions. If such compensatory motor activity does not "kick in" normal cycles, the next stage occurs: paroxysm of urine outbursts. It can be compared with a transmission in the car. If automatic transmission does not work, manual "kick in", "start" should follow.

To sum up, the act of urination performs a compensatory function in the first stage of the disease. If this level of compensation is not enough to switch sleep stages, the problem can evolve to the next level-breathing paroxysms (eg. nocturnal asthma).

The third level consists of breathing paroxysms (such as asthma) and other vegetative paroxysms. We are in agreement with the "arousal model" up to this point. The arousal effect appears to apply to enuresis occurring in "dead" sleep, which is related to deep NREM. The problem is that behaviorally "dead" sleep is not necessarily "deep" NREM. Moreover, "dead" sleep corresponds primarily to stage 2 or to transitional sleep stages not classified by classical sleep architecture. Clinically, the "arousal" hypothesis can be used to explain the "simple" or "epileptoid" forms of enuresis with Type A disorganization. Children with the "neurotic" forms of enuresis with Type B sleep disorganization who have "restless, shallow sleep" can be observed to sleep deeper both behaviorally and polysomnographically following an episode of enuresis.

Our compensatory model of enuresis includes the arousal effect as one among many compensatory effects of paroxysmal urination. Different clinical forms of nocturnal enuresis have both different clinicophysiological dynamics and different compensatory mechanisms which should be investigated in further research.

Thus, the physiological function of urination in sleep seems to be fundamentally compensatory. The compensatory model of nocturnal enuresis can explain some of the paradoxes of the problem. Viewing enuresis as a compensatory mechanism of sleep disturbance provides an answer as to why these children should not be awakened from sleep. This is because a forced awakening will not create a conditioned response, nor will it correct the distortions in the sleep pattern which are the physiological cause of the enuretic symptom. Moreover, it leads to even greater disorganization of the child's sleep pattern. This is why the awakened child urinates again as soon as he falls asleep. Up to a certain age, a child seems to need the enuretic act, and most attempts to eliminate it will fail. When the sleep mechanism matures, enuresis disappears spontaneously since it is no longer needed, and spontaneous recovery ensues. If the sleep mechanism does not mature by a certain period, decompensation takes place under the influence of increasing strain on the total organism.

The compensatory model takes into account the fact that periods of normal sleep following bedwetting and paroxysms before and during bedwetting tend to normalize the patterns of sleep. We are in agreement with Dr. Rapoport that there is no difference in terms of the statistical parameters of sleep stages between enuretics and normal children.

Problems concerning the nature, pathogenesis, and treatment of nocturnal enuresis remain. It is important to stress the fact that pathological changes of biorhythm are the basis of this disease, and that the key to its treatment lies in the means and the methods used to regulate and normalize sleep structure. Nocturnal enuresis is not a monosymptomatic disease but a complicated syndrome that consists of a number of essential and associated symptoms.

1. Essential features include:
   a. Spontaneous involuntary wetting during sleep;
   b. Disturbances of sleep;
   c. Changes in levels of wakefulness;
   d. Resistance to direct therapeutic intervention and spontaneous remission.

2. Associated features:
   a. Family pattern of inheritance;
   b. Coexisting daytime enuresis;
   c. Somatic, endocrinological, neurological, urological symptoms;
   d. Coexisting emotional, relational and behavioral symptoms.

Essential Features of Nocturnal Enuresis

Spontaneous bedwetting. The picture of nocturnal enuresis is different from daytime wetting. At night it is a paroxysmal (sudden) outburst usually of a large quantity of urine. The act of urination is accompanied often by a short cessation of breathing, twitching of the minor muscles of limbs and body and, in boys, by erection. All of these indicate that bedwetting is a spontaneous and involuntary act, and that complex functional systems of the brain are involved. Children do not awaken, and there may also be associated motor-vegetative paroxysms such as nightmares and quivering. Spontaneous urination in sleep can be predicted because it happens as the climax of a complex pattern of behavioral and electrophysical phenomena, both preceding and following the act of enuresis itself. The clinical forerunners include assuming specific positions in bed, simultaneous increase or decrease in cardiac and respiratory rates, and erection in boys. If a normal sleep cycle does not resume after the first act of enuresis, a series of repeated urinations will ensue.

Disturbances of sleep. In spite of a great deal of contradictory data about connections between enuretic episodes and stages of sleep, our experience shows quite clearly that there are differences in the sleep-wake patterns of enuretic children in comparison to those of normal children. They consist of deviations in falling asleep and awakening, deviations in the "depth" of sleep, deviations in positioning during sleep, and the simultaneous occurrence of other sleep disorders. Taken as a group, difficulties of falling asleep, the depth of sleep (behaviorally), and awakening were observed in most patients (95.3 percent). All patients had at least temporary sleep abnormalities. Abnormalities of falling asleep included the prolongation of the sleep latency period up to a few hours, or the shortening of sleep latency when children fell asleep while eating or playing. As for depth of sleep disturbances, the parents claim they observe so-called "dead" sleep in their children, when the children do not move during sleep for unusually long periods of time. It is very difficult to wake them up and hear them breathing.

The child sleeps on his back or, more rarely, on his stomach. The child looks "dead", and parents report being scared and reacting by checking the child's breathing many times every night. After bedwetting, the child with "dead" sleep continues to sleep while wet. Upon forceful awakening the child may become disoriented, with psychomotor signs such as one would see in night terror. About 26 percent of our patients had restless "very shallow" sleep, with episodes of night terrors, nightmares, sleep talking, and exaggerated movements such as jerks and even falling out of bed. In 3.9 percent there was an alternation of these two patterns: "dead" and "restless" sleep. Simultaneous multiple sleep abnormalities were noticed in 13 percent. It is important to emphasize that in about three-quarters of the children night sleep has been disturbed since infancy by phenomena such as screaming, crying without visible causes, and inversion of the sleep-wake cycle (sleepiness during the day, and night wakefulness).

The sleep positions of enuretics differ from those in the control group. The variations range from simple alternation in the time spent in any position to the appearance of many strange positions. Enuretic children also exhibit a preference for the back or stomach positions. These children slept longer in one position. An enuretic act was observed most commonly while patients slept on their back (81.5 percent) or, much more rarely, on their stomach (18.5 percent) and never when sleeping on their side.

Sleep research shows that there are three types of sleep structure disturbances in enuretic children. The three variants represent typical disturbances in the stages of sleep for children of this age who suffer from enuresis.

The first type of distortion (Type A) is characterized by prolongation of the first cycle of sleep, although the average duration of sleep stages approximates normal. The second type (Type B) involves the reduction of deep delta sleep (Stages 3 and 4), and the predominance of light sleep. The third type (Type C) involves extreme prolongation of sleep and a severe reduction of the REM sleep to 7.5 percent (from the norm of 26.6 percent). Clinically, the following patterns are observed. In Type A there is instantaneous falling asleep, "dead" sleep, and difficult awakening. In Type B there is "restless" sleep and frequent urination. This is a more aggravated form of the disorder. Type C is the most severe form. If there is alternation between the features of Type A and Type B, it often occurs in combination with other sleep disorders such as sleep terrors and nightmares.

Changes in levels of wakefulness. Our research reveals changes in levels of alertness as well as in the sleep pattern. These changes manifest themselves as sharp variations in daytime motor activity including hyperactivity and motor abnormalities, emotional instability and extreme alternations in energy levels. These include fits of drowsiness during the day, alternating with excitability in the evening, and variations in the level of motivation, the so-called "paradoxical drowsiness" which occurs in 49.7 percent.

Resistance to direct therapeutic intervention and spontaneous remission. The resistance to almost any kind of treatment has been described by many clinicians and researchers. Fifty-seven percent of our patients have shown clear evidence of such resistance. Those who work with enuretics share the feelings of helplessness we experience when the best efforts at treatment fail. It took a long time to realize that resistance to treatment and spontaneous remission are integral features of this affliction and part of its normal course. Sixty-nine percent of enuretic patients between the ages of 10-11 stopped bedwetting within a short period of time. We want to emphasize, on the other hand, that the disease in 11 percent of children between ages 10-16 deteriorated sharply, with many additional symptoms appearing such as sleep terrors, somnambulism, and asthmatic attacks. This we call decompensation.

Associated Features of Enuresis

Family pattern of inheritance. About 15-20 percent of children with bedwetting have close family members with a history of enuresis. The prevalence of nocturnal enuresis in the general population is about 2.7 percent. However, approximately 39 percent of the parents of our patients also suffered from bedwetting as children. Abnormalities in the gestation, prenatal, and neonatal periods were noticed in 62.2 percent of all cases. Somatic diseases such as pneumonia, endocrine diseases, etc., were noticed in 40.5 percent of cases.

Among other associated factors, psychosocial disorders such as marital difficulties, parental alcoholism, family conflicts, and single parent families were less often encountered as causes than the biological factors.

Enuresis Illustration by a child showing the problem of bedwetting.

Emotional disturbances such as poorly defined fright responses and morning anxiety were also observed. Associated sensory symptoms included increased sensations of thirst and appetite (bulimia). Behavioral symptoms included the development of conduct disorders (including an inclination for theft), and running away from home. Only 61 patients (16.7 percent) displayed severe emotional reactions such as suicidal tendencies and actual suicide attempts. We consider the indifference of the patient toward his or her affliction to be a rather important clinical manifestation of the pathology in the emotional sphere. Most children afflicted with enuresis recognize their illness and initially accept the idea of treatment. However, 296 (81 percent) of the 365 patients we observed did not follow through. Four types of personality profiles were described in bedwetters: 1) stubborn, inflexible, and emotionally rigid; 2) shy; 3) hysterical, acting out to attract attention, and 4) impulsive, hyperactive. Each type fits into different forms of enuresis.

Forms of Enuresis

Many questions and confusion about treatment could be resolved if we accept the known clinical fact that bedwetting can be a product of many underlying diseases and subsequently needs to be treated differently depending on the underlying cause. Five forms of enuresis can be subclassified depending on the clinical picture, type of sleep architecture, and treatment response:

1. "Familial": The most common, predominantly males, many bedwetters in the family. Sleep: "deep", Type A. Imipramine responders, alarm resistant.

2. "Diathetic": Predominantly females, non-familial, many psychosomatic symptoms, allergies, urinary tract infections; small urinary bladder. Sleep: restless, Type C. Imipramine and alarm resistant. Benzodiazepines responders.

3. "Reactive": Usually post traumatic ("secondary"), both sexes. Sleep: restless, Type B or C. Imipramine resistant, alarm responders.

4. "Endocrinopathic": Overweight, both sexes, exaggerated emotional responses. Imipramine responders, alarm resistant. Sleep: restless, Type B.

5. "Organic": History of neurological problems (epilepsy, head trauma, dysmorphysms, etc.) Predominantly males. Sleep: restless, Type C. Imipramine and alarm resistant.

Steps in the Management of Bedwetting

Step 1: Start a diary. Record daytime and nighttime episodes as well as other events, medications taken, naps, etc. Indicate if this diary can be used to evaluate the frequency of episodes, associations with water intake, weather or emotional factors. It allows us to analyze the sleep-wake cycle including daytime sleepiness or hyperactivity, follow the dynamics of the condition, control the effects of treatment, and correct the problem. Below is an example of a weekly log that we use for children with bedwetting and other sleep disorders.

NAME_____

Date	Medications	Daytime events	Nighttime events	Comments

Step 2. Put together a history of the problem for your own use and your pediatrician's. Most importantly, try to recall when you started to be concerned, the length of the child's dry period, and factors leading to increased or decreased frequency of enuresis (include food, water, weather, emotional events, sleep deprivation, sickness, etc.). Separate nighttime bedwetting and daytime accidents describing how these relate to toilet training. Are there any allergies or difficulties in nasal breathing? Describe the family history of bedwetting, and/or other sleep problems.

Step 3. When you present the diary and the history of the problem to your pediatrician, he or she will probably order a series of basic lab tests including urine analysis and urine culture. This should be done to rule out any problems in the urinary system. Quite likely those tests will indicate no abnormality. X-rays and invasive cystoscopy are recommended only if the urinal analysis turned in abnormal results or the doctor found indications of deformation during a physical examination (for example, pelvic or spinal deformations).

We found it highly productive and simple to record fluid intake and output of urine for a few days, or over a weekend, as is shown in the following chart.

FLUID INTAKE _(soups, drinks, etc.)_		OUTPUT _(amount of urination)_		COMMENTS
Date	Time	Date	Time	

This helps to identify excess water intake and its effect, as well as changes of biological rhythms of the urinary systems.

Step 4. Identify the most probable type of bedwetting your child has. Not all children fit perfectly into one form of the problem. It might be a mix, but generally it is possible to identify the type by answering the questions below.

1. One or both parents were bedwetters:

___yes ___no ___don't know.

If the answer is "yes" - most are familial or endocrinopathic types.

2. My child was toilet trained during the day, but was always wet in sleep. He has never been dry more than 3-4 months in a row:___yes ___no ___don't know.

If the answer is "yes" most are familial, endocrinopathic, or organic types. Go to the next question.

3. If episodes of bedwetting are "on and off", were those episodes provoked by emotional or school stresses:___yes ___no ___don't know.

If the answer "is yes" - most are reactive types. If the answer is "no" for emotional stress, maybe the cause lies in environmental factors such as weather or water intake. This is common for diathetic type.

4. My child has daytime enuresis and urges to urinate:___yes ___no ___don't know.

If the answer is "yes" - most are diathetic types, periods of soiling are a signal to seek professional help.

Step 5. After you and your doctor identified your child's probable type of bedwetting, you can have a better idea of what treatment might be beneficial. (See Table: *Treatment Responses Among the Different Types of Enuresis*) Keep this in mind and try several strategies.

Strategy 1: Bathroom trips

Rationale. Suppression of nocturnal voiding in young children has a great deal of age variation. It is also possible that urination itself has some function in addition to being a stimulator of the central nervous system. Attempts to help the child to stop urinating in bed seem to be appealing to many parents.

Technique. The small child is gently carried to the bathroom and placed on the toilet seat. Note: A sleeping child, even a small one, is heavy. Carry the child in an upright position with his head over your shoulder and his arms hugging you. Let the water run with little noise. If the child does not urinate you can induce the act by using the so-called sacral reflex: gently tickle the area in the bowl just above his buttocks. After urination gently bring the child back to bed and put him on his side. Do not wake the child. A dry bed raises a child's self esteem.

Down sides. This is not a treatment. It is designed solely for keeping the bed dry. It is difficult to use this technique for older children. Of course, the child could be walked into the bathroom even though it is sometimes a difficult task. Nevertheless this technique is an extra burden on parents, who may have a difficult time falling asleep after a fight with their teenager over this trip.

Strategy 2: Positional training

Rationale. The majority of children with nocturnal bedwetting problems wet in certain positions, predominantly on their back or stomach. Changing the position of the child from their back or stomach to their side between 60 and 90 minutes after the onset of sleep, helps to make sleep lighter, to switch stages, and thus possibly prevent involuntary urination. My practice shows that this technique might be quite helpful even for older children and adolescents.

Techniques. Turning the child from his back onto his side might not be easy. The child, especially an adolescent, is heavy, sleeps very deeply and flips right back into his previous position. The best way is to bend the child's knees, put them together, and turn them to the side toward his face. The closer the child's knees are to his chin the better.

Downsides. This technique may be difficult for older children and adolescents. Also, it is good preventing enuretic episodes in the beginning of the night, because constantly changing the position of the child would be difficult for parents. The child can be trained under hypnosis or meditation to have enough self-awareness of his position to change it. Passive positional training can be done by having your child wear shorts that have tennis balls fixed on the back. In our lab we developed an electronic trainer which tickles the child enough to want to scratch and change position. Do not wake up the child.

> ### Strategy 3:   *Increase presleep awareness and motivations*

Rationale. Specialists in enuresis agree that increasing presleep awareness and motivation is good treatment. But the reasoning and methods may vary to the point of not being beneficial. The idea that nocturnal urination is a learning process spreading from daytime control to nighttime control helped produce elaborate training programs. Despite claims of success, our experience shows a number of cases where the child was under the impression that he was wet. The idea that dryness is the child's responsibility produced a whole new set of instructions for self cleaning and punishments. This strategy is good for "reactive" types, but not for others.

Technique. After much searching for the best technique, we came up with a simple one, called "presleep play". Parents may ask children if they worry about being wet, and then, depending on the answer, try to rationalize the child's problem in a positive way. If the family is religious, they may suggest that the child pray for a good night's sleep with pleasant dreams, and for awakening dry. If the family is not religious and would prefer a more scientific approach, they can say to the child that he will have good dreams if he concentrates and tries to have an image of the dreams that he would like to have. Instilling this idea increases the probability of pleasant dreaming.

Conclusion. Bedwetting is a disorder of sleep and behavior. It is a troublemaker for the child, exhausting for parents and a serious problem for medical science. Treatment of enuresis hides among the methods and means of improving sleep mechanisms. Understanding of bedwetting will enhance our understanding of sleep and its other deviations.

Differences in Treatment Responses Among the Different Types of Enuresis

TREATMENT Type:	1	2	3	4	5
Sleep Hygeine and Diet					
Restriction of water and salt	-	-	++	+	-
Aerobic exercise half hour before sleep	+	++	-	-	-
Sleeping on a hard mattress	++	+	-	+	-
Hot application on the back	-	-	++	-	++
Psychotherapy					
Supportive Stars	-	++	+	-	-
Charts	-	++	-	-	-
Alarm Device	+++	+	-	+	-
Bladder exercises	+	-	+++	-	+
Autosuggestion	+	+++	-	+	-
Hypnotherapy	++	+++	-	+	+
Medication					
Tranquilizers	-	+	+	-	-
Stimulants	++	-	-	+++	-
Antidepressants	+++	++	-	+	++
DDAVP® Nasal Spray	+++	+	++	+++	+
Others	+	++	++	+	+

Description:
- None
+ Minimal
++ Some
+++ A great deal

"*Enuresis was born with the dawn of civilization and is still with us. Its history is long and colorful with a prognosis for a longer and more exciting life before its problems are, if ever, resolved.*"
— Lucille B. Glucklich

———— •••• ————

"*Urinating in bed is frequently predisposed by deep sleep; when urine begins to move, its inner nature and its hidden will (resembling the will to breathe) drives urine out before the child awakes. When children become stronger and more robust, their sleep is lighter and they stop urinate.*"
— Avicena, *Canon of Medical Sciences*, 1012 A.D.

PART
6

PREVENTION OF POTENTIALLY LIFE-THREATENING SLEEP DISORDERS

Sudden Infant Death Syndrome and Other Life-Threatening Events

Sleep Apnea in Children

She Falls Asleep Whenever She Laughs (About Narcolepsy)

Injurious Sleep

SUDDEN INFANT DEATH SYNDROME AND OTHER LIFE-THREATENING EVENTS

Sudden death of a healthy infant in sleep is one of the biggest mysteries in medicine and the biggest tragedy in the family. Imagine, you put your baby in the crib, and watch him fall asleep peacefully. In the middle of the night something makes you wake up. It is not a noise. It is not the baby crying. Nothing! In a second you realize that the thing that makes you jump out of bed is that *nothing!* Dead silence. You hear nothing from your baby, no usual sounds of moving, no sounds of breathing. Too quiet! A sense of something terrible, spreading doom comes upon you. You rush to the crib. Terrified, you see a cold, still baby with a smile on his face.

This is not a made up situation. It is a real story told with great pain by a mother who lost her three month old baby several days earlier.

In the prologue of this book, I described my first direct encounter with the death of a sleeping baby. Twenty-two years ago, in October of 1972, a pediatrician from Upstate Medical Center in Syracuse, Dr. Alfred Steinschneider, made history in the medical field with a landmark paper in the journal of pediatrics about multiple cases of Sudden Infant Death Syndrome (SIDS). This paper became one of the most widely listed papers providing support for the theory that some cases of the disorder may result from an inborn abnormality, characterized by prolonged apnea—loss of breathing during sleep. Ten thousand seemingly healthy infants die each year from SIDS for unknown reasons.

Society accuses parents of murdering their children, and this terrible accusation lies heavily on their shoulders, coupled with their own bewilderment and torments of guilt. A terrified mother recently brought her child who almost died of SIDS to the hospital. She was accused of an attempted murder after hours of questioning. This disease behaves so strangely that many doctors who do not have direct experience with SIDS do not believe in its existence. The problem is further complicated by instances of child abuse disguised as SIDS. Doctors and SIDS researchers face serious difficulties dealing with child abuse and murder when SIDS is blamed for children's deaths.

Remember, we talked about Alfred Steinschneider, who wrote the landmark paper on a case of sudden infant death in a family? This paper recently made news again as Exhibit A in a murder case. In March of 1994, prosecutors brought murder charges against Waneta E. Hoyt of New York. This is a 47-year-old mother of children whose deaths Steinschneider described in his paper. Twin siblings, M.H. and N.H. have been identified by prosecutors as Manly and Noah Hoyt. Strange matter. The doctor made a special note in the paper because three siblings of M.H. and N.H. had previously died as infants. He monitored the two babies very closely and repeatedly admitted them into the hospital for observation. Here is how he describes M.H. in an incident which occurred soon after she was discharged from the hospital. "At 8:15 A.M., the baby awoke, was disconnected from the apnea alarm, bathed and fed without difficulties. Mrs. H. placed her in the crib and left the room for a minute to get something. When she returned, M.H. was apneic and cyanic. She was given mouth-to-mouth resuscitation without success. One year later the story was repeated with Noah Hoyt with strange, surprising details.

These tragic events led doctors to conclude that some SIDS-prone babies may be born with abnormalities, characterized by apneic episodes. If so, some SIDS' deaths may be prevented by checking for abnormal respiration. Further research on SIDS cases did not confirm that apnea was the cause of death; therefore, apnea is no longer associated with these deaths.

Could the deaths of the two babies have been prevented if the doctor did not believe the mother from the start? Linda Norton, a forensic pathologist, and former forensic medical examiner for Dallas County, Texas, read this paper about M.H. and N.H. She and prosecutor William Fitzpatrick compared this description with many other murders of infants. Waneta Hoyt finally was charged with the murder of her children.

Now we are more familiar with SIDS symptoms and have a much better way of differentiating murders from disease. Children who died from SIDS are usually boys three or four months old, that had a slight cold two to three days, without any major medical problems otherwise. They died *in their sleep* around 1 to 4 A.M. Apnea alarm is of no help for SIDS. Note, that not all children who suffer sudden unexpected death have SIDS. Several different life-threatening events, called ALTE may lead to sudden death in children. Apnea may be one of these, so can septicemia (infections of the blood), cardiovascular problems, seizures, congenital abnormalities, etc. Those are known and identified problems. They are chronic problems which were serious before, and might cause sudden death. There are different forms of unexplained death, collectively called SIDS in cases eliminating murder as a cause. In 1979 we proposed a paradoxical hypothesis of SIDS. This hypothesis suggests that our system "sets up" sudden physiological responses as biological tools to serve specific adaptive functions. The paradoxical set is a condition in which adaptive flexibility of the body is lost, and response to external stimuli is reversed. For example, when breathing is going fast, the heart rate also increases. Paradoxical relationships can occur between the chest and abdomen, for example, when increased expiration causes a decrease in the heart rate. These paradoxical relationships, very common in normal infant sleep, especially in REM sleep are not usually dangerous. However when the child is prone to paradoxical responses, they may become a threat. The difference between heart rate and breathing may increase, and the child may suffer from hypoxemia. There are some data available about heart rate in children with SIDS that seems to confirm the possibility of this hypothesis. Specialists from UCLA studied heart problems in children who later on died from SIDS, and they described the coordination between respiration and heart as dysfunctional. Thus, the cause of SIDS is not external but internal. The cause might be explained by the immaturity of the nervous system responsible for coordination. The most significant factors, we know so far, are chronic prone positions, smoking during the pregnancy, and doing so right after delivery. The majority of children who died from SIDS were not breast fed.

Sudden unexplained death does not claim only infants. There is another kind, called sudden unexplained nocturnal death, "SUND", which takes young adolescents and young adults in a way similar to SIDS. There is no known disorder which might reveal the cause of these deaths. SUND occurs more commonly in South East Asian countries. It is common in Japan where they call it Bokkiri. Although cardiac problems were found in many cases, this alone does not explain the mystery SUND.

In conclusion, Sudden Infant Death Syndrome is still an enigma. It has a tremendous influence on the future of the family's life. It is a tragedy, which may be prevented. But the more we know about SIDS, the more cases we study and the more we learn from parents, the more optimistic we become that finally the answers can be found and children will be saved.

"At last, tired to death, Varka does her very utmost, strains her eyes, looks up at the flickering green patch, and listening to the screaming, finds the foe who will not let her live.

That foe is the baby.

She laughs. It seems strange to her that she has failed to grasp such a simple thing before. The green patch, the shadows, and the cricket seem to laugh and wonder, too. The hallucination takes possession of Varka. She gets up from her stool, and with a broad smile on her face and wide unblinking eyes, she walks up and down the room. She feels pleased and tickled at the thought that she will be rid directly of the baby that binds her hand and foot....Kill the baby and then sleep, sleep, sleep....

Laughing and winking and shaking her fingers at the green patch, Varka steals up to the cradle and bends over the baby. When she has strangled him, she quickly lies down on the floor, laughs with delight that she can sleep, and in a minute is sleeping as soundly as the dead."

From: *Anton Chekhov Short Stories, Sleepy, 1888*

"Sleep is the twin of death."
— Homer, *The Iliad*

SLEEP APNEA IN CHILDREN

Breathing disorders during sleep are common in both children and adults. Loud snoring was thought to be normal. Not anymore! It is actually a symptom of upper airway obstruction. Abnormalities in breathing during sleep have a profound influence on physical and intellectual development and may result in significant morbidity or even sudden death. Extraordinary effort has been made to analyze mechanisms of breathing during sleep and causes of their failure. Stopped breathing (apnea) is not the cause of Sudden Infant Death Syndrome (SIDS) as it has been thought before. Complicated desynchronizations between breathing, heart, and other systems cause SIDS.

Now we know that respiratory and heartbeat patterns during sleep are different from those during wakefulness. During NREM sleep, respiratory rate is decreased with a monotonous regular pattern. This breathing pattern appears to be due to the reduction of the number and levels of activity of respiratory centers in the brain. Resistance to air flow increases due to the decrease in the upper airway muscle tone. Oxygen saturation drops. It is important to know that the respiratory response to inner stimuli is significantly different in children than in adults. For example, in contrast to the basic stimulation of respiratory drive to hypoxia (oxygen deficiency) in adults, newborns, and premature babies parodoxically stop breathing when the oxygen level drops. Some newborns respond to hypoxia in the biphasic manner, meaning an increase in respiration and a decrease in breathing, because the central nervous system is not mature enough to overcome hypoxia. The clinical spectrum of disordered respiration in sleep is quite broad.

1) Premature infants suffer *Apnea of Prematurity* (AOP) periodic breathing with prolonged pauses. The more premature the baby, the more frequent are occurrences of apnea. Exact mechanisms of apnea in premature infants are not fully understood, but are mainly attributed to immaturity of central and peripheral chemoreceptors and pulmonary reflexes. Fetus-type periodic breathing in premature babies could be a type of maladaptive adjustment.

Known causes of apnea in premature babies are hypoxia, metabolic abnormalities, gastrointestinal reflux (reversed peristaltic of esophagus—a tube that connects the oral cavity with the stomach), anemia, seizures, congenital abnormalities, etc.

Apnea of Prematurity is a very serious condition that is potentially life-threatening for infants and can cause developmental problems. Successful treatment is possible with a good prognosis for the child's future.

Apnea disappears by the 36 week postconceptional age in most cases, but periodic breathing may persist up to 3 months past the 40 week mark. Full-term infants (older than 37 weeks gestational age) also may have pathological apnea, now called *Apnea of Infancy.* Apnea of Infancy is diagnosed when periods of cessation of breathing are 20 seconds or longer, or pauses are shorter, but are associated with one of the following symptoms:
• Decrease in the heart rate (bradycardia)
• Cyanosis (blue baby)
• Sudden paling
• Profound muscle hypotonia (the child gets limp)

Contrary to *Apnea of Prematurity,* no explanation can be offered for apnea in normal full-term infants. This makes it very difficult to predict and determine treatment for life-threatening apnea in infants. Among the known causes are maternal smoking, drug misuse, and seizures.

Apneic episodes are very frightening to observe and often need resuscitative efforts. After a few shocking experiences, many parents learned CPR and saved their babies' lives. According to the 1986 National Institute of Health Consensus Development (NIHCD) Conference statement on Infantile Apnea and home monitoring, Apnea of Prematurity (AOP) and Apnea of Infancy (AOI), should not be confused with Sudden Infant Death Syndrome (SIDS). There was a suggestion to call AOP and AOI Apparent Life-Threatening Events (ALTE) to avoid misleading associations with SIDS.

Most infants with ALTE will not die and can be treated. Children with SIDS do not have a history of ALTE. The term ALTE describes a clinical syndrome where a variety of identifiable diseases (e.g., systemic infection, gastrointestinal reflux, upper airway obstructions, etc.) can cause such episodes.

Apnea in Older Children differs significantly from AOP and AOI, and also from apnea in adults.

Apnea is divided into two basic types: Central (when the brain "forgets" to control breathing) and Peripheral (due to obstruction of airways). Pure central apnea most commonly is congenital. Breathing stops as soon as the child falls asleep. This condition is called the Ondina Curse Syndrome. Respiratory disturbances in older children are primarily obstructive and commonly overlooked.

Apnea in children is as common and dangerous as in adults, or even more so, due to its influences on psychomotor development.

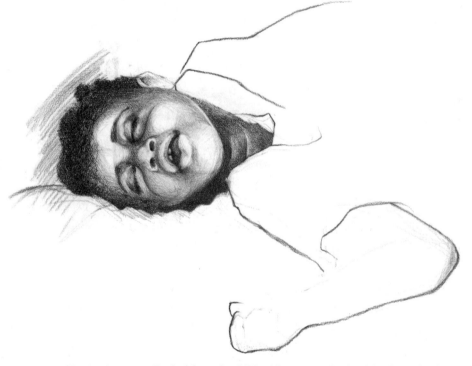

Sleep Apnea   Typical face of a child with apnea: the head is thrust far back, the child's mouth is opened widely. Bulbous, parched lips. The teeth are spaced wide apart, the tongue is abnormally large, and her nostrils are unusually large. The girl's eyes are puffed.

TABLE 6.1: PROBLEMS CAUSED BY OBSTRUCTIVE SLEEP APNEA IN CHILDREN

NOCTURNAL (NIGHTTIME) PROBLEMS

Snoring—loud, raspy, squeaky
Breathing pauses and snorts
Heavy, irregular breathing
Very restless sleep
Too deep, unarousable sleep
Profuse sweating in sleep
Severe bedwetting
Bad dreams (nightmares)
Sleep terrors
Sleep with open mouth
Automatic behavior in sleep
Nocturnal chest pain
Cardiac arrhythmias in sleep

DIURNAL (DAYTIME) PROBLEMS

Learning problems
Excessive daytime sleepiness
Severe hyperactivity
Rage reaction and often unusual aggressiveness
Pathological shyness
Attention span problems
Morning headaches
Developmental problems
Obesity
Frequent upper airway infections

Snoring is the hallmark of obstructive sleep apnea. Sonorous breathing is often associated with pauses and snorts. Many nocturnal symptoms develop due to obstructive apnea - difficulty in breathing, heavy sweating, bedwetting, morning headaches, night terrors, and nightmares. Significant medical problems including life-threatening symptoms have been reported. Daytime problems are also very serious: learning problems, abnormality of behavior, short and long standing personality changes are all symptoms of apnea.

What causes obstructive apnea in sleep? Hypertrophic tonsils and adenoids, changes in facial bone structure: a small chin or one that is too far back, long soft palate, large tongue, teeth positions, obesity, anemia, burns to the head and neck, metabolic abnormalities, etc. It is important to remember the vicious circle. For example, central apnea induces deep muscle relaxation and blood stoppage which stimulates the growth of the adenoids and tonsils. Large adenoids and tonsils block the airway making the child wake up. At first, small obstructions might be adaptive but soon make the apnea worse. It is important to remember that large surgery with removal of too much tissue might be counterproductive. Besides surgery, there is another treatment called CPAP (Continuous Positive Airway Pressure). CPAP was a life-saver for many children who were treated before the surgery *tracheotomy* —"temporary hole in the trachea". If you remember the history of sleep medicine, it started with a successful treatment of two children with obstructive sleep apnea. Potent respiratory stimulants have been used experimentally on AOP patients with good results. Nortryptiline is used for older patients.

The treatment of severe apnea is a serious concern for sleep science and practice. Early resolution of sleep apnea may accelerate physical growth and mental development of the child, and prevent life-long problems.

SHE FALLS ASLEEP WHENEVER SHE LAUGHS
(ABOUT NARCOLEPSY)

The story of the 11-year-old, slightly overweight, but very charming girl is about her laughter. Whenever she starts to laugh she suddenly looks weak and limp, as if she has fallen asleep. And she has. Jill is very well liked by her classmates, and they do not make fun of her when she falls asleep at school during tests or in the lunchroom. Her friends shake her to wake her up. Her case was studied by a pediatrician who feels that she is exhausted and has side effects from asthma medications. The straw that broke the camel's back and forced her grandmother to seek help with a sleep clinic was an embarrassing incident; when she fell asleep snoring loudly at her uncle's funeral a month before. It took her grandmother some time to wake her up, but the girl looked confused, frightened, and could not move for a few seconds.

Described episodes of sleepiness became more noticeable and grew progressively worse. It looked strange to her relatives. She would suddenly fall asleep in the middle of a dinner or a conversation, while laughing or talking excitedly. She would lose her balance and almost fall. Weakness in her legs became a new symptom. She felt weak in the morning. Fully awakened, she couldn't move. She tried to scream, but the sound wouldn't come out of her throat. Recently she lost her appetite, but she still gained weight.

Questions about her family history revealed that three members of the family had sleep attacks during the day. This family also had "family bad luck": repeated car accidents as a result of the driver falling asleep behind the wheel. In fact, the uncle whose funeral Jill attended died in a bad car accident involving several cars. He was known for falling asleep at the wheel, and he complained of excessive daytime sleepiness to his family doctor one month prior to his deadly accident.

Jill has a disease. It is called *narcolepsy*, and she has all four major symptoms of it:

1. Excessive daytime sleepiness and sleep attacks.
2. Sudden weakness of muscles, called cataplexy. This is the most troublesome symptom. It comes whenever

the person gets excited. That is why laughing, anger, and crying provoke weakness in the muscles.

3. Frightening visions before sleep, called hypnogogic hallucinations or in the morning, called hypnopompic hallucinations.

4. A symptom called sleep paralysis which makes her incapable of moving or uttering a sound.

The word *narcolepsy* is a combination of two words: *narcos*, which means "induced sleep" and *epilepsy*. In the past it was believed that this disease is a version of epilepsy. Now we know that it is not true. Narcolepsy is a genetic disorder, resulting from a certain biochemical deficit that affects the brain mechanisms for turning "on" and "off" REM sleep.

Now we know a lot about this previously mysterious disease due to animal research (see Part 2). In 1984, a large study in Japan discovered that the majority of patients with narcolepsy are affected by Human Leucocyte Antigen (HLA known as DRw15). First, this disease, thought to be exotic is surprisingly not so rare. It is as common as Parkinson's disease, Multiple Sclerosis or Hemophilia. Several famous people have it, like the comedian, Lenny Bruce, or computer software pioneer, entrepreneur, and philanthropist, Joseph A. Piscopo, and even renowned physician, orthopedic surgeon for the Los Angeles Dodgers, Dr. Frank Jobs. According to the American Narcolepsy Association one in every thousand people has narcolepsy.

The second important point is that narcolepsy starts in childhood. Mild, but growing symptoms of excessive daytime sleepiness are often misinterpreted as fatigue, laziness, daydreaming, manipulation, or depression. Dr. Roger Frank pointed out in his book, <u>Sleep Disorders: America's Hidden Nightmare</u> that on the average, "It takes examination by about five different doctors and passing of nearly fifteen years before a narcoleptic is properly diagnosed and can begin to receive treatment." In our clinic, we identify narcoleptic children as early as the age of ten. We also screen relatives, especially children, of already identified narcoleptics. And we have been impressed by how many sleep disorders exist in families of narcoleptics in various forms. During the night, it might be bedwetting, headbanging, sleepwalking, etc. During the day, children can be chronically tired, irritable, inattentive, daydreaming, unusually anxious, dropping things, often falling or hurting themselves. The classical tetrad will develop later.

How do we diagnose narcolepsy? A formal diagnosis of narcolepsy can be done by sleep evaluation using all night sleep study. Two findings speak strongly for the diagnosis: 1) The first REM period starts unusually soon (short REM latency). If in normal healthy adults the first REM starts in about 60-90 minutes, in a narcoleptic it is usually within the first 20 minutes. 2) Disorganized sleep architecture. Again, short REM latency and disorganized sleep architecture are not specific for narcolepsy, and may be seen after significant sleep deprivation and in severe depression. So these data should be checked against the clinical picture and the family history.

The Multiple Sleep Latency Test, MSLT, was designed, interestingly enough, by one of the pioneers in pediatric sleep medicine, Dr. Mary Carskadon. This test consists of several polysomnographic recordings when the person is asked to lie down in a dark room during the daytime. The time of falling asleep and the initial stage of sleep are recorded. Then the person is awakened, and in about one hour repeats the process. If the person falls asleep quickly (within ten minutes) and goes immediately into REM sleep, narcolepsy can be diagnosed at once, excluding psychological or environmental factors.

Narcolepsy is a disordered "transmission" in the brain which causes REM sleep at inappropriate times. The MSLT is a proven method, but it is long, cumbersome and difficult for children. New diagnostic methods such as Pupilometry, are now being developed.

If you have a family member who episodically feels weak and has sleep attacks, or if your child develops sleep and daytime problems, it is worthwhile to remember the possibility of narcolepsy and check with your pediatrician or a sleep clinic.

Treatment is available. Treatment with stimulants, commonly used for narcolepsy, is also commonly used for children with the opposite condition of hyperactivity. It means that treatment is available and safe if applied professionally. It also indicates that two extremes, excessive daytime sleepiness and excessive alertness and motor excitement may have something in common: an underlying problem with the basic biorhythm, the sleep-wake cycle.

Today we cannot cure narcolepsy, because the cause lies too deep in genetic roots. But even now, before genetic engineering gets to narcolepsy, we can alleviate symptoms in children and minimize this potentially life-threatening disease in young adults.

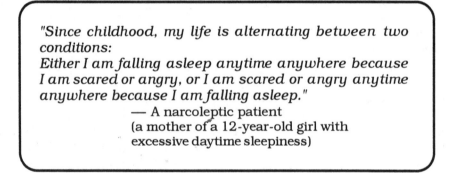

"Since childhood, my life is alternating between two conditions:
Either I am falling asleep anytime anywhere because I am scared or angry, or I am scared or angry anytime anywhere because I am falling asleep."
— A narcoleptic patient
(a mother of a 12-year-old girl with excessive daytime sleepiness)

INJURIOUS SLEEP

Just a few years ago, the phrase "injurious sleep" sounded absurd. But the more we learn about sleep and the more sophisticated and specific are the methods we have to differentiate behaviors, the more we are amazed at how many phases of sleep have related disorders. To prove this point, let us start with cases of highly publicized homicide in sleep. As recently as on Sunday, June 23, 1994, David Poole, 31, while sleeping, jumped out of his bed, grabbed a gun and started randomly shooting at the wall. His neighbor, an 8th grader, was shot four times, narrowly escaping death. Poole had a bad dream, thinking that someone was after him, intending to kill, and he "defended" himself. He had a history of pathological somnambulism. There are a few typical situations when fatal nocturnal aggression occurs: abrupt, confused arousal from sleep, somnambulism and REM behavior disorders. There are other less severe but nevertheless very serious injuries, such as broken bones, hitting, slapping, slamming doors, breaking furniture, bruises, and cutting—all of these injuries associated with the sleep apnea syndrome, nocturnal enuresis, headbanging, nightmares, night terrors, nocturnal dissociative conditions, etc.

Dr. Broughton from Canada found the first documented case of a murder committed while in sleep. It happened in medieval times. A Silesian woodcutter, Bernard Schedmazing, woke up abruptly after only a few hours of sleep, thought he saw an intruder at the foot of his bed and picking up his ax, killed his wife lying beside him. There are a number of well documented homicides in association with sleep conditions, most commonly, related to sleepwalking or sudden and abrupt arousals in the morning or in the middle of the night. Homicidal episodes associated with REM behavioral disorders have not been reported so far, but severe and multiple injuries to oneself and others are very typical. Here are some examples: a colonel shot a guardsman on patrol and his own horse. A servant girl stabbed one of her master's children to death during a sleepwalking episode.

These cases are different from child abuse cases related to confusional conditions due to sleep deprivation, described first by Chekhov. We are talking about murders committed by people during nighttime sleep. A lot of publicity was given to a London housewife who in her sleep threw her infant out of the window. Recently there was a case where the father, during a sleepwalking episode, pulled his infant out of the crib and hit his head against the floor. The infant was brought back to life after a prolonged hospital stay, but the father committed suicide. A fireman awoke to find himself beating his wife's head with a shovel and immediately fainted. Upon regaining consciousness, he realized she was dead and attempted suicide. A mother who was taking some medications arose from her sleep and beat her daughter to death. The cases are the result of so-called pathological sleepwalking or "somnambulism". Sleepwalking is usually associated with funny stories about people walking on the roof. In actuality, it might have a not-so-funny ending. It is interesting that sometimes a person's behavior in his sleep is the opposite of his daytime temperament. For example, a "perfect husband" strangled his wife, or another situation involved a person who stabbed to death his dear friend, staying overnight at his house. A person who was suffering from a phobia of "hights" jumped out of the window of a four story building in his sleep.

Dr. Schnak has recently reviewed the stories of hundreds of patients with sleep related severe injuries. It is very important to understand such cases medically as well as legally (in terms of voluntary control of such situations). This would help us understand the nature of violent behavior in sleep.

The team of internationally known sleep researchers including Dr. Broughton, from Canada; Castaut from France; and Dr. Cartwright from Chicago studied the case of Kenneth P. is a 22-year-old "perfect" son. He trampled his wife to death and assaulted his father-in-law in the early morning. He was charged with first degree murder of his wife and an attempted assault on his father-in-law. Based on the careful evaluation of his history in multiple sleep revelations, the diagnosis of pathological sleepwalking was diagnosed, and after a highly emotional trial, it was concluded that Kenneth P. committed a violent act unconsciously and under a severe medical condition.

The nature of sleepwalking and related legal defense became more complex and serious. Somnambulism represents a remarkable state, combining an apparent level of consciousness "self awareness" but having also symptoms of sleep. It is an organized behavior that sometimes is very similar to wakefulness because of its complexity and apparently goal-oriented appearance. Although in sleepwalking episodes the eyes are typically open, the individual does not fully incorporate environmental stimuli. Shakespeare fully recognized this in describing Lady Macbeth's sleepwalking. The Doctor remarked on observing Lady Macbeth that "her eyes are open", to which the Lady-in-Waiting who had observed many such episodes answered, "Aye, but their sense is shot."

It is in general not possible to distinguish somnambulistic behavior from the person's usual behavior during the daytime, because unconsciously this behavior is pre-programmed and has to "run itself out." There is no evidence that during sleepwalking episodes a somnambulist can either execute a conscious intent from prior wakefulness, or can create an intent. There is no evidence to believe that a sleepwalker can actually do what he wants to do during the daytime or fake certain conditions. Phenomenologically indistinguishable complex behavior, not remembered afterwards, is seen in a number of medical conditions in which conscious awareness is absent or impaired to permit such behavior. This includes some so-called psychotic fugue stages. Any dissociative stage includes the fugue stage, drug-related dissociated stage, trance states or epileptic seizures, and some others. (See Part 7 on Dissociative Conditions). From a medical and legal viewpoint, the requirements of the legal word "automatism" are satisfied, because the behavior is unconscious and involuntary. This is summarized in the ruling of the Supreme Court of Canada, which quoted from a statement of Mr. Justice Dickson in R. versus Rabey. "Although the work of automatism made its way but lately through the legal stage, it is a basic principle that absence of volition in respect of the art involved is always a defense to the crime."

The question is whether sleepwalking in this case should be considered as insane or as non-insane automatism. This classification is a matter of importance to the legal outcome of the trial. If the classification of sleepwalking is that of non-insane automatism, the accused is entitled to full acquittal, and is therefore set free, which happened in the case of Kenneth P.   However, if the automatic acts in question are considered to spring from mind disease, they are classified or considered as insane automatism, and the individual should be sent to a mandatory institution for the criminally insane for an *indefinite* period of time.

The legal concepts for "mind disease" and "insanity" are not precisely similar to medical science. The concept of mind diseases based on the idea of the continuing danger, means that these conditions create a current danger to the public from this person.   If sleepwalking is considered to be a mind disease, the person should be put into an institution for an indefinite period of time, because of the likelihood of recurrent violence and somnambulistic episodes.   But like in the above described case, the sleepwalking was very rare and was triggered by a highly unusual combination of severe sleep deprivation and overwhelming stress.   Thus, the likelihood of curing this type of behavior is very low.   It was also stated that there is no existing specific medication for the treatment of somnambulism.   The avoidance of precipitating factors, such as sleep deprivation and stress, normal sleep-wake cycle, plus drug treatment would facilitate sleep.

Another point against this idea is that there is no documented case of repeated violence of somnambulism in literature, so that its recurrence in general is very exceptional, if tragic.   Therefore somnambulism is not considered insanity. It should not be considered as a mind disease either, because this also holds the idea of recurrence from external factors, let us say, from head trauma, or from drug intake. If the person did not show any symptoms of mind disease during wakefulness, then sleepwalking itself is not a disease, but is a disorder of sleep. Specifically, during sleepwalking, the brain does not awaken, and the state of mind at the time is that of being asleep, which is a normal condition. The most important thing is to prove volition on the part of the accused, which is not the case with sleepwalking.

So if automatic violent behavior during somnambulism is considered a mind disease, the person should be sent for treatment for a long period of time. If it is considered insane automatism, the person should be set free. Different countries and courts have made different decisions. The Supreme Court of Canada found sleepwalking to be a form of non-insane automatism, which means the person who displayed violent behavior is set free. In England, unfortunately, the Court of Appeals, ruled on the same issue of violent somnambulism in favor of insane automatism, and the person was sent to an institution for many years. The main concern of law makers is whether somnambulism can be easily faked. If so, one might expect a flood of defenses on this basis. We should say that it is almost impossible to fake it. First, it should be noted that for more than a century, somnambulism has been generally classified and known, and no rush of such defenses occurred. Secondly, it is extremely difficult for anyone to create a convincing and verifiable personal and family history of somnambulism. Most importantly, objective polysomnographic features characterize these conditions. Someone who would try to simulate an episode would almost certainly report a feature incompatible with this diagnosis, and by definition, somnambulism occurs in extremely deep stages of sleep, easily verified by objective methods.

REM behavior disorder is another remarkable condition in which the person experiences highly emotional dreams and reacts to them behaviorally. In REM sleep, muscles are paralyzed normally and a person does not react. The essence of the disorder is a loss of control over muscles when the person is moving violently, defending himself from enemies, while actually hurting himself or his loved ones.

Agitated arousal is the most common cause of injuries. As an example, a family in which four members are anorexic and two are headbangers described how they tried to awaken the father using a broom, because of his agitation and aggressive reaction to touching or forceful awakening. This ended with multiple blunt traumas to two members of the family, when the 260 pound man inflicted injuries to his wife and older son while they tried to wake him up and forgot, on this occasion, to use a broom. Killing in sleep is quite dramatic and not very common, but life-threatening injuries and traumas are extremely common and present significant public health issues. Broken fingers, broken furniture, bruises, cuts, hurt animals, runaways or urination on somebody occur much more often than you can imagine.

We can assume that murder and self injuries are important issues for adults and less important for children. This is not true. The real answer to this is that injurious behavior is very common in children too.   Children and adolescents often run away in their sleep.   They have headbanging episodes, pull hair, and hurt themselves. The following are just a few typical examples: a 12-year-old girl ran out of her house into the street and caused a car accident. Result: multiple bruises and a head trauma.

An 11-year-old boy jumped out of his bed.   He fought with his grandmother who was trying to stop him. Result: she broke her leg.

A 10-year-old bed wetter urinated in the closet.   On the way back he bumped into the wall. Result: he had prolonged nose bleeding.

A five-year-old girl headbanger accidentally poked her eye with a screw on the bed headboard.

These problems are usually associated with arousals from sleep and also with so-called *parasomnias* (See Part 5).

The whole other set of self-injurious behavior is related to dissociative conditions and confusional situations. Confusional situations relate to the person's decreased level of alertness or fragmented alertness due to sleep deprivation, or due to medical and psychiatric conditions. One example of that is thumb sucking when the child sucks his fingers and damages the skin. As we described above, many serious bed habits can be conceptualized as self-injurious behavior related to the pathology of alertness.

There was a recent study on children who repeatedly hold their breath or adolescents with repetitive hanging. They actually choked themselves due to the urge to get into these confusional states of mind with the world looking like a dream. These adolescents did not want to commit suicide, and they were not depressed, but some of them accidentally choked themselves to death.

It is amazing that sleep—which is supposed to be the quietest and healthiest state—might be the most agitated, brutal, and dangerous to the sleeper and to others. According to Dr. William Dement, who collected statistics for the Congressional Commission on Health, mortality and morbidity are related to disorders of sleep

and alertness and can be compared to war. Our mission is
to prevent this war.

> *"In sleep, what difference is there
> between Solomon and the fool."*
> — Proverb

PART 7

SLEEP RELATED DAYTIME DISORDERS OF ALERTNESS

Problems of Morning Awakening and
Daytime Wakefulness

Excessive Daytime Sleepiness;
Disorders of Daytime Alertness,
Their Origin and Treatment

Dissociative Conditions

Bad Habits

PROBLEMS OF MORNING AWAKENING AND
DAYTIME WAKEFULNESS

Morning might be sometimes as bad as bedtime. Many children sleep so deeply in the morning that waking them up for school is a big challenge for parents. It may turn into an ugly fight. Yelling, screaming, and fighting ruins the whole day for all family members.

Several causes can lead to unusual difficulties in awakening. The most benign is the so-called "phase delay syndrome". The person goes to sleep and wakes up much later than socially acceptable. Some people are "early birds". They go to bed early and wake up early. Some of us normally have the opposite tendency; go to sleep later and wake up later, they are "owls". This difference is in our biological clock, and we have to live with it. If our inner clocks, inner biological rhythms of the sleep-wake cycle coincide with social rhythms and social clocks, so-called "social zeitgebers", we are fine. But if social clocks are too different from our biological inner clocks, it might put too much stress on our adjustment and our adaptability. And if this adaptability is exhausted—we are deep in trouble.

In children, however, the type of biorhythm is not fixed yet, and is pretty flexible to go either way. The child can be trained to fall asleep earlier or later. If an adolescent, for example, goes to sleep later and later every night, he or she ends up having a sleep-wake cycle incompatible with their school schedule. This is also the phase delay syndrome. The gravity of the problem of late awakenings and their affect on school performance is not yet adequately appreciated and addressed.

Another reason for late awakening may be a sleep disorder with multiple awakenings or other deviations of quality and quantity of sleep, causing sleep deprivation. The third cause of difficulties in awakening is not a widely known fact: some normal children and children with sleep problems, called *parasomnias*, have reversed distribution of NREM cycle. People with this problem have their NREM sleep in the morning instead of the first half of the night. It means, actually that they sleep deeper in the morning. This happens to children with bedwetting problems. Investigation and understanding of problematic morning awakening and insufficient alertness may be quite complicated due to technical and terminological problems. In many sleep labs, the sleep recording stops and the patient is awakened by the technician at a certain time in the morning, even if the subject is very sleepy. When we in our lab let the child sleep as much as he wanted, we found a lot of interesting data.

Terminology is also somewhat confusing. Awakening is equated with arousal. There is a very popular theory by Dr. Broughton and Dr. Gastaut that sleep disorders in children are disorders of arousal. Disorders of arousal may mean awakening with incomplete arousal. It means that problems are on the border between sleep and awakening. Incomplete arousal can cause anxiety and aggression. This term is good when applied to night problems, but not adequate when some altered states of consciousness appear during morning wakefulness. When a child is aroused forcefully he may become agitated, aggressive and violent. Dr. Gudden in 1905 and Dr. Epstein in 1925 independently named this type of problem as "sleep drunkenness".

Dr. Wernike, who discovered the center of speech in the brain in 1900, described a special syndrome of feelings of loss, bewilderment, as separate phenomena from psychotic disorders. A special study of this bewilderment syndrome was undertaken by Dr. Ann Belenkaja. She stated that some otherwise normal people feel lost getting into a dream-like state. Their psychic activity is then determined by inner subjective experiences, not by external circumstances, although the connections with the outside world remain intact, and the person can continue to perform his duties. At the same time, their external world seems to be alien, unrelated, and strange. The person perceives a new significance in routine events. This phenomenon is frequent during periods of fever, sudden forceful awakenings, and it looks similar to sleepwalking and sleep talking episodes during the nighttime. It is also common in younger children during forceful awakening after bedwetting. A person with the syndrome of bewilderment has a very short attention, ability to focus is low. This attention is not focused. They give answers, missing the questions, during such times children and adolescents complain of tiredness but cannot fall asleep if they go to bed. In the morning, these children are still sleepy and continuously see dreams while getting dressed, eating breakfast, on the bus, or even at school. These dreams are sometimes frightening, but at the same time, children recognize them as dreams, although the images may be superimposed by reality. We wrote earlier about the girl who "saw" her teacher's dark hair as red, exactly the way she saw it in her dream. She heard the teacher's talk about her dream. In the child's description, in her mind she shut off the real sound of the teacher's voice and turned on the inner voice which she heard in her dream. Another form of difficult awakening was described by Dr. Pfister in 1902 as "sleep paralysis" when the person is completely awake and has re-entered the external world but is unable to move or talk. These symptoms are typical for a disease called narcolepsy. (See Part 6) It is also very common in normal children, especially adolescents, after sleep deprivation or alcohol intake.

The above problems of awakening and alertness happen on the border between sleep and wakefulness, and they are phenomena of transitional altered states of consciousness. Metabolic activities are also probably altered at this time because people can have different body reactions. Those are not diseases but if they become too frequent they should be addressed seriously, because they may be symptomatic of future problems.

The younger the child, the more difficult it is to analyze these deviations. The state of awakening fluctuates in children. Symptoms may be viewed as problems if they are very different for this particular child or appear at an unusual time. Another important phenomenon is "paradoxical sleepiness", when the child is very sleepy but becomes capricious, agitated, and hyperactive. Fluctuations occur from very high levels of activity (hyperactivity) to daydreaming and sleepiness and back again during the day.

Another form of deviation in the sleep-wake cycle is "inversion" of sleep-wakefulness which means that the child is extremely sleepy during the daytime and not sleepy during the night. It might be a normal situation, seen in normal children. It is basically a regression to the early form of the biorhythm, but in certain psychological, psychiatric, neurological, and somatic conditions, the inversion of sleep and wakefulness may be an early sign of upcoming disease. After trauma, and in the first stage of recovery, children frequently have inversion of the sleep-wake cycle.

EXCESSIVE DAYTIME SLEEPINESS;
DISORDERS OF DAYTIME ALERTNESS,
THEIR ORIGIN AND TREATMENT

In January of 1989, a 17-year-old young man from New Hampshire was in the newspaper headline nationwide. He received the National Student Safety Driver Award. Just seven months later in July, this young man was dead, having fallen asleep at the wheel. His car drifted into a head on collision, also killing his friends and the driver of the other car.

This was not an accident, strictly speaking. It was the inevitable consequence of inadequate sleep. In Part 3 we described other examples of tragic events resulting from excessive daytime sleepiness. The major cause of excessive sleepiness during the day is sleep deprivation. As we stated many times in the previous chapters, night sleep and daytime wakefulness are two strongly connected and balanced states of alertness. Any disruption of sleep will inevitably have a rebound effect on the daytime activities. It is important to emphasize that in children and adolescents, disruption of alertness has many causes, often hidden and presented with various symptoms.

Sleep-wake schedule deviations. Growing children have a wide range of individual variations in their need for sleep. Some children need a lot of sleep, some do not. There is also a wide range in the need for sleep in the same individual, depending on emotional events, social and family schedules, etc. When the child is emotionally overwhelmed, worried about his upcoming tests, or physically exhausted, his need for sleep is drastically increased, while his actual sleep is usually decreased due to concern, excitement, or agitation. This is a basic, but commonly overlooked part of growing up. When the need for sleep increases, behaviorally and subjectively the child responds in the opposite way. Every parent is familiar with the situation when a small child who is usually calm during the daytime becomes extremely feisty and hyperactive, and raises a big fuss when it is time to go to bed. He fights about going to bed, even though his eyes are almost closed.

An 8th grader cannot fall asleep, concerned about the next day's school test or too tired to sleep after studying late. A teenager tells you that he feels fine after sleeping four hours last night. This is the first rule for parents: children do not feel sleep loss the way adults do, and respond to it with agitation. Sleep deficiency can accumulate, and sometimes blow up with different problems. In other words, sleep loss has a cumulative effect. It is our responsibility to help the child get enough sleep.

How do you balance the natural flexibility of a child's activity with firm control? The practical rule of thumb is simple: an everyday routine. The child's sleep schedule can vary, say one hour at the most. But during emotionally overwhelming days, late birthday parties or stress at home and school, parents' attention to the child's sleep should be increased. This is the time when the parent should be less permissive. If it is impossible to put the child to bed earlier the same day—say he came home too late,—the best strategy would be not to let the child sleep too long the next morning, but wake him up no later than one hour after his usual time and make him go to bed one hour earlier the next day. This suggestion is based on the fact that our biological clock sets our biorhythms. It resets in the morning, so we should keep our wake up time as fixed as possible.

The next group of causes are related to medical causes of sleep disruption. The majority of our children are generally healthy. Children's sleep problems related to chronic medical problems like asthma or acute problems like otitis are discussed separately later on, but there are many minor short-lived problems which nevertheless might severely disrupt sleep and, subsequently, alertness the next day. Such problems include the following.

1. *Difficulties in nasal breathing*. We found that during the night when the child cannot breathe through the nose and his sleep is very restless, his bedwetting might relapse, and apnea might reoccur. This child also has morning headaches. Recent research discovered that breathing through the nose does not only cool and clean the incoming air. Nasal breathing is an interesting process, called in humans nasal cycling. The air goes through the nostrils unequally, predominantly through the right nostril for a few minutes and then through the left nostril. Alternating breathing is involved in the regulation of what we call the "brain tonus". Tonus means the stability of

functioning. As an example, nasal breathing, coupled with tears, serves as a regulator of emotional stability. If you cry it makes you feel better, but if you cry too long, you will feel exhausted. Especially in children, nasal breathing is part of the physiological mechanism of wakefulness. It is an interesting mechanism of stabilizing the developing brain. Changes in nasal breathing can lead to changes in the sleep positions and other movements in sleep as well as in sleep stages. Drops of normal saline, oil drops, are usually helpful for dryness. Do not use over-the-counter medication, because antihistamine components may over-dry the mucous secretions. This can cause a shift in nasal breathing, hindering it.

2. *Earaches*. These are common for small children. By pressuring in the middle part of the ear, you can recognize an earache from the child's reactions. Ear drops usually work to solve the problem, but earaches are very serious causes of sleep disruptions in small children. They might induce multiple awakenings, headaches, bedwetting, and other psychosomatic symptoms.

3. *Teething*. You can tell that this is the problem if the child cries for several nights in a row. The pain disrupts the phases of the sleep-wake cycle and causes excessive irritability in the daytime. Give them Tylenol® or Benadryl®, one teaspoon before sleep.

With older children, in the vast majority of cases, instability of the sleep-wake cycle takes on different forms.

1. *Daydreaming*. Intensive and prolonged vivid images block out the external world. Such a child stays in his own world, responds to it, lives in it, and shuts himself off from the reality. This may disrupt his school learning activity and relationships with peers.

2. *Hyperactivity*. Surprisingly, hyperactivity in some cases may be considered as a sleep-alertness disorder. The highly alert child who is always active and running around, may actually have deviated arousal patterns. There are periods of fragmented sleep, attention hyperactivity disorder (ADHD), that is formally defined as a disorder of arousal (a physiological term for the word "alertness"). Dr. Stephen Sheldon and other researchers analyzed the need for sleep in children. They found that children with the attention deficit disorder, and with hyperactivity had symptoms like motor restlessness and increased sleep pressure. Increased sleep pressure was

objectively manifested by early sleep onset latency (time between going to bed and actually falling asleep). It showed evidence of frequent micro sleep disorders during the daytime. One of the investigators, a parent, noted that kids run around to stay awake like sharks who are always moving to get enough oxygen. This is a striking comparison but it may have some truth.

3. *Specific dissociation.* Dissociation, fantasy worlds are normal and necessary to the health of the young people. It is brain gymnastics. It is a source of great activity. Getting out of hand, the dissociation might become fixed, and instead of a healthy and helpful phenomenon, it can be transformed into disruptive bad habits. Imaginary friends are a normal phenomenon, but if they are fixed, this may also acquire some pathological features. Dissociation might lead to multiple personalities. Abnormal sleep, out-of-body experiences may lead to psychotic behavior. Many medical problems start as prolonged disorders of dissociation. Psychiatric problems also start with dissociation prior to psychotic breaks.

Dr. Dement's Safety Principles for Everyone:
• Sleepiness kills! A nap can save your life.
• Your urge to sleep may be disguised or hidden.
• When your sleep debt is large, a sleep attack can occur without warning.
• If you feel drowsy, it is almost too late.

———————•••———————

"A sudden wave of drowsiness should be treated almost as seriously as chest pain."
— Dr. William Dement

DISSOCIATIVE CONDITIONS

Psychiatrists recognize a class of phenomena called "dissociation". Dissociations are unclear states of mind when thoughts, feelings, and memory are not integrated with each other. It is based on the decrease in the level of alertness, and the fragmentation of the stream of consciousness. It is part of a normal physiological and psychological process, if it happens at the right time, in the right place, and in the right degree. These dissociations are usually normal during pre-sleep and in the process of awakening. Dissociations as normal conditions also include a fantasy world and creative thinking. In other words, dissociative conditions for the most part, are normal, healthy and welcome.

Dissociative conditions manifest themselves in a number of ways, such as:

(1) *Depersonalization*, when the person experiences strange sensations or disproportions in his own body;

(2) *Derealization* —where the room or the whole world look strange, twisted in time or space.

(3) *Deja vu* or *jamais vu* —this is related to the feeling when something familiar looks like something very new or what is new looks like something already seen;

(4) *Living in a fantasy world, daydreaming* —this is a condition familiar to everyone, when the person dissociates himself from reality and becomes absorbed in his own world;

(5) *Imaginary friend* —this is another very common situation when young children pretend to have a friend who they talk to. They know the imaginary friend's name and play with him. A little less common are phenomena of pre-dream illusions or hallucinations, when the person is going to sleep and sees an awesome figure. All these phenomena are a normal part of dissociation between perceptual organs—eyes, ears, etc.—when a real external object can be misperceived. The condition worsens when the person is deprived of sleep. All of us become dissociated sometimes but dissociation may also become a sickness. It plays a major role in psychopathology.

Another more serious form of dissociative phenomena is the hypnoid stage, sudden obsessions, and out-of-body experiences. Still, it can be a rather frequent consequence of deprivation. About 70 percent of people experience transit dissociative conditions quite often. The dissociative condition can be fixed as deep symptoms and cause significant problems. They may become serious enough to call it a disorder. Psychiatry recognizes five disorders primarily based on fixed and deep dissociation:

(1)   Psychogenic amnesia —sudden loss of the person's memory, his previous life, including his own name;

(2)   Depersonalization syndrome —fixed feeling that the person is different;

(3)   Psychogenic fugue stage —when the person suddenly travels far away, and wakes up in an unknown place without any memory of how he or she got there and why;

(4)   Multiple personality —when the person has several identities, switching from one to the other; and

(5)   Atypical or mixed form.

Many of these disorders are characteristic of adolescents, but they may be seen in younger children as well. Dissociation may be part of a larger group of other mental disorders, such as post traumatic stress disorder. It is a generally known fact that chronic trauma during childhood, including abuse, can lead to multiple personality conditions. Eating disorders, commonly seen in adolescents, demonstrate dissociation as a significant part of their clinical picture.

An intensive research of dissociation in young patients with psychological disorders resulted in the development of a scale identifying how the child is dissociating, when normal daydreaming transforms into unproductive dissociation. For those who are interested, a modified and simplified test on dissociation is included in the book at the end of this chapter.

The physiological basis of dissociation lies in the relation of sleep and alertness. Dissociative condition is one of the many exciting, transitional stages in the wide spectrum of the sleep-wake cycle. The highest level of genius and the ultimate self-destruction in mental disorders can both be due to dissociative conditions. The secrets of our destiny and the destiny of our children determine in which direction our children will grow: toward productive fantasy which will change the world for the better, or unproductive dissociation from reality toward illness and violence. This destiny is rooted in our types of sleep and alertness. Let's look into their roots.

CHILD DISSOCIATIVE CHECKLIST
(Revised from Frank Putman, M.D.)

Below is a list of behaviors that describe children. For each item that describes your child NOW or WITHIN THE PAST 12 MONTHS, please circle **2** if the item is VERY TRUE of your child. Circle **1** if the item is SOMEWHAT or SOMETIMES TRUE of your child. If the item is NOT TRUE of your child, circle **O**.

0 1 2   1. Child does not remember or denies traumatic or painful experiences that are known to have occurred.

0 1 2   2. Child goes into a daze or trance-like state at times or often appears "spaced out". Teachers may report that he or she "daydreams" frequently in school, is draggy, fatigued, and sleepy.

0 1 2   3. Child shows rapid changes in personality. He or she may go from being shy to being outgoing, from feminine to masculine, from timid to aggressive.

0 1 2   4. Child is unusually forgetful or confused about things that he or she should know, e.g. may forget the names of friends, teachers or other important people, loses possessions or gets disoriented easily.

0 1 2   5. Child has a very poor sense of time. He or she loses track of time, may think that it is morning when it is actually afternoon, gets confused about what day it is, does not remember when something happened.

0 1 2   6. Child shows marked day-to-day or even hour-to-hour variations in his or her skills, knowledge, food preferences, athletic abilities, e.g. changes in handwriting, memory for previously learned information such as the multiplication table, spelling, use of tools, or artistic ability.

0 1 2   7. Child shows rapid regressions in age-level of behavior, e.g. a twelve-year-old starts to use baby talk, sucks thumb or draws like a four yr. old.

0 1 2   8. Child has a difficult time learning from experiences, e.g. explanations. Normal discipline or punishment does not change his behavior.

0 1 2   9. Child continues to deny misbehavior even when the evidence is obvious.

0 1 2   10. Child refers to himself in the third person, or at times insists on being called by a different name. He may also claim that things that he did actually happened to another person.

0 1 2   11. Child rapidly changes physical complaints such as headache or upset stomach. For example, he may complain of a headache one minute and seem to forget all about it right away.

0 1 2   12. Child is unusually sexually precocious and may attempt age-inappropriate sexual behavior with other children and adults.

0 1 2   13. Child suffers from unexplained injuries or may even deliberately injure himself at times.

0 1 2   14. Child reports hearing voices that talk to him. The voices may be friendly or angry and may come from "imaginary companions" sounding like voices of parents, friends or teachers

0 1 2   15. Child has vivid imaginary companion or companions. Child may insist that the imaginary companion(s) is (are) responsible for things that he has done.

0 1 2   16. Child has intense outbursts of anger, often without apparent cause, and may display unusual physical strength during these episodes.

0 1 2   17. Child does not react to his name being called several times.

0 1 2   18. Child has unusual nighttime experiences, e.g. sleepwalks, may report seeing "ghosts" or other things happening at night .

0 1 2   19. Child frequently talks to himself, may use a different voice or argue with himself at times.

0 1 2   20. Child watches TV for hours on end including commercials, or plays "Sega Genesis" for hours, not expressing any interest in playing with peers.

Interpretation of total count:

10-19   To be concerned.

≥ 20 Serious problem; recommend medical attention.

BAD HABITS

The deep and intimate relationship between habits and sleep is not easily seen on the surface. It is hidden and indirect. At the same time, it is extremely important to understand this relationship because the origin of many habits is rooted in sleep. If we know this relationship, we may have a better chance to control our habits. Habits are specific, stable, repetitive patterns of behavior, feelings and thoughts. Habits might be simple or very elaborate; they may appear spontaneously or be consciously developed. Habits are a normal and necessary part of our functioning but may be transformed into unnecessary and sometimes unhealthy rituals.

Parents are frequently concerned about their children's behavioral patterns, especially if they become too repetitive, or stereotyped. These are legitimate concerns. Stereotyped patterns are presented in a lot of cases as bad habits. Habits as such are very common in normal and even gifted children and adolescents, but some may be extremely irritating and oftentimes dangerous. Habits may be the result of multiple psychological or medical causes. At the same time, they may in turn cause multiple problems.

What is the nature of bad habits? We have to admit that the genesis of bad habits is very complex and not entirely understood. But there are some data suggesting a possible connection between sleep and bad habits.

As we suggested earlier, sleep and alertness are two intimately connected sides of biological, circadian rhythms. During their individual evolution, sleep mechanisms developed first, followed by the development of alertness. Sleep stages and alertness are unstable and fluctuating states of wakefulness. In other words, our vigilance is always vibrating from one extreme to the other, from slowing down and sleepiness, to flaring to excited levels. The metabolism of our body also follows these changes of wakefulness, but it is not that easy for the body to follow our biorhythm. As we mentioned above, our habits are "switches" and "stabilizers" of the state of alertness, making our biorhythms work automatically and smoothly. If these switches from one stage to another are broken, the next level of unhealthy habits will develop. Our lives are made up of habits. They are seen at any and all stages of alertness, but the most common of them are "at work" before sleep, in sleep, in the morning, or during the day in altered states of consciousness.

Take thumb-sucking for example. Small children have a difficult time falling asleep. Thumb-sucking before sleep helps them to calm down and to fall asleep. However, sometimes the child begins to suck his finger when he is bored, but has to stay awake and focused. This habit might occur in the stage of sleep to maintain a level of alertness, or as a means of calming himself down. While sucking his finger, the child is staring unblinkingly into space. He does not hear his name being called, and he does not remember what he was thinking about when asked later.

When children's alertness is unstable, there is an urge to find something to keep it up or to calm it down. The urge for stimulants or tranquilizers of any kind can include a loud sound or a flashlight. Urges are signals of needs for an external "pacemaker" to stabilize someone's biological rhythm. There are so many bad habits. We have spoken the most about the common ones earlier (See Parts 6 and 7). The most frequently encountered bad habits are nail biting, head rocking, headbanging, hair pulling, and some others including self-injurious behavior.

7.1   Development of Habit Disorders

Prenatal 0 3		9 mos. 3	6	9 -Years 12	18

Hand Sucking
Foot Kicking
Thumb Sucking
Headbanging
Head/Body Rocking
Pica
Nose/Skin Picking
Nail Biting
Breath Holding
Habitual Cough
Teeth Grinding
Hair Pulling
Tics
Tourette's
Firesetting
Obsessive Compulsive
Bulimia
Kleptomania
Self-Injury
Gambling

As you can see from table *7.1*, different ages are associated with different habits. But once they appear, habits, by definition, have a tendency to stay for a long time. The more deviated the habits, the stronger they seem to stick to the person. Many of them appear during transitional, confusional, or sleepy times.

What traits do habits commonly have? First, it is a clear and dramatic presentation. Second, it appears in transitional stages of alertness. Third, there is no underlying organic or pathological reason fully explaining even the most horrible habits, such as hair pulling (although in some cases it might be due to genetic predisposition). Four, habits are very resistant to changes, even with therapy (exhibiting so-called therapeutic resistance). Five, despite therapeutic resistance, habits can disappear by themselves, for no obvious reason. Adolescents and older children who can verbalize their feelings, describe habits as a process of experiencing some kind of internal tension. They feel that the world or they themselves are not real. They live with some exceedingly unpleasant sensations and confusing thoughts. Their condition can be compared with a popping balloon. When their ears are cleaned with water and their mind becomes clear, this brings them back to the real world. It sounds as if the habit helps them to go from an altered state of consciousness back to reality. Physiologically they feel a little dissociated while this is going on. Some of them hyperventilate, and the EEG demonstrates that their level of consciousness is different.

Searching for inner principles of habits, we spent a lot of time talking to parents about the history of habits and going back to what we call the pre-morbid pre-habit stage. What we found is that habits have natural stages of development. The first stage is called the "undifferentiated" stage. The child is emotional, his sleep patterns are increasingly unstable, but no particular habit has yet developed. Pre-habit period, or the "undifferentiated" period is a time of high risk.

In contrast with this, during the next period, a specific bad habit gets clearly differentiated and crystallized as an identifiable symptom. Other symptoms of general instability subside during that time. This period is, for lack of a better term, called "crystalization". Later bad habits stick to the person for quite a long while. This is the "monosymptomatic" phase. Parents would say that the child has tics or is pulling his hair, or has some other kind of bad habit, but otherwise, the child is okay. Professional analysis quickly uncovers many other symptoms during that time, combining into what we call syndromes. But a bad habit at this stage overshadows any other less visible, bothersome symptoms. The next critical stage is called "determination." To get rid of bad habits at this stage is crucial, or things will get worse and the existing habit will change to a more serious one. Other bad habits may appear, or old bad habits may become combined.

Knowing the nature of their development can help to shape good habits and reshape bad ones. The key to controlling habits is understanding where they came from. Habits are our external "pacemakers", changing and stabilizing our stage of alertness. Thus, we have mentioned the five stages in natural habit development: undifferentiated stage, crystallization, monosymptomatic stage, and, finally, determination with spontaneous cure or the deterioration phase.

We already talked about different habits being related to the person's age or specific sleep disorders. Many habits are formed during the pre-natal stage, such as hand sucking, or lip sucking. When a baby is born, he has a few episodes of so-called startled responses. The infant may have instances of lip sucking and head rocking. A one year old child has thumb sucking, and lip sucking. A little more on thumb sucking. People used to believe that this behavior has a pleasurable aspect. About 50 percent of children between 18 months and two years have thumb sucking. At the age of three, 30 percent of American children still have some thumb sucking. This repetitive behavior is culturally sensitive. For example, thumb sucking is not reported in Eskimo children. In European countries, thumb sucking is considered socially unacceptable and disappears much earlier. People believe that prolonged thumb sucking causes malocclusions. Also, severe laceration of skin on the hands of the child. Lip sucking and biting is a variation of thumb sucking, and also might be caused by stress or dry skin.

Masturbation for many years was considered to be a normal phenomenon, which is very common for almost all children. Recently we arrived at the conclusion that the whole issue of masturbation was a little bit exaggerated in previous literature.

Head rocking and head banging are very common bad habits before sleep, and we discussed these when we talked about rhythmic movements in children (See Part 5). Very serious self-injurious habits are much more common among children and adolescents than we had thought before. It is not just benign nail biting or nose picking, but it sometimes might have serious effects also, such as nose bleeding. But there are many other self-destructive behaviors, such as severe headbanging against the wall during the daytime, and hair pulling, so-called trichotillomania. Another example is self-hanging or self-cutting behavior. It might be related to a breathing problem such as a habitual cough or breath- holding spells in young children. In conclusion, bad habits are a very interesting and large field of medicine which has now developed into a special field of science called "Habitology."

"A bad habit never disappears miraculously, it's an
undo-it-yourself project."
— Abigail Van Buren

PART
8

SLEEP SICKNESS AND SICKNESS IN SLEEP
SLEEP IN MEDICAL DISORDERS AND
MEDICAL DISORDERS IN SLEEP

Sleep and Medical Conditions

Sleep After Traumatic Brain Injury

Sleep Disorders in Children After Burn Injuries

Sleep in Children With Life-Threatening
Viral Infections and Cancers

Allergies, Nocturnal Asthma and Sleep

Sleep and Other Medical Problems

Sleep in Children With Special Mental Needs

Sleep Patterns in Learning Disorders

Hyperactivity and Sleep

SLEEP AND MEDICAL CONDITIONS

In general, hospitalized children, especially if they are very young, develop more problems in their sleep. Hospitalization has three effects on the child: The first one is the *Psychological effect* (the so-called "hospitalism"). This phenomenon was common in the old days when psychological needs were not addressed. It is related to psychological regression, depression, withdrawal syndrome, and developing bad habits, such as head rocking, headbanging, etc. The second effect is related to the *decreased amount of sleep* of children staying in the hospital. Dr. Hagemann found that hospitalized children ages 3-8 years old lose a fifth to one third of their normal sleep time because of the delay in sleep onset. Children who are distressed are awake longer before they are able to fall asleep. It is interesting to note that when parents are present at bedtime, and the children listen to a parent reading a story, they fall asleep later compared to those children who listen to a "stranger" or one of the staff reading to them. It is probably due to the fact that parents in the hospital have more worries, are more tense, and may "overdo" the bedtime ritual.

This is contradictory to popular belief that parents should sleep at the child's bedside. For example, a survey of 400 psychiatrists conducted by Dietropinto in 1980 found that 44 percent of psychiatrists believed that the mother should sleep in the hospital in the child's ward whenever possible. (Did any of them try to do so? I did in my role as a father—no fun and no help.) A helpful suggestion for hospitalized children to sleep better, may be to establish a more structured activity at bedtime, and rotate the responsibility among parents (if there are several children in one room). The purpose of this would be to modify the hospital environment (e.g. dim the lights, reduce noise, turn the TV off) to reduce its interference with sleep.

Medications like Benadryl® are reported to have marked improvement on sleep in terms of faster onset and increased duration of sleep. The third effect of hospitalization on sleep is the nocturnal *deterioration of many acute medical conditions*. Sleep might even induce a medical crisis. It is common knowledge that the pain increases during the night, especially in acute crises.

Children with sickle cell anemia have a crisis during the nighttime called vaso occlusive crisis (VOC). Many other medical problems, heart and stomach problems might deteriorate during the nighttime. Some such medical conditions will be presented later in more detail.

SLEEP AFTER TRAUMATIC BRAIN INJURY

Traumatic brain injuries are known to cause many behavioral and sleep problems, not only during the most dramatic acute period, but for many months or years afterwards. Our experience with children who have post-traumatic brain injuries suggests that sleep disorders are very important symptoms, and are not sufficiently appreciated, though they can often occur as a consequence of even a mild head injury. Also, sleep disorders might be the only objective symptomatology allowing us to verify the condition in cases of litigation.

After a head injury, a few types of sleep disorders may commonly develop:

(1) *Disorders of the phases of sleep.* People have different sleep-wake schedule. Children do not have a stable schedule; especially in adolescents; their sleep-wake schedule fluctuates from one extreme to the other. A head trauma may have a profound effect on immature centers of biological clocks. The children's sleep pattern may be shifted significantly up or down to the point of a disease. Some children, especially those of an early age, respond to trauma by an advanced phase of sleep. They go to sleep too early, and likewise wake up early. During the daytime they get irritable and have difficulty staying awake, or get hyperactive. Some children, especially adolescents, respond to trauma by phase delay, or the complete disorganization of sleep. Phase delay means that they go to sleep extremely late and wake up equally late. Needless to say, both these changes in sleep can bring about many social, medical and behavioral consequences.

(2) Trauma *increases the likelihood of many parasomnias* which are not desirable during the sleep: bedwetting, night terrors, nightmares, sleepwalking, headbanging, and other sleep symptoms.

Sleep disorders are not isolated symptoms. Sleep disorders are usually accompanied by many medical symptoms, and have a tendency to accumulate at certain times within circadian rhythms. Morning headaches, afternoon dizziness, reversed time of increased appetite, afternoon nausea, night sleep respiratory difficulties, etc., are some such symptoms.

It is very important to keep in mind that post-traumatic sleep injuries lead to significant changes in the level of alertness during the daytime. Attention usually decreases, which causes problems at school. Children experience excessive daytime sleepiness, fatigue, and behavior problems including irritability, outbursts of rage, and violence.

If you notice significant changes in your child's sleep and behavior during the daytime, it is recommended that your child have a psychological and physiological evaluation, especially in cases where trauma was not apparent, but possible.

SLEEP DISORDERS IN CHILDREN AFTER BURN INJURIES

Burn injuries are another type of trauma. Sleep disorders are a common result of burns. The difference in the speed of the healing process may depend on the severity of sleep disruption. Sleep makes a major difference in burn injuries. Sleep is a healthy state. Healthy hormones, especially the growth hormone, cortisol, and thyroid hormones are released during specific phases of sleep through the night. Significant and chronic disruptions of sleep stages may delay or cause changes in hormonal release, and this may hinder the healing process of tissue regeneration.

Sleep disorders can also be viewed as an "alteration of coping". This hypothesis was confirmed in the study of sleep of 82 children and adolescents in the burn units in Dallas and Boston. Even after good care, children (especially two year olds) suffered from frequent episodes of nightmares, night terrors and sleepwalking. This may be considered as attempts to cope, but such manifestations of coping, originally adaptive, may cause problems later. Our experience in the burn unit at Cook County Hospital confirmed that burn injuries can lead to acute sleep disorders both in the post surgery, and during the prolonged recovery state. Sleep has a profound effect on the speed of the healing process.

After burn injuries, while being treated in intensive burn care units, children may suffer from significant sleep deprivation. Sleep deprivation may be caused by bright light, noise, temperature changes (particularly low temperatures), or other disruptive effects of the burn unit or intensive care unit environment. Low air temperature is good for adults with burns, but children react to low temperatures as if they had chills. Pain, itching, and an uncomfortable position are also significant factors leading to disorganized sleep. Patients may experience episodes of sudden agitation and anxiety, with attempts to throw out tubes and dressings. In the hospital room children often have significant difficulties falling asleep, due to itching, dull pain (even after they are medicated appropriately), and difficulty in finding comfortable positions for sleep.

A team of physicians and psychologists worked on individual plans to decrease destructive and disruptive environmental factors and improve the children's sleep. Long term consequences of sleep deprivation after burn injuries are also very significant. During the recovery period nightmares, flashbacks, sleepwalking and bedwetting continue. In the daytime, children experience flashbacks, dissociated episodes, and anxiety about going to bed, expecting fires to break out while they are asleep. In addition there is the cosmetic effect of burns, loss of different functions, or tragic loss of family members and many other psychological problems.

The following are some recommendations for you, if you happen to have a child with burn injuries:

(1) Pay attention to the child's sleep. Good sleep signifies a good, healthy and quick recovery. Bad sleep delays adaptation and the healing process, and may develop into long term psychological and behavioral disorders.

(2) Avoid the child's going to sleep late as much as possible. Human hormones are released during the first half of the night.

(3) Talk to the child before he goes to bed. Tell him that his good dreams can speed up recovery. Try to come up with examples of good images in sleep or things he would like to see in his dreams. (For details of techniques, see Part 6.)

(4) Be sure that you take care of itching, stuffy nose, frequent urination, and other causes of sleep interruptions.

(5) Carefully observe your child's behavior during the daytime. If you notice increased irritability of mood and motor activity, short naps prior to 4 P.M. are usually helpful if you are still able to keep approximately the same bedtime.

SLEEP IN CHILDREN WITH LIFE-THREATENING
VIRAL INFECTIONS AND CANCERS

Unfortunately, children having blood cancer and viral infections including AIDS and HIV are not uncommon anymore. The reason we are talking about these life-threatening disorders in a book for parents, is to show that sleep may be the way to reveal the secrets of treatment of different life-threatening disorders in children.   The immune system goes through intensive changes during the nighttime. Night pain and crisis in sickle-cell anemia, HIV, and other viral related disorders have their peak during the nighttime. Sleep is altered very drastically, and knowing these principles, we can influence sleep and synchronize our body's systems to achieve a healthy reorganization of sleep.

Let us consider HIV infections. Children may be born with HIV or become infected during blood transfusions. At the present time several hundred children are diagnosed with AIDS, but many more are HIV positive. Mothers infect their fetus in the first trimester. Newborns with AIDS and other inborn viral infections usually have characteristic faces. (Incidentally, in medicine, there are many types of specific faces. For example, children with fetal alcohol syndrome have very specific facial characteristics. We discussed the adenoid face, anorectic face, etc.   Viral infections, blood cancers and some other life-threatening conditions are associated with hormonal changes, mostly occurring during sleep. Sleep during viral infections and blood cancer has not been researched until recently.   But some interesting daytime research has already been done. As compared with control groups, sleep in these children has three important differences:

(1)   Slow wave NREM sleep is increased.

(2)   Predominantly slow wave NREM sleep is seen in the morning rather than at the beginning of the night which is normally the case.

(3)   REM sleep is also increased, as well as multiple awakenings.

Sleep architecture in life-threatening disorders is drastically altered. Such altered sleep is typical of viral infections, life-threatening cancers, severe burn injuries, and can be also observed during the post surgery period.

Sleep disturbances are very early signs of severe burn injury, viral infection, and cancer. This suggests that changes in sleep physiology may be early symptoms of problems with the central nervous system during immune deficiency mobilizations. Sleep features can be considered for early diagnosis and used to work out a therapeutic strategy.

ALLERGIES, NOCTURNAL ASTHMA AND SLEEP

Allergies, asthma, and other breathing problems are interconnected with sleep disorders much more closely than was thought before. There are at least three factors that unite allergies, breathing problems, and sleep disorders.

The first, is the chronobiological factor. As we know from Part 2, many disorders have a circadian rhythm in variations of symptoms as a response to diagnostic tests. Allergy and asthma are strongly influenced by biological, especially circadian, rhythms. Symptoms of allergic rhinitis, such as sneezing, running and stuffy nose, are much worse in the morning, causing early awakenings, morning headaches, and difficulties in breathing. The diagnosis of allergy is based on the so-called cutaneous tests—skin response to histamine and other allergens. The worst reaction occurs at bedtime and during sleep—not during active day hours. This means that lab results done during the working hours may underestimate the severity of the allergy. Effects of anti-allergic medications are also varied, depending on the time they are taken.

The second factor is nasal breathing. We talked earlier about the importance of nasal breathing. Allergy, specifically allergic rhinitis, can cause a stuffy nose and nasal obstruction, forcing the child to breathe through the mouth. Dr. Marx of the pediatric allergy clinic in Jackson Memorial Hospital in Chicago demonstrated that 60 percent of allergic children breathe through the mouth compared to 20 percent of non-allergic children. Breathing through the mouth causes bruxism and nocturnal teeth clenching. A dry mouth in someone who breathes through the mouth is associated with allergic itching or irritation of the palate, and changes in the flow of saliva. During mouth breathing, Dr. Marx found intermittent allergic edema of the mucous in the Eustachian tubes, channels from the mouth to the ears on either side. This condition leads to ear infections. Dryness of the mouth during mouth breathing influences tissue growth and causes multiple dental problems, such as malformation. Dr. Loesel, who studied the causes of glands and adenoid growth, found that nasal allergy and nasal obstruction are significant factors in adenoid growth. Mouth breathing also causes hyperemia, (chronically red throat), the collapse of dental arches, teeth malocclusion, obstruction of breathing, enuresis, and a number of other symptoms.

The third factor is the sleep-wake structure. The sleep-wake biorhythm itself is a function of development. If the sleep-wake cycle has not matured, due to different factors, the sleep-wake cycle becomes fragmented, inverted, and deviated. It can, by itself, change the sensitivity of tissue to the external factors. All three factors are considered to be chronobiological. Nasal breathing and sleep structure are closely interrelated and may be the basis for different medical and psychological problems. In our research of relationships between these three factors in allergic children, we found that among a hundred children coming to the allergy clinic at Cook County Hospital in Chicago, 22 percent have sleep apnea, compared with one percent in children without allergies. Thirty-two percent have sleep-related asthma with disruption of the sleep structure. Bedwetting was a symptom in 24 percent compared to the normal seven percent. Extremely restless sleep—26 percent versus 8.5 percent which is the norm. Approximately 40 percent snored loudly compared to three percent of non-allergic children. 30 percent talked in their sleep compared to the normally found 12 percent, and 24 percent suffered from nightmares compared with 14 percent in normal children. A severe combination of more than four symptoms at the same time was present in 16 percent versus the normal 12 percent. Serious sleep problems, needing urgent attention were found in six percent of allergic children. The lesson of these statistics is very simple: allergy, breathing problems, and sleep disorders are strongly related to each other, and therefore their treatment should be connected with means and methods of regulating sleep.

What is asthma? Asthma is a type of allergic hyper-sensitivity of air ways to external chemicals or inner factors that cause breathing distress. Like other allergies, asthma is strongly influenced by chronobiological factors. The time when the patient is least vulnerable to attack is between noon and 5 P.M. The time he is most vulnerable is during sleep at night. The risk of having asthma attacks during the nighttime while asleep is a hundred-fold greater than during daytime activity. Nasal breathing is also crucial for children with asthma. Breathing difficulties significantly increase in children whose nasal passages are obstructed. The relief of nasal breathing should be an important part in the prevention and treatment of asthma. Asthma attacks occur in 5-10 percent of children, being predominant during nocturnal sleep. In New Zealand, asthma reached epidemic proportions and became the leading cause of death in children.

Families that have children with asthma are very familiar with the stress of being awakened many times by the scary sounds of the children's wheezing and coughing. They are familiar with the look of fear on the child's face, the rush for medications, the terrible fits of coughing. In children, asthma is much more severe than in adults. Associated features of nocturnal asthma are: poor sleep, daytime fatigue, irritability, stomachaches, low appetite. Asthma attacks are more common in the second half of the night, and they may happen in any stage of sleep, but predominantly in transitional states, between stage 2 and REM.   Pulmonary function tests show decreased oxygenation and increased inter-chest pressure immediately before and during the attacks.

Observations that many asthmatics wheeze at night are common. Even in 1698 Dr. John Floyer, an asthmatic himself, wrote: "I have observed the fit always happens after sleep in the night. At first awakening at about one or two o'clock at night, the fit of asthma more evidently begins. Breathing is very slow. The diaphragm seems stiff and tight.   Despite the clarity of this description, two and half centuries passed before nocturnal asthma received serious attention. Nocturnal asthma is the product of many factors (as is an allergy). One of them is bronchoconstrictions. The previously held view that asthma could be fully explained by the release of mast cells, mediators which cause bronchial spasms, needs to be modified. It seems that several different mechanisms are involved in the genesis of asthma.   The neural mechanisms may contribute to (or significantly modify) inflammation and bronchial spasms. Autonomic nervous systems control airway inflammation, and this neural control is quite strong and complicated. Body chemicals, such as substance P, neurokinin, calcitonin may be released by the local autonomic reflexes. Coupled with the direct inflammatory mediator, bradikinin, it can trigger or delay vasoconstriction and bronchial constriction.

Autonomic reflexes are in the skin and in the gut. They may spread or decrease the constriction of blood vessels and, by so doing, treat bronchial spasms. Emotional influences on asthma are well-known. They are studied by psychoimmunology that has enough data to confirm it. Dr. William Orr demonstrated the significant role of the gastro-intestinal reflux in sleep, introducing symptoms of nocturnal asthma.

Implications of treatment. Prevention and treatment of nocturnal asthma should be based on the three factors described above: chronobiological dependency, the improvement of nasal breathing and the normalization of sleep structure. Sleep regime is an important measure. The child's schedule should be structured, and the sleep environment should be arranged carefully. To improve sleep, a moderate level of rhythmical physical exercises before sleep may be helpful. A fan and humidifier should also be considered to improve nasal breathing. A helpful procedure at home would be to put regular saline in the nose. If you do not have it handy, just make very light salty water and put drops in the child's nose. But first, try it on yourself. It should not be too salty, or it could make the mucus lining too dry. In terms of medication, the chronopharmacologic aspect is very important. It is not necessary, as was previously thought, to give the child medication at regular intervals: once a day at a specific time is best. Theophylline is usually good before sleep. Research shows that hormones should be given in the morning, and if needed, between lunch and 3 P.M. If nocturnal asthma is associated with other sleep problems, and indicates that there are deep sleep abnormalities such as bedwetting, sleeptalking, sleepwalking, nightmares, or other parasomnias, consider giving the child tricyclics such as Tofranil® or Norpramine® QHS. It is important to remember that sometimes asthma medication has side effects such as irritability from theophylline and suppression of adrenal glands from steroids. We know a case of a very severe nocturnal asthma with multiple respiratory and cardio respiratory arrests, successfully treated as a sleep disorder.

The patient, a 10-year-old Caucasian female, has been an asthmatic since the age of four. On July 3, 1989 she awoke from her sleep because of acute shortage of breath, as a result of associated wheezing. Shortly thereafter, she, according to her mother, collapsed with cyanosis. No pulse or respiration could be detected. Her mother initiated CPR and took the child to the hospital. In the emergency room they gave the child an injection; however, the intubation attempt was unsuccessful, and the patient began to breathe spontaneously much later. The child was hospitalized for further observation and treatment. Her case history revealed that she had eaten peanuts six hours prior to this incident. Skin tests for allergies were repeated many times, and showed that she was, in fact, allergic to peanuts and soybeans but they could not have caused such a severe allergy with respiratory arrests.

Very intensive cardiophysiological evaluation was initiated throughout the fainting spell as a possible cause of cardio-breathing arrest. However, cardiology evaluation showed no heart problems. Later the girl continued to have episodes of sleep apnea even when taking a daytime nap. The patient's mother noticed that the child did not react to any stimuli during the actual asthma attacks when she stopped breathing. She developed nocturnal and morning headaches as well as irregular pain. Bedwetting episodes, which previously were very sporadic, now dramatically increased. In addition, the patient was very irritable in the morning with no recall of attacks that occurred during the previous night. The patient's clinical status continued to deteriorate. Episodes of bedwetting, and sleep apnea, happened at least two or three times every night, accompanied by confused and agitated arousals. The result of this frequent life-threatening event, was an increase in tension and anxiety at home with her parents keeping a constant vigil at her bedside. Much work was done to determine what provoked these apnea episodes but no answer was found. The dose of prednisone was increased to the maximum, as well as the dose of theophylline, but the severity and the frequency of the child's asthma attacks and apnea also increased.

A test was also performed to reveal that her cognitive performance was in the high average range with a slight superiority of functions mediated by the right hemisphere of the brain. And while the tests indicated low self-esteem, her overall neuropsychological evaluation revealed an intellectually normal child. The girl's and the family's sleep history proved that both she and a number of family members had multiple sleep problems, such as bedwetting, sleep talking, nightmares, strange positions in sleep, convulsive sleep movements. There was also a strong family history of other sleep disorders. Two uncles were reported to have died in their sleep. Thorough night sleep studies were performed to rule out sleep apnea syndrome. Central apnea, obstructive apnea, and general deviation of the sleep structure were found. Based on sleep studies, the diagnosis of the sleep apnea syndrome with parasomnias was suggested. A trial period for Norpramine® was recommended in conjunction with a tapered dose of prednisone. After two or three weeks, the frequency and severity of respiratory arrests and apnea decreased, and they eventually disappeared. Steroids were tapered, and then discontinued. Three months later the medication was discontinued, and prednisone started to improve the girl's asthma. However, the episodes of apnea reappeared, and prednisone had to be discontinued. The child was started on Norpramine® for another four months.

During the two and half year follow-up period, there were no apnea episodes. The child's bedwetting decreased to about one episode in two months. She was using albuterol and cromolyn sodium inhalers; however, during the following six months, she had no episode of wheezing or apnea.

This is a case of asthma with a current respiratory arrest that was successfully managed as a sleep disorder. This case demonstrated the complex relationship of asthma and sleep disorders, and the need for sleep evaluations. The role of medication for the treatment of patients with nocturnal asthma was defined. Some asthma medication can destroy the sleep structure, specifically the switches between the stages of sleep. In these cases, asthma attacks play the role of such compensatory switches, similar to parasomnias (bedwetting and breath-holding spells). This hypothesis may equally explain why apnea, bedwetting and other parasomnias increase with larger dosage of medication (see Part 5).

In conclusion, internal asthma, especially asthma with recurring respiratory life-threatening attacks, is difficult to manage. Recent research in sleep medicine suggests that alterations in sleep mechanisms are involved in nocturnal asthma attacks. Tricyclics, for example, may have positive effects in controlling nocturnal respiratory problems. The approach to nocturnal asthma as a sleep disorder is promising, and requires further research.

SLEEP AND OTHER MEDICAL PROBLEMS

Sleep and behavior disturbances in children can be found in many other disorders, such as, for example, atopic dermatitis. Scientists from John Hopkins University, Baltimore, Maryland and the University of Pittsburgh, studied sleep in patients with severe dermatitis. This study presented a compelling evidence, of being an excellent model of chronic sleep problems for at least five reasons:

(1) Intensive itching, called *pruritus* ("the hallmark of dermatitis"), can be a drastic interference with the process of falling asleep in many children.

(2) Compulsive scratching through the night and throughout all stages of sleep causes repetitive sleep disturbances.

(3) Since dermatitis begins after infancy, and has chronic and recurrent causes, many children experience significant sleep disturbances throughout their early development.

(4) Parents have an extremely difficult time with their own night sleep because it is difficult to ignore a child's constantly scratching, awakening many times in tears as well as having to apply treatment throughout the night. Specific sleep disturbances are not only children's problems, but are a serious concern for parents, siblings and the entire family.

(5) In addition to the direct disturbances of sleep due to dermatitis, there are disturbances of alertness. Altered states and altered nighttime behavior since early childhood can lead to adaptive and maladaptive (meaning bad) sleep habits, and very deviated and maladaptive, self-comforting behaviors.

Thus, children with dermatitis suffer from chronic sleep deprivation, and this changes the development of sleep-wake habits and entails severe sleep interruption for the entire family.

The influence of sleep disorders on the child's development and family dynamics is not taken seriously enough. The results of studies confirm that children with acute dermatitis are more restless during sleep, have more headbanging, bedwetting, more frequent and agitated awakenings with sitting in bed or running around. Such children take a very long time before they are able to fall back to sleep after awakening. They make more frequent nighttime trips to the bathroom and their total sleep time is significantly decreased. As a result of sleep deprivation, these children have difficulty waking up in the morning, and staying awake, especially in the afternoon. They are irritable, and their behavior is more aggressive. They also daydream more, and their attention span at school decreases. They also have a serious fear of the dark and are nervous to go to bed, displaying the so-called anticipatory anxiety of a bad night.

In conclusion, dermatitis is an example of how chronic sleep disruptions can lead to significant behavior, school, and family problems. Treatment of dermatitis as well as other chronic problems should include an evaluation and treatment of sleep.

SLEEP IN CHILDREN WITH SPECIAL MENTAL NEEDS

Children with different forms of developmental disabilities and mentally handicapped children have a much higher rate of sleep disorders compared to intellectually normal children. About 80 percent of parents of handicapped children with developmental disabilities report that their children experience significant sleep difficulties, and 23 percent of parents report that these difficulties are severe. According to the *Health Psychology Journal*, sleep problems in mentally handicapped children are similar to those in normal children but start much earlier and last much longer. Different groups of mentally handicapped children have a somewhat different spectrum of problems. For example, Dr. Meyer in 1979 reported that among autistic children, 49 percent have extremely disturbed sleep. These problems cause undue stress for parents and caregivers, especially if many of those children have nocturnal wanderings. Given that, the solution to sleep problems is often amenable to behavioral techniques.

Bedtime tempers are frequent and very stressful problems in this population. The recommended treatment is a positive bedtime routine, conditioning the child to go to bed routinely and quickly. Dr. Wolfe, with his colleagues, described a successful treatment of bed tantrums used on an autistic child: the child's bedroom door was closed at bedtime. A well-favored bedtime procedure with a positive response is reported to increase nighttime sleep, decrease excessive bedtime sleepiness and nocturnal wanderings.

Our personal experience shows that, unfortunately, treatment of sleep disorders in mentally handicapped children is not that simple. We take the opportunity to express our great admiration for parents who are struggling with both their child's multiple sleep problems and their own sleep deprivations. Many mentally handicapped children suffer from obesity and excessive tissue growth, like adenoids and tonsils, which prevents them from normal breathing and flexible positions during sleep. It is known that children with Down's Syndrome are more predisposed to sleep apnea syndrome which causes pulmonary hypertension. Rapid improvements were observed in a group of such children after tonsillectomy and adenoidectomy. So the treatment of sleep and behavior problems in mentally handicapped children might be somewhat more complicated, but it is available.

SLEEP PATTERNS IN LEARNING DISORDERS

What are the relationships between sleep maturational and cognitive processes? Reading disability is probably the most debilitating of developmental disorders due to its personal, social, and behavioral consequences: Estimated prevalence is 5-15 percent of school age population. Despite the increased attention given to these disorders over the past 30 years, the problem remains controversial. Possible causes of learning disabilities include a maturational delay of areas in the left brain hemisphere which is responsible for language processing, or the undeveloped brain regions responsible for reading. As a result, asymmetry of the brain is reversed, and the fundamental basis for reading and learning is undeveloped.

The most direct evidence of a neurobiological basis for learning, and specifically reading disabilities, has come from brain imaging studies of dyslexic individuals with cortical and structural asymmetry. As is usually the case, research of their behavior and cognitive functions is focused on the symptoms during wakefulness. Studies of sleep, however, could provide useful information regarding sleep in cognitively normal children and sleep patterns related to various developmental factors.

Sleep medicine collected data allowing us to differentiate specific organic entities such as sleep in autism, sleep in hyperactivity, sleep in children with minimal brain dysfunction and sleep in the mentally retarded. Parameters involve the number of rapid eye movements, slow wave sleep, and the time between falling asleep and the onset of the first REM period. All of these have been found to decrease with age in normal children and have been linked to the maturation of the central nervous system.

An unexpected parameter which was found, surprisingly, in learning disabled children, is that they do not have the usual "first night effect", which means customary sleep disturbances in strange and novel situations of the sleep laboratory. This is not because children get upset, but rather because they need to get used to the laboratory setting. For example, hyperactive children are very used to having a lot of evaluations, but nevertheless, they are very sensitive to their first night in the sleep laboratory. Researchers believe that this is probably due to the children's specific cognitive process. Those children did not care. Sleep in learning disabled children with reading disorders, is much deeper, and they have fewer dreams. Their REM latency increases (REM starts later), and the general amount of REM decreases. Basically, this means that their dream sleep decreases and moves to the very end of the night. All of these are symptoms of maturational delay. Slow wave sleep (stage 4) is a restorative sleep for physical and also for cognitive functions. A decrease in the amount of slow wave sleep represents a deficit of restoration, specifically restoration of the cerebral functioning. One part of slow wave sleep (stage 2) is also changed in children with learning disabilities. There are data accumulated in research demonstrating that changes of stage 2 are connected with neurological conditions such as autism and brain damage.

In conclusion, sleep processes in children with learning disabilities, are very immature, and finding some ways of changing that sleep, making it age appropriate, may help improve children's daytime learning abilities.

HYPERACTIVITY AND SLEEP

Paradoxically, many children labeled as "hyperactive" have significant sleep problems. Dr. Bergman in 1976 described a seven year old boy who was diagnosed with attention deficit hyperactivity disorder (ADHD) when, in fact, he had significant sleep disorders, resulting in deviation of daytime behavior with hyperactivity. Instead of his being placed on Ritalin®, his problem was treated successfully by focusing on his sleep difficulties. Later many studies were reported about the close association between ADHD and sleep disorders. Together with Dr. Stephen Sheldon, we performed a study EEG during the daytime in ADHD children. The finding was that hyperactive children had micro sleep episodes during the daytime, despite their hyperactivity. Treatment of sleep problems seemed to improve daytime performance.

Dr. Marc Weissbluth found that infants who had extremely restless sleep and developed poor sleep habits in infancy are more likely to develop hyperactivity disorders. He strongly believed early childhood sleep disorders might be the cause of the striking transformation of the colicky infant with a difficult temperament, into a hyperactive school age child. Our experience with the treatment of hyperactive children, focusing on their sleep difficulties is quite promising. Several children have been able to move from a class for children with special needs to the regular class or even to advanced programs. Hyperactivity is a disorder of arousal. This condition is formally accepted in many books, and viewing hyperactivity as a sleep and behavioral deviation would be very helpful in terms of understanding the nature and treatment of the attention deficit hyperactivity disorder in children.

"Sleep hath its own world,
and the wide realm of wild reality."
— Lord Byron, *The Dream*

PART
9

SUMMARY

PRACTICAL TIPS FOR PARENTS OF CHILDREN WITH SLEEP PROBLEMS
(COOKBOOK OF SLEEP)

There are times when parents need practical guidance as to what to do, and then a quick reference from a source they can trust comes in extremely handy.

Parents may have this need for immediate help at any hour, sometimes in the middle of the night. Below you will find a list of the most common problems and available remedies in the shape of a short "rescue" guide. In addition to some helpful practical tips to relieve your anxiety, you will find references for details in relating parts of the book.

I.   Presleep

1) Sleep hygiene
2) Limit setting
3) Bedtime agitation and anxiety
4) Difficulties falling asleep
5) Unusual bedtime rituals
6) Nocturnal leg cramps
7) Sleep starts
8) Terrifying Hallucinations

II.   Problems in Maintaining Sleep

1) Quiet awakenings
2) Multiple disturbed awakenings
3) Colics
4) Nocturnal feeding
5) Excessive nocturnal fluids
6) Extensive crying, moaning and thrashing in sleep
7) Rhythmical movement disorders
8) Periodic limb movements
9) Night terrors
10) Bedwetting
11) Quiet sleepwalking
12) Sleeptalking
13) Agitated sleepwalking (somnambulism)
14) Teeth grinding (bruxism)
15) Injurious sleep and sleep violence

III. Problems with Different Body Systems

1) Nocturnal regurgitations and spitting up
2) Nocturnal eating/drinking syndrome
3) Sleep related abnormal swallowing syndrome
4) Sleep related laryngospasm
5) Primary showing
6) Sleep asthma
7) Sleep related breathing arrhythmias
8) Excessive sleep sweating
9) Sleep related painful erections

IV. Problems of Morning Awakening

1) Awakening too early
2) Sleep paralysis

V. Sleep Related Parental Problems

1) Pregnancy associated sleep disorder
2) Parents' sleep deprivation

I. PRESLEEP

Problem and its Description	What to do
SLEEP HYGIENE Sleep complaints associated with inadequate sleep hygiene are varied. They include: confusion of night and day by infants, multiple midnight awakenings, excessive daytime sleepiness or hyperactivity (including the so-called Attention Deficit Hyperactivity Syndrome), sleep deprivation, academic problems at school, difficulties in associating with peers, and, in extreme cases, development of serious sleep disorders.	Depending on the child's age, it is important to establish designated times for going to bed, waking up, having daytime naps, times for play, meals and study. This also includes specific times and sequences of having medication or doing exercises as part of treatment for different problems. The key point is fixed times of awakening, which sets the child's biological rhythms. Even at an age when the child assumes greater responsibility for determining his sleep schedule in adolescence, it is important that parents prevent irregular bedtimes and awakenings inasmuch as possible. When this is unavoidable, your child may get up one hour later the morning after a late night out, and try to go to bed one hour earlier that same day. The sleeping environment should be cozy and conducive to sleep. The child's bed should not be cluttered or used for other activities (especially doing homework in bed, eating and watching TV in bed). The temperature should neither be too warm nor too cold. Parents should also make sure that the child has a comfortable bed. For more, see Part 2 about Biological Clocks and Part 3 about Causes of Abnormal Sleep and Alertness.

LIMIT SETTING

Limit setting sleep problems are common during childhood and may be associated with other manifestations of behavioral deviations or mistakes of parenting. Excessive sleepiness might be the result of the failure to set limits on bedtime, leading to a decrease in sleep. Parents often state that their child refuses to go to sleep at a time they have established. The child frequently gets out of bed, asks for another drink of water or a bedtime story, or finds some other excuse to stall bedtime. The parents finally give in to the child's demands and rarely set limits on the child's behavior.

To avoid limit setting sleep problems, start setting limits more assertively, although it is not so easy. The first step is to refuse to buy into all the pretexts the child may have in avoiding going to bed on time. Of course, as parents, we should always use an age-appropriate approach in dealing with our children. It would be ridiculous, for instance, to start disciplining a three month old infant who is unable to fall asleep and gets the family frustrated with his incessant crying. When the baby is six months old, however, we can start being somewhat more adamant about bedtime and wake up hours.

For older children, the rule of thumb is not letting them sleep too late after establishing their sleep schedule. This may destroy their established sleep pattern.

When limits are set and enforced, the child is able to fall asleep within a reasonable period of time and gets a sufficient amount of sleep for his age. Both the quantity and quality of sleep are improved, and symptoms of excessive daytime sleepiness disappear. For more, see Part 2 and Part 3.

BEDTIME AGITATION AND ANXIETY

This is very common in children and generally affects children between the age of one and six years old. Sometimes it is associated with late parties or travel.

Three important components need to be kept in mind: hyperactivity, emotional anxiety, and the need for special rituals. Some children have a tendency to get all the more agitated and active, the more tired and sleepy they are. This is by no means abnormal. Our goal is to know this trait of our child's and help him overcome it. Our children, particularly adolescents, are often prevented from falling asleep by mental and emotional anxiety about a forthcoming test or exam, or an important event they are planning to attend.

Young children who become agitated and anxious at bedtime need parental reassurance. If it happens prior to one year of age holding, rocking and lying down together might help. Children at this age are unlikely to be spoiled. At the age of three and especially six, putting the child to bed might be a real problem. Careful analysis of the possible causes of anxiety and agitation is important before parents choose a "soft" or "firm" approach.

Sleep onset is associated with certain objects (e.g., a special blanket, pillow, or pacifier), being held in the parent's arms, rocking, nursing, or being carried. Children are often asleep when placed in the crib or bed. Characteristic is the ability to fall to sleep quickly once the right associations are provided for the child.

Hyperactivity can be helped by channeling activity in controlled forms, such as dancing, aerobics, walking outside, etc. for 20-30 minutes one hour prior to sleep, followed by a warm shower and then light sweet juice. Anxiety, on the contrary, needs physical contact from parents, such as hugging and patting. Prolonged explanations about anxiety are ineffective. However, having your child share his or her worries or the reasons for their concern, can often bring them relief and calm their fears. So a friendly bedtime talk will often help your child peacefully fall asleep.

(For more, see Part 1, 2 and 4).

DIFFICULTIES IN FALLING ASLEEP

BIRTH TO 4 MONTHS

This is a time when the external world disrupts inner clocks, and the child tries to adjust to new demands. Typical problems are: confusion of night and day, difficulty in switching smoothly from wakefulness to sleep, and struggles and agitation at bedtime.

5 MONTHS TO 9 MONTHS

It is a time when a newborn's schedule of feedings and naps is switching to a more mature one. At this age your child may develop new problems in going to bed and falling asleep. This may be expressed in frequent demands for food and drink at bedtime, fussiness and hyperactivity, or demands to be held and rocked late into the night. Colic could be a serious reason preventing your baby from falling asleep. (For details, see Colics).

At this age you will witness a great increase in your child's motor development. He will learn to sit, crawl and stand and sometimes practice these skills at night.

Tips to help your child fall asleep:

Introduce a love object such as a blanket or stuffed animal. Try to develop a routine where the child receives a full night of sleep.

Wean your baby of nighttime feeding. This can be done by increasing the amount of nourishment given during the day and extending the period of fasting at night. Do not forget how extremely important it is to keep the baby's nose clean for proper breathing.

Minimize the baby's anxiety. If there is a baby sitter, have the sitter play with the baby so that the two get to know each other. Make your baby's bedtime pleasant. Comfort the baby by talking to him in a comforting, relaxed way. Use more touching. Do not be afraid of spoiling the baby at this age. (You'll have a chance to be tough soon.)

To prevent loss of sleep, practice these skills with children as often as possible during the day.

10 MONTHS TO 18 MONTHS	
At this age, children usually have problems sleeping alone. A typical example of bedtime problems would be a demand to lie next to the parents while falling asleep or being held for a long time. Co-sleeping is a controversial issue. (See more in Part 4: Sleep Problems in Newborns).	To help your toddler fall asleep alone, use the love object. Use a fun bedtime routine, including snuggling with the love object, tucking the toddler in, and saying good night in a soft comforting voice. Make sure the child does not fall asleep during feedings. Play games with your child so he realizes that you are not gone while he is asleep. Make sure your child is sleeping in his own bed. Unless he is ill, and you are using co-sleeping as a temporary measure. Try to ensure that your child falls asleep by himself. If the child wakes up and cries for his parents before morning, reassure him, but don't pick him up and be as brief as possible.
TEETHING is an important cause of bedtime irritation	If teething causes distress, the child can get comfort from chewing on a pacifier or teething rings.
18 MONTHS TO 3 YEARS	
The major cause of difficulty falling asleep at this age is general anxiety or specific fears (e.g., darkness, thunderstorms, lightning, monsters).	To help your child overcome fears: Consider having your fearful child share a room with a brother or sister. Buying a pet, maybe just a fish, could sometimes be of help. Remember the security object and nightlight. Keep reassuring the child and build self-confidence. Help your child to overcome any fears; never confirm these fears. Try to find out what is scaring the child and discuss it during the day.

TRAVELING at this age is not as easy as it was before.

When traveling, keep the following guidelines in mind:
Prepare the child for departure a couple of days before you leave.
Bring your child's love object, a book or two and several of his toys with you for familiarity.
Always set aside an hour or two for a nap.
Be aware of the adjustment your child will be required to make because of the change in time zones.

3 YEARS TO 5 YEARS

Welcome to the beginning of the bedtime war! Your child is now smart enough to cause you more troubles than ever before. At this age parents can prevent or create problems. This is an age when habits, including habits of regimen, have a tendency to be fixed. For instance, it is nice to have visitors or family members play with your child, but if it is too late and happens too often, the child will become agitated and have difficulties falling asleep.

Enforce bedtime. This happens to be a common problem among preschoolers. Now it is the time to show that you can be strict.
Create regular bedtime by figuring out how much sleep your child seems to need by averaging sleep over a period of two weeks or so.
Be sure that your child is actually tired when you put him to bed.
Be consistent about the bedtime routine.
Encourage the child. Do not lose your temper.
If your child is toilet trained, make sure he uses the toilet before you tuck him in.

6 YEARS TO 12 YEARS

The major causes of sleep disruption include school related stress. For example, a child may feel anxiety adjusting to a new school teacher, worrying about a difficult test or exam, etc.

The parent must maintain the typical routines of sleep and not let them fade away. Routine is the best stabilizing factor. Let your child share his anxiety with you. This often helps him get it out of his system. Bedtime stories or fairy tales can do wonders in helping your child fall asleep.

13 YEARS TO 18 YEARS (Adolescence)

The major problem is a discrepancy between an increasing need to sleep more and a decrease in actual sleep time.

It is easier to give advice than to actually control an adolescent. Nevertheless, try to convince your big boy or girl that:
Wake up time should be as fixed as possible and as early as possible.
Oversleeping is as dangerous as undersleeping.
Sleepiness can translate into tiredness and boredom.
The best "high" produced by sleep is not by drugs.

MENSTRUAL ASSOCIATED SLEEP PROBLEMS

This includes either prolonged difficulty falling asleep and/or significant daytime sleepiness. Symptoms of this problem usually appear one week before the onset of menses and continue for at least three consecutive months. In the middle of the period the sleep is normal.

This problem is quite disruptive and is accepted by the parents of the teen after a prolonged period of accusations of laziness. Bright light in the morning is one of the proven ways of treatment. If the situation grows worse, a doctor might suggest birth control pills or other means of stabilization of the menstrual cycle.

UNUSUAL BEDTIME RITUALS

Some children develop special bedtime rituals when they have a problem falling asleep. Rituals can be individual requests, like requests to scratch his back, or elaborate habit like covering the head with a blanket or asking grandma to rhythmically press it. Many other unusual things are sometimes done by the child in order to fall asleep, such as masturbation, or hair pulling, or other self-injurious behavior. These rituals are attempts to relieve tension and ensure the onset of sleep.

Elaborate rituals need medical attention for an evaluation of the causes. The general strategy is to switch them from more complicated to simpler ones. Active rhythmical squishing of a soft ball, for instance, may help headbanging or self-injurious habits. Behavior modifications and medications supervised by professionals are strongly recommended in these situations.

NOCTURNAL LEG CRAMPS

Although this problem has not been described during infancy, children may be awakened at night by leg pains and cramps. Their history may reveal occasional nighttime awakenings or early morning arousals and difficulty returning to sleep.

Both upper and lower leg muscles may be involved. Nocturnal leg pains and cramps must be differentiated from those of clear organic origin, including but not limited to arthritis, arthralgia, metabolic disorders, dystonia, seizure disorders, peripheral neuropathies, and myelopathies.

Rubbing or massage of the affected area may relieve the discomfort. Because leg pain is usually associated with other types of pain, it would be wise to see your doctor to find out the possible underlying causes.

SLEEP STARTS	
Sleep starts are usually benign and run an uneventful course. They are considered normal events. When severe or frequent, however, sleep starts may result in chronic difficulties with falling asleep. A massive, brief, single contraction of the legs (and occasionally, the arms and head) occurs at sleep onset and results in arousal. A conscious perception of falling, or a visual dream, or even hallucinations often occur. If sleep onset is delayed significantly, sleep deprivation (and its resultant symptoms) can follow. Your child may occasionally get bruises from hitting a foot or hand against a fixed object (bedpost, nightstand).	This symptom is very benign in teens. A warm shower and a warm blanket are reportedly quite helpful.

If your child's symptoms persist, and you notice regular bruises on his legs or arms, you may want to seek your pediatrician's advice. |
| **TERRIFYING HALLUCINATIONS** | |
| Frightening dreams are common during early and middle childhood but are usually associated with nighttime sleep. Frightening dreams at sleep onset may be terrifying to the child, and may have a hallucinatory quality. They may also be associated with other sensory misperceptions, vague thoughts, and illusions. Mumbling, screaming, and body movements may occur. Fear or anxiety-laden awakening is common in such cases. The sleeping environment may be involved in provoking such dreams. | Episodic hallucinations are benign but if they become persistent they might be frightening to the child and parents. A psychological evaluation might help uncover emotional problems. A medical evaluation is also recommended to rule out possible medical problems. Treatment with medication is available. |

II. PROBLEMS WITH MAINTAINING SLEEP

QUIET AWAKENINGS

In early childhood nighttime awakening is part of a normal problem of sleep consolidation. In preschool, children awakenings might also be a natural part of establishing nocturnal urinary control.

Such nighttime awakenings can become a problem if your child is unable to fall asleep again for a long while. But you should bear in mind that most young children are "self-soothers", and are able to fall asleep on their own with the help of sleep aids, such as pacifiers, their fingers or lulling sounds.

Quiet awakenings have some interesting effects on parents. Those of them who are overly sensitive and protective, jump up to check the child whenever they suspect he may be awake. This only serves to prolong his awakening and converts quiet awakenings into crabby ones. The best approach would be just to wait a few minutes and let the child go through this period and find his way back to sleep. If not, a brief, reassuring but firm intervention usually solves this problem. (See Part 4 for details)

MULTIPLE DISTURBED AWAKENINGS

This is common during childhood and generally affects children between the ages of six months and three years. Complaints of difficulty falling asleep at the beginning of the night are infrequent. Most complaints center on nocturnal awakenings and an inability of the child to go back to sleep on his or her own after waking at night.

Those children receiving excessive fluids at night seem to wake up more frequently and have a harder time falling asleep again.

In the first year of the baby's life, it is important to distinguish between multiple awakenings as a problem for the *infant* and a problem for the *parents*.

If a young child is unable to return to sleep and cries for a long time, and this is repeated many times through the night, this could be caused by both internal (medical) and external (environmental, feeding) problems.

After 18 weeks, disturbed awakenings can be caused by what is known as separation anxiety (the child's or the mother's hospitalization, etc.)

This problem relates to the transition between developmental stages. When this transition is too long and too disturbing the treatment becomes a challenge. This is a time when firm, but flexible approach and parental patience can create peace at home.

Research shows that intervention should be considered very carefully during that period. Sometimes first reducing the number of afternoon awakenings reportedly had adverse effects on the infants' later development.

COLICS

This problem characteristically occurs at two to three weeks of age and does not usually last beyond four months of age. These otherwise healthy children experience paroxysms of inconsolable irritability that can last for more than three hours per day. Violent screaming and relatively uninhibited movements occur during a paroxysm, and infants have been described as hypertonic during such episodes. The infant may grimace and appear to be in pain. Attacks typically occur in the late afternoon or evening (5 P.M. to midnight) but may occur from 7 P.M. to 2 A.M. Rarely are episodes randomly distributed throughout the day. Symptoms resolve spontaneously in almost all infants by four months of age. Complaints of sleeplessness due to colic persisting beyond four months of age are usually a result of parental mismanagement of the sleep problem during the colicky period. In such cases other causes for sleeplessness should be sought.

Try to establish and maintain a regular sleep schedule, despite the frequent crying. The infant's crying may be continuous. Because of the irregularity of their sleep and alert states, it is difficult to schedule their sleep. It is often hard to understand when they are hungry, fussy, tired or in pain.

To help soothe a colicky baby:
Touch, hug, and rock the baby. A pacifier on a short ribbon is very helpful. If your baby doesn't like it, give a substitute. Place a warm water bottle on the baby's abdomen. Cover the baby's hands with a soft blanket, and put his head against a soft crib bumper.

If you are exhausted place the baby on your chest with his abdomen toward you so the baby can feel your warmth, your heartbeat and breathing.

Heartbeat sounds in a teddy bear can sometimes soothe your baby.

You can also try turning on a fan. The sound of running water or the vacuum cleaner may be equally soothing.

Your smile can sometimes stop the baby's crying. Remember that a crying baby might be just tired. Sometimes it's better to do nothing and let him fall asleep.

Many experts believe in the "Let him cry" attitude. Some psychologists take the opposite attitude. They believe that parents should never be encouraged to let their child cry for fear of encouraging neglect. Both extremes are wrong.

Here is a practical guide in this controversial issue: Be sensitive to "I need you" crying, but remember that the first sound doesn't mean that the baby needs to be picked up immediately.

NOCTURNAL FEEDING

Feeding in the middle of the night. This is another big controversial issue dividing parents who feel the need to feed an infant and experts who believe that it is wrong.

You must remember that more babies are "self-soothers" and will put themselves back to sleep if they should awaken at night. This pattern should be encouraged by parents in every way.

Those babies who are "signalers" and finally arouse their parents in the middle of the night require a different approach, including nocturnal feeding to help them facilitate sleep.

It should be emphasized, however, that many researchers are now inclined to believe that multiple feedings at night might actually increase the frequency of nocturnal awakenings.

Follow your baby's call. He is temporarily the leader. You can't spoil a baby prior to four-five months of age, because his sleep, wake, hunger are controlled by inner mechanisms. After 5-6 months you should observe the child's response to feeding. There are times when the child tends to become alert and playful after feeding and times when he falls asleep. As a general guidance, nocturnal feeding is not the best treatment for nocturnal awakenings. (For more, see Part 4.)

EXCESSIVE NOCTURNAL FLUIDS

This problem is common during infancy and early childhood. Parents complain that the child has frequent nighttime awakenings, which are sometimes prolonged. The child may awaken three to eight times per night, and sleep returns only after the ingestion of four to eight ounces of fluid. The child may consume 12 to 32 ounces of fluid across the night. The amount of fluid differentiates this disorder from sleep onset association disorder, since in the latter only small volumes of fluid are consumed, and the problem is related more to associating the nipple and suckling with sleep than to consumption of fluids. The baby is usually fed just before bedtime. Awakenings are also more frequent than with sleep onset association disorder. Diapers are often soaked in the morning, or frequent nighttime diaper changes are required.

This problem might be seen sometimes when the parents give too much fluid in an attempt to soothe the baby, when the baby wakes up many times. The problem might be solved by a consultation with your pediatrician concerning an appropriate amount of fluid intake and slowly decreasing the frequency and amount of night feedings.

EXTENSIVE CRYING, MOANING AND THRASHING WHILE SLEEPING	
This problem could be caused by a multitude of reasons: sleep disorders, including apnea and other breathing problems, could cause excessive crying, moaning and thrashing. This symptom is typical for young children from six months to six years old.	Be sure that the child doesn't injure himself or doesn't have a breathing problem. Let the episode run its course. It will help your child, and make you feel better if you hold the child, gently rub or pat or rock him. Loving touching is the best medicine. Try not to wake the child. You may cover him with an extra blanket or lie down with the child hugging him from behind until he calms down and falls back asleep. If your child is over two years old, it could help to ask in a quiet voice what he is dreaming about. Make sure that the child gets enough sleep. Start a diary to find out the possible stresses your child might have prior to bedtime. Remember that the most common cause of nocturnal crying is nasal obstruction. With your doctor's permission you can use medications for a short time.
RHYTHMICAL MOVEMENT DISORDERS	
Complaints of rhythmical headbanging, head rocking, body rocking, or body rolling are characteristic. These sleep disorders are common during infancy and childhood and tend to resolve spontaneously as the child matures. The behaviors can also occur during wakefulness but tend to cluster around times of sleep onset and persist into light stages of sleep.	It is quite difficult to treat headbanging and rocking. Punishments and physical restraints are more harmful than helpful. Rhythmical activity at bedtime, soft rhythmical noise during sleep and early awakenings might be helpful. (For more details, see Parts 5 and 6.)

NIGHTMARES

In contrast to night terrors, the child usually has nightmares during early morning hours (typically the last third of the sleep period). Nightmares are less intense that sleep terrors and are associated with significantly less autonomic arousal. Verbal reports of the frightening dream are common and have a story-like quality. The dream content that causes fear and anxiety in your child may not be considered disturbing by others. Nightmares are part of the normal process of growing up. The more nervous the child, the earlier he is bound to have scary dreams. As a parent you should not get unduly alarmed and should remember that injuries due to nightmares are infrequent, and children respond well to parental efforts to comfort them. However, return to sleep may be significantly delayed.

If the child is crying in his sleep but not awake, you might wait for a minute, because the bad dream might not last too long. If it does, gently change the child's body position, correcting his blanket, and pat his back softly. Touching his forehead and speaking to the child in a low, quiet voice reassures him.

If the child wakes up, do not try to rationally convince him that his fears are not real. (Bad dreams are a child's reality.) Just comfort him, make a bathroom trip and sit next to his bed for a while. If your child has nightmares more than once a week, or they influence daytime behavior, these are legitimate reasons for a consultation with your pediatrician. (For more details, see Part 5 on Nightmares and how they differ from night terrors.)

BEDWETTING

Bedwetting might occur due to a variety of reasons. There are at least five different types of functional nocturnal enuresis (bedwetting) different in their genesis, clinical picture, and treatment and prognosis. See Part 5, chapter on the Secrets of Bedwetting, which also describes in detail steps that are helpful in the management of this problem, which is so frustrating to parents. Young children don't seem to mind having this problem but because it tends to be perceived as socially unacceptable, older children suffer greatly from bedwetting. They fear both physical punishment and being despised by adults and by their peers. Psychologically, bedwetting can badly hurt your child's self-esteem and cause long standing personal problems in the future.

Strategy 1: Increase presleep awareness and motivation using presleep playtime.
Strategy 2: Positional training.
Strategy 3: Bathroom trips.
Strategy 4: Parental hypnotic suggestions.
Strategy 5: Daytime training of the functional capacity of the urinary bladder.
Strategy 6: Awakening during urination alarm techniques.
Strategy 7: Medication treatment. Each form of bedwetting might be helped by different classes of medication which should be carefully selected by you and your doctor.
Strategy 8: Alternative techniques, such as physical therapy, herbal therapy, biofeedback, acupuncture and reflex therapy can be very beneficial if based on careful evaluation. (For details of the techniques, and which of them should be selected, based on the type of your child's bedwetting problem, see Part 5 on Secrets of Bedwetting, where you will find a description of all five types of nocturnal enuresis, its paradoxes, and steps in managing this problem.

QUIET SLEEPWALKING	
This can occur at any age from toddler to late adolescence. The child may sit up in bed or move quietly, or make a trip to the bathroom or urinate in inappropriate places. This problem presents no danger to the child and reflects a normal stage in the child's development.	If you see your child sleepwalking, calmly tell him or her to return to bed. Wait until they stop at the bathroom to urinate. Don't try to wake the child up because they could be confused or agitated. If the child wakes up and is angry or embarrassed, try to comment, matter-of-factly, and let the child go back to bed. Avoid discussing the episode in the morning unless your child asks you about it or you plan to see a doctor. Make sure you have taken safety precautions to avoid your child getting injured while walking outside of the home or falling down the stairs. Contrary to popular belief, sleepwalkers are very clumsy and can easily hurt themselves.
SLEEPTALKING	
Generally it is characterized by clear speech, vocalization, moans, or other utterances. Episodes may occur spontaneously or be triggered off by other factors. Sleep talking may be quite annoying sometimes, and its content is often associated with other family members.	This problem does not usually require special treatment. You may stop the episode in case of increasingly loud speech with symptoms of agitation by changing the child's position or rubbing the child's face with a warm, damp towel.

AGITATED SLEEPWALKING (SOMNAMBULISM)

Children may leave the house, and injury in cases of sleepwalking is quite common. Episodes may occur as frequently as several times a week, or they may be rare and take place only when precipitating factors are present (e.g., fever, sleep restriction, certain medications, bladder distention). Agitated sleepwalking may also be associated with obstructive sleep apnea syndrome.

Children awakened from a somnambulistic episode often appear confused, disoriented, and frightened. Sleeptalking may occur during sleepwalking episodes, but the speech is often mumbled and incoherent.

Attempts to restrain the child may increase and prolong agitation. Nevertheless, this has to be done if the situation is getting dangerously out of hand. Keep your distance. Have safety precautions for the child and for family members. Remember that the agitated child is as strong as an adult. Wait until the child has calmed down. Agitated sleepwalking is a serious enough reason for seeking medical evaluation and help. Keep a diary of such episodes and precipitating events to find out the best way to handle the problem. (See more in Part 5 on Sleepwalking and on Injurious Sleep.)

TEETH GRINDING (BRUXISM)

Loud, unpleasant sounds are generated by the child forcibly grinding and clenching his teeth. The sound is unmistakable. Bruxism appears to be not as bad as was thought before. Bruxism might be one of the symptoms of sleep apnea syndrome.

When you hear these very specific teeth grinding sounds, try changing the child's sleeping position. Often if the child lies on his side, bruxism disappears. Evaluation of bruxism is important to rule out gastroinfection or dental causes of teeth grinding. Consultation of an orthodontist is recommended, and he might prescribe some protective teeth rubberings. (For details, see Part 2 and Part 6: Sleep Apnea in Children.)

INJURIOUS SLEEP AND SLEEP VIOLENCE

Sudden partial arousals from sleep occur with apparent association with dreams. Punching, swinging, leaping out of bed, running around the room, and loud vocalizations are often signs of this disorder, which can be seriously injurious for the child and other family members.

Nocturnal aggression can be manifested in different forms: abrupt, confused arousal from sleep in a state of somnambulism results in injuries, such as broken bones, bruises, cutting, hitting, slamming doors and breaking furniture.

There are also known cases of murder or serious injury associated with sleep conditions.

The child at these times is quite strong and it is difficult to restrain him. The best approach would be to insure a safe environment, by closing the windows, stairways, removing sharp objects, and removing other children in the vicinity. The episode will usually subside by itself in a minute. Medical, psychiatric, and sleep evaluations are important.

(For details and treatment suggestions, see Part 6 on Injurious Sleep.)

III. PROBLEMS WITH DIFFERENT BODY SYSTEMS

NOCTURNAL REGURGITATIONS AND SPITTING UP

Sleep related regurgitations can occur in infants, and childhood correlates may exist. Infants awaken frequently at night and often appear to be in pain. Symptoms may be easily confused with colic. Older children may complain of stomachache, chest pain or tightness in the chest. Nocturnal wheezing or spasms of the larynx can occur, and infants may have episodes of apnea, as an apparent life-threatening event. Daytime symptoms of this problem may be present, and frequent spitting up or regurgitation may develop into a chronic problem. In severe forms, signs of failure to breathe may be prominent.

Nocturnal regurgitations are difficult to handle, first of all, because this problem is difficult to diagnose and secondly, parents do not know what to do.

We found that the best and easiest approach is to treat the symptom as if it is a pain. Place a bottle of warm water onto the abdomen. Contact your pediatrician if the symptom does not go away. Carefully selected medications might really help.

NOCTURNAL EATING/DRINKING SYNDROME

This syndrome is characterized by frequent nocturnal awakenings. Digestive and endocrine rhythms are affected, and the child's eating and drinking pattern remains at a more infantile level (e.g., feeding every three to four hours). The child cannot return to sleep without eating or drinking significant amounts, and the sleep-wake pattern is there fore disrupted.

This syndrome is seen in older children when they make trips to the refrigerator in the middle of the night and do not remember them in the morning. Behavior modification techniques under the professional supervision of a psychologist, pediatrician or child psychiatrist is needed.

SLEEP RELATED ABNORMAL SWALLOWING SYNDROME This problem is rare in infants and children, but it may exist, especially in cases of central nervous system disturbances that interfere with the gag reflex and swallowing of pooled secretions. Sleep is restless and interrupted. The child awakens suddenly with coughing, gagging, and choking. These episodes tend to follow periods of gurgling sounds during sleep. Significant apnea is not present, although some of its symptoms may occur. Awakenings are typically of short duration, and return to sleep is rapid.	This rare, but serious symptom, needs immediate medical attention. The best strategy is to contact your pediatrician at once and learn techniques to prevent suffocation.
SLEEP RELATED LARYNGOSPASM A sudden awakening from sleep occurs and is accompanied by respiratory difficulties, an intense feeling of choking and suffocation. Episodes are brief and resolve spontaneously after a few minutes. Children may panic during the episode because they feel unable to breathe. Differentiating sleep-related laryngospasm croup may be difficult, and spasmodic croup may be a childhood variant of this sleep disorder.	This is a very serious symptom. In acute situations call an ambulance and try to wake the child up, using a fan or cold water. Some may use an anti-asthmatic spray. Immediate medical consultation is the best strategy.

PRIMARY SNORING

Primary snoring refers to loud, sonorous upper airway breathing sounds. Apnea, hypopnea, and hypoventilation are notably absent.

Family members usually complain of being kept awake by the noisy breathing. At times the child is aware of the snoring at sleep onset or after a brief awakening. Excessive sleepiness or insomnia are not present.

Snoring in children occurs rather seldom and is usually a symptom of some underlying medical problems. Difficult nasal breathing might cause bedwetting, awakenings, and learning problems.

It should be kept in mind that snoring can be the hallmark of obstructive sleep apnea.

Because snoring in children is usually a symptom of some underlying medical problem, it is best to go for a professional evaluation of its causes.

Do not forget how important it is to keep the child's nose clean for good breathing, and take proper care of mouth hygiene.

Consultation with a local sleep center is recommended if the symptoms persist.

SLEEP ASTHMA	
It is a very threatening and dangerous disease. The genesis and treatment of nocturnal sleep asthma in many ways is different from daytime asthma. (For details, see Part 5 on Allergies, Asthma and Sleep Disorders.)	You can help to minimize and relieve nocturnal asthmatic episodes by: Presleep breathing exercises. A warm shower. Good ventilation and use of a fan during summer. Use of a humidifier when heat comes on. In case of an asthma attack, comfort the child who is anxious and breathing too fast. Try to calm his breathing by breathing in synchrony with him and holding your breath. If you hear loud and fast breathing try to: Gently change the child's position (usually breathing normalizes on the side). Lift the child's head. If it is not helpful, gently awaken the child. Make a bathroom trip and give him an extra blanket in the winter and a fan in the summer.
SLEEP RELATED BREATHING ARRHYTHMIAS	
This is a disorder characterized by a sudden increase in respiratory rate of more than 20% above base-line waking level. These episodes begin at sleep onset, persist throughout the sleep period, and resolve spontaneously immediately on awakening. Excessive daytime sleepiness is the child's usual complaint.	In small children, these changes are uncontrollable, so the best way to help is usually to change the body position to the side. In older children, breath-holding spells are partly voluntary and associated with pain/pleasure sensations. Treatment in these cases should be done by professionals.

EXCESSIVE SLEEP SWEATING

Symptoms include profuse sweating during sleep, which may result in arousal or awakening because of the discomfort. Daytime sweating may or may not be present.

Sleep sweats may occur during illnesses or may be associated with autonomic nervous system dysfunction (e.g., familial dysautonomia). Excessive night sweating may be associated with other disorders, such as seizure disorders, hyperthyroidism, head injury, hypothalamic lesions, and diabetes.

Excessive sweating during sleep is also common in patients with obstructive sleep apnea syndrome and certain mental disorders.

Excessive sweating is a symptom which should be brought to your doctor.

Meantime, it is important to change the child's pajamas in sleep. It does not usually disturb the child, because he sleeps soundly.

Contrary to popular belief, a warm blanket is good, but an air conditioner or fan is not good. Some parents reported good effects from rubbing the skin with alcohol.

SLEEP RELATED PAINFUL ERECTIONS

Prepubertal boys often wake up in the second half of the night crying and complaining about pain in the penis, which is hard, erect, and sometimes red. Mothers usually don't know how to react to this and are ashamed to bring it up with a pediatrician. They may believe that their child masturbates.

Adolescent boys also experience painful erections not associated with sexual dreams. This might be a normal part of sleep, if it is mainly episodic. If recurring, it should be brought up to a pediatrician, because painful erections can be a possible side effect of some medications and a symptom of other medical problems. Such erections have no association with sexual dreams or sexual dysfunction.

Take this complaint seriously.

First help the child to urinate, because it is very difficult at this moment.

Wet a towel with warm water, wring it, and apply to the groin area for a few minutes. If not enough, repeat it with cold water. The child should be in a vertical or seated position. It is better if the child does this by himself.

Reassure him that it is normal and nothing to be ashamed about, and he should feel comfortable to tell his parents, if this happens again.

It is important to wake the child up completely. The child is usually wet with sweat, so it is helpful to take a shower.

IV. PROBLEMS OF MORNING AWAKENING

AWAKENING TOO EARLY

A short sleeper habitually sleeps substantially less (less than 75%) than is the norm for his or her age group. Parents may complain that their child has a very short nocturnal sleep period. Symptoms usually begin during adolescence but may appear earlier. Short sleepers sleep continuously at night. Sleep onset is not delayed, although the time of sleep onset may be later than expected, and early morning awakenings occur. Children are unable to sleep longer, despite opportunities or attempts. Sleep is refreshing. Daytime symptoms are absent, and the child functions well during the day. Complications occur when attempts are made to extend sleep artificially with medications.

If awakening too early is associated with normal functioning during the day, it reflects specific developmental stages. It is still difficult for parents who are sleep deprived, but they should try to avoid resolving the problem by giving the child sleep medication.

SLEEP PARALYSIS

Children, adolescents, and adults can be affected. Although sleep paralysis is one symptom of the classic tetrad of narcolepsy, it may occur in an isolated or a familial form.

Symptoms of the isolated form of this disorder typically occur at sleep offset. Although awake and alert, the child cannot move his arms, legs, body and head. There may be a sensation of an inability to breathe. Eye and respiratory movements remain intact, however.

Attacks usually last only a few minutes and end spontaneously. Episodes can occasionally be stopped by the child rapidly moving his eyes. Familial sleep paralysis (and the sleep paralysis of narcolepsy) tends to occur at sleep onset and follows a more chronic course.

Early medical and psychological evaluation is recommended for this symptom to rule out underlying causes. Medical treatment is possible.

V. SLEEP-RELATED PARENTAL PROBLEMS

PREGNANCY ASSOCIATED SLEEP DISORDER

This sleep disorder can occur in pregnant women of any age. Insomnia generally begins toward the end of the second trimester and is characterized by frequent nocturnal awakenings. Sleep onset is delayed, and waking up after sleep onset becomes more frequent as term approaches.

Sleeplessness can be profound, and it may be related to an inability to assume a comfortable sleeping position, back pain, baby movements, small functional bladder capacity, and urinary frequency.

Sleeplessness may persist after delivery, and child care activities may prolong the sleepless periods. Symptoms may gradually subside.

During pregnancy the sleep-wake cycle becomes more controlled by inner hormones than external social clues. Thus, the mother-to-be should trust her body and stop trying to accommodate social demands. You should try to get sleep when you can. Of course, it is difficult if you have a full-time job, other children and a husband who seems to need you now even more. The bottom line is that naps are crucial. If your husband or other family members can take care of the children during the night or early morning, it would be the best help they can give you.

(See Part 4 on *Pregnancy and Sleep* for more details)

PARENTS' SLEEP DEPRIVATION

This problem has become a serious public health issue. Emotional and physical exhaustion, irritability, angry outbursts, and loss of concentration may lead to family problems, depression, poor job performance, falling asleep at the wheel, and potential child abuse. The most difficult part is the recognition and acceptance of the fact of sleep deprivation which is usually denied. Tiredness and anger are the earliest signs of sleep deprivation. Parents' sleep deprivation is the most difficult to treat. Parents' disorders should be a special field of medicine. (See more in Part 1 on Bedtime Wars...and Harm My Child? Oh, no!)

We cannot change the reality of life but there are many ways to adjust. One is an alternation of sleep time between parents. Administrators on the job or at school might be helpful in rescheduling if appropriately informed. Recommendations of your family doctor might help to prevent health deterioration in terms of headaches, blood pressure, etc.

"When patterns are broken, new worlds can emerge."
— Tuli Kuperberg

———————◆◆◆———————

"When I thought I had all the answers, they changed all the questions."
— Landau, (Physicist)

EPILOGUE

The world of children's sleep is vast, and it is far more boundless than we thought before. This world has its own mountains. The child is growing in sleep, maturing in his physical and emotional strength and preparing himself for productive hours of alertness during the day. But this world also has dangerous storms, when the child sleeps in terror and his normal physiological and emotional processes are in turmoil.

The world of children sleep knows exciting dreams and brutal deaths. The way is paved from peaceful childhood sleep to productive alertness of the adult. This road is not easy to travel. We presently know more than a hundred deviations and disorders of sleep and alertness. We have described only some of them. The goal of this book is to bring together parents, doctors and the entire community to recognize the significance of this world and to unite their efforts for the treatment and prevention of tragedies of the night and the day. If this book raises more questions than it is able to answer we feel that our goal has been achieved.

Many important things were left out on account of space and other considerations. A lot of very significant things about sleep and its disorders in children have been uncovered since this book was sent to print. The book is not finished because not all of our questions have been answered. It will not be finished until our children can sleep normally. We are asking parents, relatives, friends, and colleagues to continue sharing with us their concerns, their questions, stories, and any helpful hints they may have related to sleep and daytime disorders in children.

Every night, and for 1001 nights the beautiful Scheherazade from the famous Arabic Epos told the angry sultan a wonderful fairy tale uncovering her secret. Every night sleep medicine is telling us a beautiful tale, revealing yet another secret and offering a new mystery. This book is just the first night's story. There are a thousand others ahead of us...

> *"The reward for work well done is the opportunity to do more."*
> — Jonas Salk, M.D.,
> Inventor of the Polio vaccine

Appendix 1

Helpful Organizations for Concerned Parents

The American Narcolepsy Association
1139 Bush Street, Suite D
San Carlos, CA 94070-2477
(415) 591-7979

The American Sleep Apnea Association
2700 East Main Street, Suite 206
Columbus, OH 43209-2536
(614) 239-4200

The American Sleep Disorders Association
1610 14th Street N.W., Suite 300
Rochester, MN 55901
(507) 287-6006

The Association of Sleep Disorders Centers
P.O. Box 2604
Del Mar, CA 92014
(619) 755-6556

Center for Healing Fairy Tales
Nemchonok, Irena and Peppard, Victor
Division of Modern Languages and Linguistics
CPR 419
University of South Florida
Tampa, FL 33620

Foundation for Children's Sleep Disorders
4200 W. Peterson, Suite # 109
Chicago, IL 60646
(708) 368-6799

National Commission on Sleep Disorders Research
Dr. William C. Dement, Chairman
Stanford Sleep Disorders Center
701 Welch Road, Suite 2226
Palo Alto, CA 94304
(415) 725-6484

National Organization for Rare Diseases
P.O. Box 8923
New Fairfield, CT 06812
(203) 746-6518

National Sleep Foundation
122 South Robertson Blvd., 3rd Floor
Los Angeles, CA 90048
(213) 288-0466

National SIDS Resource Center
8201 Greenboro Drive, Suite 600
Mc Lean, VA 22102
(703) 821-8955

Sleep & Behavioral Medicine Institute
Alexander Z. Golbin, M.D., Medical Director,
4200 W. Peterson, Suite # 109
Chicago, IL 60646
(312) 736-2424

Sudden Infant Death Syndrome Alliance
10500 Little Patuxent Pkwy., Suite 410
Columbia, MD 21044
(800) 221-SIDS

REFERENCES AND ADDITIONAL READING:

Appendix 2

Bedtime Reading for Children

Ayelsworth, Jim. *Tonight's the Night*. Chicago: Albert Whitman & Company, 1981.

Barrett, Judi. *I Hate to Go to Bed*. New York: Four Winds Press, 1977.

de Paola, Tomie. *When Everyone was Fast Asleep*. New York: Holiday House, 1976.

Katzwinkle, William. *The Nap Master*. New York: Harcourt Brace, 1979.

Larrick, N. *When the Dark Comes Dancing: A Bedtime Poetry Book*. New York: Philomel, 1983.

Mayer, Mercer. *There's a Nightmare in My Closet*. New York: Dial Press, 1968.

Morris, Terry Nell. *Goodnight, Dear Monster*. New York: Alfred A. Knopf, 1980.

Plath, Sylvia. *The Bed Book*. New York: Harper & Row, 1976.

Rice, Eve. *Goodnight, Goodnight*. New York: Greenwillow, 1980.

Seuss, Dr. *Dr. Suess's Sleep Book*. New York: Random House, 1962.

Showers, Paul. *Sleep is for Everyone*. New York: Thomas Y. Crowell, 1974.

Simon, Norma. *Where Does My Cat Sleep?* Chicago: Albert Whitman & Company, 1982.

Stevenson, James. *We Can't Sleep*. New York: Greenwillow Books, 1982.

Ward, Andrew. *Baby Bear and the Long Sleep*. Boston: Little, Brown, 1980.

Wells, Rosemary. *Good Night, Fred*. New York: Dial Press, 1981.

Zolotow, Charlotte. *Wake Up and Goodnight*. New York: Harper & Row, 1971.

Appendix 3

Books About Children's Sleep for Parents

Behrstock, Barry and Trubo, Richard. *The Parent's When-Not-to-Worry Book.* Harper & Row, 1983.

Cartwright, R. and Lamberg, L. *Crisis Dreaming.* New York: Harper Collins, 1993.

Cuthbertson, J., and Schevill, S. *Helping Your Child Through the Night.* New York: Doubleday, 1985.

Dotto, Lydia. *Losing Sleep.* New York: Stoddart Publishing, 1990.

Ferber, R. *Solve Your Child's Sleep Problems.* New York: Simon & Schuster. 1985.

Fritz, Roger. *Sleep Disorders: America's Hidden Nightmare.* Naperville, IL: National Sleep Alert, 1993.

Garfield, Patricia. *Your Child's Dreams.* New York: Ballantine, 1984.

Hales, Diane. *The Complete Book of Sleep.* Reading, Massachusetts: Addison-Wesley, 1980.

Heins, M., and Seiden, A. *Child Care • Parents Care.* New York: Doubleday, 1987.

Huntley, R., and Kerr, K. *The Sleep Book for Tired Parents.* Parenting Press, 1991.

Keith, L.G., Papiernik-Berkhauer, E., and Keith, D.M. *Multiple Pregnancy: Epidemiology, Gestation and Perinatal Outcome.* London: Parthenon Publishing Group, 1994.

Michaels, Evelyne. "How to Handle Your Child's Nightmares." *Chatelaine Magazine,* July 1983.

Milter, Elizabeth A. and Merrill M. *101 Questions About Sleep and Dreams.* Del Mar, California: Wakefulness-Sleep Education and Research Foundation, 1990.

The Parent / Child Sleep Guide. Washington, DC: Sleep Products Safety Council/ Better Sleep Council, P.O. Box 13, Washington, DC 20044.

Scharf, M. *Waking Up Dry: How to End Bedwetting Forever,* RSCS, 1986.

Sears, William. *Nighttime Parenting: How to Get Your Baby and Child to Sleep.* New York: New American Library, 1987.

Sheldon, S., Spire, J.P., and Levy, H. *Pediatric Sleep Medicine.* W.B. Saunders Co., 1992.

Spock, Benjamin. *Baby and Child Care.* New York: Pocket Books, Simon & Schuster, Inc., 1992.

Spock, Benjamin. *Dr. Spock on Parenting.* New York: Pocket Books, 1988.

Sturane, Eileen. *The Dream World of Pregnancy.* New York: Stationhill Press, 1994.

Weissbluth, Marc. *Healthy Sleep Habits, Happy Child.* New York: Ballantine Books, 1987.

Wiseman, Anne Sayne. *Nightmare Help - for Children, from Children.* Berkeley, CA: Ten Speed Press, 1989.

Scientific Reading

For a complete list of references including these subjects: enuresis, sleep in animals, stereotyped rhythmic movements in sleep, normal sleep and biorhythms, abnormal sleep and alertness disorders, dissociative disorders, somnambulism, hyperactivity, injurious sleep, narcolepsy, sleeptalking, or other areas, please contact:

Sleep & Behavioral Medicine Institute
Alexander Z. Golbin, M.D., Medical Director,
4200 W. Peterson, Suite # 109
Chicago, IL 60646
(312) 736-2424

Appendix 4

GLOSSARY OF TERMS
(TERMS AND DEFINITIONS)

Antagonist
A compound or drug that has an opposing action.

Antidepressant
A compound or drug that counteracts a depressive state (to bring back to the normal level or function).

Antihistamine
A drug that is antagonistic to the actions of a chemical, histamine (released in an inflammatory or allergic reaction).

Anxiety
A feeling of danger and dread with tense, restlessness, and dyspnea, but no apparent stimulus to cause this apprehension.

Apnea
Lack of breathing. May be sleep-induced from the failure of the respiratory center to stimulate enough respiration during sleep. This pause may last more than ten seconds.

Arousal
An awakening or change from a deep to a lighter stage of sleep. Changes in EEG, muscle tone and heart rate increases.

Autonomic Nervous System (ANS)
The nervous system that is not under voluntary control. This includes: smooth and cardiac muscle, glands, and other involuntary organs.

Benzodiazepine
Compound or drug generally used for anxiety and neurotic states; a muscle relaxant that has sedative properties. An example includes Flurazepam, commonly used for insomnia.

Biofeedback
Training technique used to have some voluntary control over "autonomic functions". Where a thought can produce a desirable response. Can be used to regulate heart rate, blood pressure, skin temperature, and other physiological processes.

Biological Clocks
Mechanisms in the brain that are set or reset by certain environmental time cues, such as the timing of sunrise or "lights on" in the morning and sunset or "lights off" at night; in conjunction with the 24-hour wake-sleep cycle.

Cataplexy
An attack of extreme muscular weakness, usually occurring from an emotional state; like heavy laughter. Often presents as a symptom of narcolepsy.

Chronic
Long duration; a disease that has a slow or long process.

Chronobiology
The study of the timing of biological events; usually repeated or cyclic phenomena.

Circadian Rhythm
Biologic variations that usually occur with a cycle of 24 hours. Includes sleep and waking.

Chronopharmacology
The study of the effects of medication on biologic rhythms. Includes the study of biologic rhythm dependencies of medications and their mechanisms of action. Also, includes the study of the effect of medications during day to night work or travel across several time zones.

Crystallization
A proposed tentative term reflecting a critical period of appearance of jactatio.

Delta sleep
Deep sleep; "Slow-wave sleep", large and slow EEG waves (delta waves). Includes sleep stages 3 and 4 (The first 90 minutes of sleep). Amount decreases as a person gets older.

Desynchronization
A change in time structure that results in a loss of biologic efficiency. Seen when traveling across several time zones by high-speed aircraft; this is a temporary *desynchronization* of the circadian time structure, resulting in the myriad of complaints and symptoms referred to as "jet lag".

Dyssomnia
Term given to a disorder in the amount and timing of sleep. Includes: insomnia, circadian-rhythm disturbances, and excessive daytime sleepiness.

Electroencephalogram (EEG)
A recording of electric potentials (activity) of the brain; recorded from the electrodes that are placed on the scalp.

Electromyogram (EMG)
A recording of electrical currents (activity) from muscle.

Electro-oculogram (EOG)
A recording measuring the potential difference from the front and the back of the eyeball, giving certain patterns. Records changes from shifts of the eyeball position.

Excessive daytime somnolence
Sleepiness; trouble remaining awake even with adequate sleep.

Habits
Repetitive patterns of behaviors, thoughts and feelings.
Behaviors formed by frequent repetition of the same act

Headbanging
Rhythmic movement disorder. In the prone position, rhythmic lifting of the head and upper body and forcefully beating the forehead or cheeks against the pillow, fists or any surface.

Head / Body rocking
Rhythmic movement disorder. In the supine or semi-supine position; pendulum-like rhythmical movements of the head (arms and body) from side to side.

Histamine
A chemical secreted by the body during an inflammatory or allergic response that also stimulates gastric secretion, constricts bronchial smooth muscle, and vasodilates.

Hypersomnia
A condition of sleeping for a long time, but in normal intervals. (compared to somnolence)

Hypnagogic
At the *beginning* of sleep.

Hypnopompic
    At the *end* of sleep or during awakening.

Hypnosis
    An artificially induced trance-like state.

Insomnia
    Wakefulness, or the inability to sleep when sleep should normally occur.

Jactatio nocturna
    A rhythmic movement disorder. A separate class of specific individually constant sleep related rhythmical motor activities of high frequency (0.3-3/sec).

Light Sleep
    Sleep stages 1 and 2.

Metabolism
    Chemical changes that occur in the body. *Anabolism* builds larger molecules from smaller ones. *Catabolism* breaks down large molecules into smaller ones, releasing heat and energy.

Multiple Sleep Latency Test (MSLT)
    Test that measures how sleepy you are. Taken in normal waking time period while falling asleep. Used to evaluate sleep disorders and medications.

Myoclonus
    Muscle spasm or twitches of a muscle or group of muscles, may cause limb movements.

Narcolepsy
    A sudden uncontrolled sleep that occurs without warning. An abnormal sleep-stage sequencing.

Nightmares
    Anxiety-filled dreams that occur during REM sleep and can usually be recalled (compared to night terrors).

Night terrors
    (See Pavor nocturnus)

Nocturnal
    Pertaining to the dark hours.

Non-rapid eye movement sleep (NREM)
Sleep stages 1, 2, 3, and 4 of a 90 minute sleep cycle. (All sleep that does not include REM sleep.)

Parasomnia
Undesirable phenomena in sleep. Includes sleep disturbances like sleepwalking, bedwetting, and nightmares.

Pavor Nocturnus
Sleep terrors or night terrors. Occurs in deep sleep (stage 4), the child is screaming and terrified, disoriented and cannot be comforted. Difficult to awaken, and cannot describe a dream. Usually the child has no recollection of the event.

Periodic Limb Movements
Repetitive twitching, usually of the legs and feet, during sleep.

Polysomnogram
Recording of physiological activities during sleep. Includes: heart rate, eye movements, brain waves, and muscle activity.

Rhythm
First defined by its *period*, 24 hours or 28 days, for example. One of the most important periodicities is the **circadian** (24 hour) **rhythm**.

Ultradian rhythm Biologic oscillations that are shorter than 20 hours duration. For example, EEG and ECG rhythms.

Infradian rhythm Biologic oscillations that are greater than 28 hours in duration. For example, weekly, menstrual, and seasonal cycles in biologic function.

Rapid eye movement sleep (REM)
Period of increased brain activity. Dreams are associated with the period, and paralysis of muscles. Occurs about every 90 minutes.

Self-cure
A proposed tentative term reflecting the stage in the natural course of affliction with spontaneous self-extinction.

Serotonin
Major neurotransmitter of sleep. If deficiency, plays a major role in disorders of alertness and violent behavior. Also acts as a vasoconstrictor that inhibits gastric secretion and excites smooth muscle.

Shuttling
Forward-backward rhythmical movements of the whole body in elbow-knee position.

Sleep Paralysis
Unable to move voluntarily, sleep-onset paralysis is associated with narcolepsy. May be considered normal towards the end of sleep.

Somnambulism
Sleepwalking. A sleep disorder usually of the first third of the night (not during REM sleep).

Somnolence
Sleeping for a long time. Inclined to sleep; increased drowsiness and sleepiness.

Substitution
A proposed tentative term reflecting common beliefs that one form of jactatio may switch into another. Better or worse, or to non-motor or even into a psychological habit.

Sympathetic Nervous System
The "Flight or Fight" part of the nervous system that increases heart rate, dilates the pupils (to react to the environment), and other physiologic functions.

Zeitgeber
An environmental "Time giver" or cue as to what time it is. Helps the body rhythm produce a 24-hour day. Includes the light of the daytime.

ZZZZ's
All sleep researchers use this "term" to acknowledge good sleep, and we wish you to have pleasant sleep ZZZZ's.

"Sleep, the sweetest gift of heaven."
—Vergil

INDEX